Pure Christianity

*Christianity without Total Depravity
and with Fulfilled Eschatology*

SUNG-IN PARK

ARCHWAY
PUBLISHING

Archway Publishing books may be ordered through booksellers or by contacting:

Archway Publishing
1663 Liberty Drive
Bloomington, IN 47403
www.archwaypublishing.com
1 (888) 242-5904

ISBN: 978-1-4808-7599-9 (sc)
ISBN: 978-1-4808-7598-2 (e)

Library of Congress Control Number: 2019903210

Print information available on the last page.

Archway Publishing rev. date: 03/26/2019

This book is dedicated to my wife
Dr. Mi-Suk Shim and my children Moses and Ruby

CONTENTS

Preface

In these postmodern, highly charged, and increasingly polarized times, reflecting on the Christian religion with clarity becomes more and more crucial. The Christian religion, born of and represented by Jesus's teaching to the Jewish community, has never not been based on interpreted teachings. And through the years—and even in the very early years—those interpretations seem to have included distortions, misinterpretations by Jesus's disciples and followers. Such distortions are particularly visible in Paul's writings—not least because they are particularly visible. Whether intentional or unintentional, Paul's interpretations became ambiguous and equivocal when they were introduced to the broader world, outside of Palestine, to those who had no grounding in the Hebrew faith tradition.

Originally, what became Christianity was the culmination of the Jewish promise about the coming Messiah, and it was inclusive in its nature toward the world. In this Jewish hope for a messiah, there was no sense of judgment of the world as sinner.

Jesus's end of the world, associated with his second coming, was bound only to Judea and the Jewish people: the destruction of Jerusalem and Judea in AD 70 by the Romans (final destruction in AD 73 at Masada). The Gospel thus proclaimed the imminent "reign of God" or the "reign of the son of God" in association with the birth of the Church; the church came out of the sinful and man-ruled Judea and as follower of the Messiah was supposed to replace Judea. However, when the Gospel was proclaimed outside of Judea, Christianity reinterpreted Judea as the world instead of replacing Judea with the Church in its theology. As a result, sinful Judea became the sinful world, and the Church stood over and against it. Christianity then judged and condemned the world (instead of Judea), despite the fact that the world never had had a covenant with God. The Christian perspective made the world the sinner as Christians waited for the end, the final judgment of God, in association with the Second Coming of the Messiah. Unfortunately, Christianity has taken root as a world religion by virtue of judging, condemning, and threatening the world; in the process, the doctrine of Total Depravity was formulated on the basis of Original Sin and the doctrine of eschatology on the basis of the Second Coming of the Messiah. The logical and necessary conclusion was that Christianity would seek to be the exclusive, excluding winner over and against all other religions—logical on the basis of its distorted doctrines and necessary to justify its growth and expansion.

My intent is not simply to make Christianity an inclusive religion so that we might have harmony with all other religions, nor to solve an age-old problem by transforming the basic tenets of Christianity intentionally, nor to vindicate the principles of other religions without discretion. Rather, my intent is to show how Christianity was never intended to be exclusive: Christianity was originally inclusive in its nature. Neither is the purpose of this writing to diminish the authority of the Bible or to underestimate the value of Christian theology and history; instead, I hope to present the core of Christian religion and its development in a more transparent way, in light of its early context, and thereby to preserve the Christian religion in a pluralistic age for the will and glory of our LORD.

In the following sections, I examine the Christian texts to illustrate and support my perspective and to present the face of Christianity in light of its heritage and early context.

Section I
Rapid Universalizing of Christianity: Judea Became the World

To understand the Christian religion appropriately, we first must understand how Christianity was universalized in the first century, right after the movement left the soil of Palestine. On the basis of Scripture, we might say that Christianity, as a meaningful, final realization of Judaism, became a universalized religion for the world through the work of the disciples, particularly of Paul. Exactly how did Judea become the world—or did the world become Judea—in the interpretations of these communicators? What are the steps or processes by which a particular religious community and practice intentionally expands beyond a smaller sphere of influence to a larger one? I examine these questions first and then turn to the writings of Paul, who, as a teacher of the Gentiles[1] and widely circulated writer, played the most significant role in universalizing the Christian religion. By scrutinizing certain Pauline texts, as well as other biblical texts, we can see how this movement from Judea to the world proves to be a problematic and too-quickly assumed leap in the early years of the Church.

Judea became the world

In the process of universalizing Christianity, Judea became the world:

1. The sin of Judea became the sin of the world
2. The judgment on Judea became the judgment on the world: The end of Judea became the end of the world

3.   The only savior of Judea became the only savior of the world

Universalizing Christianity means that Judea became the world.
I'd like to visualize this universalization by diagrams:

The scope of the New Testament

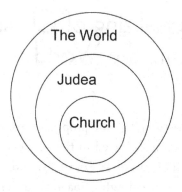

The Church, as the new Kingdom of God that is reigned over by the
promised Jewish Messiah (Christ), was primarily designed to replace or
be compared to Judea:

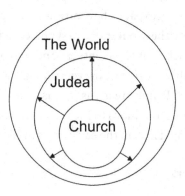

However, instead of the Church replacing Judea, the disciples expanded Judea to the world:

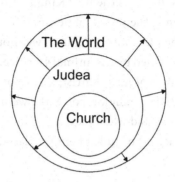

As a result, Judea became the world in which the Church was situated:

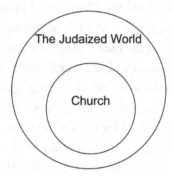

Since the Roman Empire played a significant role as a medium in which Christianity was universalized, the first-century Judaized Roman Empire was the first step toward the Judaized world:

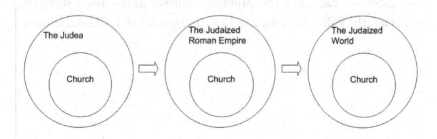

Therefore the true tenets of Christianity should be found first in the relationship between the Church and Judea since the intended role of the Church was to replace Judea as the new Kingdom of God. For example, Jesus came as the King of the Jews, but became the King of the Church; Judea was bound to the Law, but the Church was bound to the teachings of Jesus; Judea was sanctified by the animal sacrifice, but the Church was sanctified by the sacrifice of Jesus Christ, and so on. To understand the present historical Christian religion correctly, we need first to see how the true tenets were distorted when Judea expanded to the world and the world was Judaized instead of Judea being replaced by or compared to the Church.

Where does the ambiguity and equivocation of Christian theology come from? In the New Testament, we can find both Judeas: Judea being replaced by (or compared to) the Church and Judea being expanded to the world. In the Gospels and non-Pauline writings, Church is strongly replaced by (or compared to) Judea: Jesus, the Lord of the Church, was born as the promised Messiah of Judea and died as the King of the Jews. However, in the Pauline letters, Church is strongly compared to the world as it became Judaized: Jesus, the Lord of the Church, came to the world as the Second Adam and died for the sin of the world. Thus, the actual problem of Christianity does not rest upon whether the virgin birth is true or not; whether Jesus married or not. It is that Judea became the world without proper explanation. What happened in the history and tradition of Judea was applied directly to the world without any distinction between the two communities: One is much bigger than the other; one has the special covenant relationship with God and the other does not. The distortion caused by this problem occurred immediately when the gospel left the Palestinian soils and became saturated in Church history.

CHAPTER 1
The Sin of Judea Became the Sin of the World

Sin, as understood in the Judean context—that of breaking the covenant between God and his people—was redeemed by sacrifice, by the blood of animals. The sin of Judea aligned with the sin of the Church and its understanding that the sins of believers were redeemed through Christ's suffering and death. However, when the gospel left the soil of Palestine, this understanding of sacrifice / forgiveness transitioned from the sin of Judaism to the sin of the world without any clear explanation about what the sin of the world is and why or how the world is identified with Judea.

The sin of Judea/Israel[2] was collectively bound to its long-lived covenant in association with the Law and requiring the specially designed sacrifice for its redemption (particularly Yom Kipper; refer to Leviticus 16:3–34). In the Old Testament, the sin denounced by the prophets was the sin of the nation in a collective sense, not that of every individual citizen in the nation nor every individual in the world.[3] When Judea or Israel was denounced as the sinner, that did not necessarily mean that every individual citizen of the nation was a sinner nor was that true of every individual in the world. Mathematically speaking, if more than 50% of the citizens of a nation are sinners, that nation might be called sinful. Or if the representatives of a nation are sinners, that nation might be called sinful, too. However, the sinful nation does not necessarily count all individuals in a nation or the world without exception. Likewise, in the Gospels, the sin denounced by Jesus and John the Baptist was the sin of Judea or the Jews in a collective sense, not every Jew or individual in the world (Matthew 3:1–10, 4:14–17). In each case, the world and the individuals in it were left to the Justice of God. The essential problem is that when the gospel was preached to the Gentiles, the world beyond Judea, that never had such a covenant with its creator, was treated as though it did. The world that was never a recipient of the Law requiring specialized sacrifice for its breaking was treated as if it were. In this process, sin moved from the collective to the individual. The disciples denounced the world as sinful not because the majority of the world's population was sinners, or the leaders of the world were sinners but solely based upon each individual's sin. Therefore, the world and every individual in that world became doomed.

How did the sin of Judea become identified with the sin of the world? Identifying the sin of Judea with the world came about by utilizing the so-called Original Sin that deduces Total Depravity; utilizing natural Law and general revelation; and adopting the universal expressions, "world" and "all," for a group of the people. The sin of Judea should have been compared to the sin of the Church for which Jesus died. However, the sin of Judea was outwardly expanded to the world. In this chapter, I will study how the world became identified with Judea or vice versa.

A. Utilizing Genesis chapter 2 & 3 (the Original Sin) that deduces Total Depravity

If Christianity claims its authority and legitimacy based upon the Old Testament, Original Sin is a false doctrine because of myriad inconsistencies. From the Old Testament texts, if Original Sin exists, it draws out many uneasy questions. Why did God give the Law to the people of Israel through Moses without first trying to resolve the problem of Original Sin? Even if Israel observed the Law perfectly, the people would remain sinners because of Original Sin. In other words, if the people of Israel could not keep the Law due to their sinful nature (their Original Sin), why did God give them the Law and ask them to practice it (Deuteronomy 30:14[4])? Why did the prophets call for repentance as a solution when the people of God violated the given Law? It seems that repentance does not resolve the problem of the Original Sin. Further, why did God show favor to Abel right after the Fall? If Original Sin is associated with physical death, why did Enoch and Elijah not die? If Original Sin is associated with spiritual death and the inability of doing good, why was Noah called a righteous man and blameless?

The spirit of the Torah and voice of the prophets simply do not cooperate with the concept of the Original Sin. Deuteronomy 24:16 clearly states that each individual is responsible for his or her own sin: "Fathers shall not be put to death for their sons, nor shall sons be put to death for their fathers; everyone shall be put to death for his own sin."

If Original Sin is a doctrine of the New Testament, some questions remain. Why did Jesus never mention it? Matthew 1:21 proclaims that Jesus died for the sins of his people.[5] What kind of sin did Jesus die for? Original Sin or sins violating the Law or both? Are Christians the people who do not have Original Sin? If so, how about their children? When a couple become free from Original Sin by the redemption of Jesus, marries, and produces a child, shouldn't that child be free from Original Sin? In this case, Total Depravity cannot be Total. If not, why does a Christian marry and give birth to a boy or girl? In fact, they are producing sinners. Aren't Christians joyful when they hold a newborn baby? Don't Christians congratulate someone who has a newborn? If Christians truly believe in Original Sin, they should not procreate because when a baby is born, the world has one more sinner. Who knows if this baby will believe in Jesus? If Original Sin is associated with physical death, why do Christians who are resolved by Jesus still die? If Original Sin is associated with spiritual death, Total Depravity cannot be proved to be Total. One more question: Why does a Christian celebrate a birthday? Isn't a birthday a day of a birth of a sinner?

If Original Sin is true, a question still remains. How about the fate of an infant? Do they die as a sinner or not? Where is justice if a human being is born as a sinner without any choice? Nobody comes to this world because of his or her choice or will. If I were born as a sinner, then who was responsible of that birth? God, my parents, or me?

In fact, Original Sin and Total Depravity are inventions of Christian theology, developed in the process of universalizing the religion and have no legitimate biblical or rational basis.

In spite of the numerous uneasy questions and ambiguous answers, many Christians still believe these doctrines because a writer of the New Testament, Paul, utilized the Genesis accounts (chapter 2 and 3) to justify his argument that everyone is a sinner who will die, thereby needing redemption or salvation through Jesus.

Criticism on Paul's utilizing Genesis account: Romans 5: 12–21

Let us read the relevant text:

Romans 5: 12–21

12. Therefore, just as through one man sin entered into the world, and death through sin, and so death spread to all men, because all sinned

13. for until the Law sin was in the world, but sin is not imputed when there is no law.

14. Nevertheless death reigned from Adam until Moses, even over those who had not sinned in the likeness of the offense of Adam, who is a type of Him who was to come.

15. But the free gift is not like the transgression. For if by the transgression of the one the many died, much more did the grace of God and the gift by the grace of the one Man, Jesus Christ, abound to the many.

16. The gift is not like that which came through the one who sinned; for on the one hand the judgment arose from one transgression resulting in condemnation, but on the other hand the free gift arose from many transgressions resulting in justification.

17. For if by the transgression of the one, death reigned through the one, much more those who receive the abundance of grace and of the gift of righteousness will reign in life through the One, Jesus Christ.

18. So then as through one transgression there resulted condemnation to all men, even so through one act of righteousness there resulted justification of life to all men.

19. For as through the one man's disobedience the many were made sinners, even so through the obedience of the One the many will be made righteous.
20. The Law came in so that the transgression would increase; but where sin increased, grace abounded all the more,
21. so that, as sin reigned in death, even so grace would reign through righteousness to eternal life through Jesus Christ our Lord.

First, we need to define the meaning of death (θάνατος). When Paul wrote Romans, he also wrote 1 Corinthians. Let us compare an account of 1 Corinthians and this text to discern the meaning of death.

1Corinthians 15:20–26
20. But now Christ has been raised from the dead, the first fruits of those who are asleep.
21. For since by a man came death, by a man also came the resurrection of the dead.
22. For as in Adam all die, so also in Christ all will be made alive.
23. But each in his own order: Christ the first fruits, after that those who are Christ's at His coming,
24. then comes the end, when He hands over the kingdom to the God and Father, when He has abolished all rule and all authority and power.
25. For He must reign until He has put all His enemies under His feet.
26. The last enemy that will be abolished is death.

Both texts draw on Genesis. In the text of 1 Corinthians 15:20–26, death means a physical death without any doubt. Therefore we can naturally assume that death in Romans 5:12–21 means a physical death, too. If so, in verse 12, Paul relates natural death of a human being to the sin of Adam. In other words, he says, "Since Adam sinned, all (πάντας) men die." And then in verse 13, Paul says, "Prior to the Law, there was sin but sin was not considered as sin because there was no Law." Up to this point, according to Paul's logic, death should not exist before the Law because sin was not considered as sin. In verse 14, however, Paul says paradoxically, "Nevertheless death reigned from Adam until Moses, even over those who had not sinned in the likeness of the offense of Adam." Here Paul should have explained the reason people died before Moses even though they did not sin like Adam and were not considered as sinners because there was no Law. However, somehow, he does not. Maybe he is simply trying to separate sin of the Law from sin of Adam because sin of the Law does not induce a natural death that applies to all human beings, rather some death by judgment or sentence from judges. If so, he is indeed talking about Original Sin, which is considered as sin apart from the Law and has been transmitted to all human beings from one man, Adam, and thus causes natural death of all human beings. Instead of explaining the reason people died, in verse 14b, Paul abruptly connects this one man, Adam, to Jesus: "who is a type of Him who was to come." If Adam is a type of Jesus, up to this point, logic draws an assumed conclusion: "All men die due to Adam. Likewise all men live due to Jesus." However, in verse 15, Paul distorts the assumed conclusion. He changed all ($\pi\acute{\alpha}\nu\tau\alpha\varsigma$) to many ($\pi o\lambda\lambda o\grave{\iota}$): "But the free gift is not like the transgression. For if by the transgression of the one the many died, much more did the grace of God and the gift by the grace of the one Man, Jesus Christ, abound to the many." He says "death spread to all men" due to Adam in verse 12. However, in verse 15, he says "the many died" due to Adam. Regarding Jesus, he also distorts the assumed conclusion he has developed. Rather than saying, "all men live due to Jesus," he says, "the many lived due to Jesus."

This logical distortion is repeated in verses 18 and 19: "18. So then as through one transgression there resulted condemnation to all men, even so through one act of righteousness there resulted justification of life to all men. 19. For as through the one man's disobedience the many were made sinners, even so through the obedience of the One the many will be made righteous." Why did Paul change all ($\pi\acute{\alpha}\nu\tau\alpha\varsigma$) to many ($\pi o\lambda\lambda o\grave{\iota}$)? When Adam and Jesus are contrasted, if all die due to Adam, all should live due to Jesus. Paul, however, believed that some can live due to Jesus based upon their choices rather than everyone, without choice. If not, proclaiming the gospel would have no meaning. Therefore, this change or correction was inevitable to Paul.

A similar problem is found in 1Corinthians 15:20–26. As in Romans 5:12–21, Adam and Jesus are contrasted to each other to make a point about the Resurrection of Jesus. When we read verses 20 and 21, the assumed conclusion is that all die due to Adam, likewise all are resurrected due to Jesus. However, in verse 23, Paul just says that Jesus was resurrected as the first, and then those Christians would be next: "But each in his own order: Christ the first fruits, after that those who are Christ's at His coming."

What about non-Christians? Without mentioning them, Paul moves quickly to the end in verse 24: "then comes the end, when He hands over the kingdom to the God and Father, when He has abolished all rule and all authority and power." Will non-Christians be resurrected due to Jesus? Since Adam and Jesus are contrasted to each other in terms of death and resurrection, all human beings, including non-Christians, should be resurrected. If this is the case, what is the rationale for proclaiming the gospel? If non-Christians will not be resurrected, the logic Paul set contrasting Adam and Jesus becomes illogical.

Therefore, in spite of Paul's endeavor, utilizing the Genesis account to make all human beings sinners fails. Paul tried to make the point that all human beings are sinners, therefore everyone needs Jesus to be saved. Since all human beings die, Paul tried to connect natural death of human beings to primeval and primitive sin. To claim proper authority for the argument, he drew the basis of the totality of sin from the Old Testament Genesis chapters 2 and 3, the account of the first human beings. However, his writing itself reveals the logical flaw. To contrast Jesus to Adam, all circumstances must remain equal: since all die in Adam without choice, logically all should live in Jesus without choice. Even though everyone physically dies, Paul believed that only those who choose Jesus can live. Therefore, Paul immediately changed all (πάντας) to many (πολλοί) to make sense of his argument. However, this change paradoxically denies the claim that natural death is caused by the result of sin of Adam, because if some, not all, die due to Adam, then that death cannot be the natural death that affects every human being. When Paul changed all (πάντας) to many (πολλοί), in fact, he destroyed the premise he set by himself: All human beings are sinners, thus, everyone needs Jesus to be saved.

Paul's failure offers some possibilities of thought.

1. Jesus may not be contrasted to Adam.
2. Original Sin (Total Depravity) may not have any biblical basis.
3. Jesus may not be the only way to salvation.

Paul's failure forces us to think about the Genesis account itself. Is there any basis for a Doctrine of Total Depravity, set out in the Genesis account, that affects all human beings? Are all human beings really sinners due to Adam, and do they all die as a result? Some believe that sin results from Adam, directly passed on to every human being born from sexual intercourse between a male and a female. Some believe that all human beings were in Adam because Adam was the prototype of humankind, therefore, when he sinned all sinned and will die. Some believe that all are born innocent, but sin in the way of Adam and thereby die. In this case, a reason is presented for why all sin in Adam's sin, in other words, separation from God. Either way, Original Sin, or Total Depravity, insists that on the basis of Adam's sin, all human beings become sinners and, as a result, die. Even though Paul failed in his logic of contrasting Adam to Jesus, this belief forces us to examine the Genesis account itself to see if the Original Sin itself might be vindicated without Paul.

Exegetical study on Genesis 2: 1–25; 3: 1–24

Let us read the texts (NASB):

Genesis 2: 1–25
1. Thus the heavens and the earth were completed, and all their hosts.
2. By the seventh day God completed His work which He had done, and He rested on the seventh day from all His work which He had done.
3. Then God blessed the seventh day and sanctified it, because in it He rested from all His work which God had created and made.

4. This is the account of the heavens and the earth when they were created, in the day that the LORD God made earth and heaven.

5. Now no shrub of the field was yet in the earth, and no plant of the field had yet sprouted, for the LORD God had not sent rain upon the earth, and there was no man to cultivate the ground.

6. But a mist used to rise from the earth and water the whole surface of the ground.

7. Then the LORD God formed man of dust from the ground, and breathed into his nostrils the breath of life; and man became a living being.

8. The LORD God planted a garden toward the east, in Eden; and there He placed the man whom He had formed.

9. Out of the ground the LORD God caused to grow every tree that is pleasing to the sight and good for food; the tree of life also in the midst of the garden, and the tree of the knowledge of good and evil.

10. Now a river flowed out of Eden to water the garden; and from there it divided and became four rivers.

11. The name of the first is Pishon; it flows around the whole land of Havilah, where there is gold.

12. The gold of that land is good; the bdellium and the onyx stone are there.

13. The name of the second river is Gihon; it flows around the whole land of Cush.

14. The name of the third river is Tigris; it flows east of Assyria And the fourth river is the Euphrates.

15. Then the LORD God took the man and put him into the garden of Eden to cultivate it and keep it.

16. The LORD God commanded the man, saying, "From any tree of the garden you may eat freely;

17. but from the tree of the knowledge of good and evil you shall not eat, for in the day that you eat from it you will surely die."

18. Then the LORD God said, "It is not good for the man to be alone; I will make him a helper suitable for him."

19. Out of the ground the LORD God formed every beast of the field and every bird of the sky, and brought them to the man to see what he would call them; and whatever the man called a living creature, that was its name.

20. The man gave names to all the cattle, and to the birds of the sky, and to every beast of the field, but for Adam there was not found a helper suitable for him.

21. So the LORD God caused a deep sleep to fall upon the man, and he slept; then He took one of his ribs and closed up the flesh at that place.

22. The LORD God fashioned into a woman the rib which He had taken from the man, and brought her to the man.

23. The man said, "This is now bone of my bones, And flesh of my flesh; She shall be called Woman, Because she was taken out of Man."

24. For this reason a man shall leave his father and his mother, and be joined to his wife; and they shall become one flesh.

25. And the man and his wife were both naked and were not ashamed.

Genesis 3: 1–24

1. Now the serpent was more crafty than any other wild animal that the LORD God had made. He said to the woman, "Did God say, 'You shall not eat from any tree in the garden'?"

2. The woman said to the serpent, "We may eat of the fruit of the trees in the garden;

3. but God said, "You shall not eat of the fruit of the tree that is in the middle of the garden, nor shall you touch it, or you shall die.'"

4. But the serpent said to the woman, "You will not die;

5. for God knows that when you eat of it your eyes will be opened, and you will be like God, knowing good and evil."

6. So when the woman saw that the tree was good for food, and that it was a delight to the eyes, and that the tree was to be desired to make one wise, she took of its fruit and ate; and she also gave some to her husband, who was with her, and he ate.

7. Then the eyes of both were opened, and they knew that they were naked; and they sewed fig leaves together and made loincloths for themselves.

8. They heard the sound of the LORD God walking in the garden at the time of the evening breeze, and the man and his wife hid themselves from the presence of the LORD God among the trees of the garden.

9. But the LORD God called to the man, and said to him, "Where are you?"

10. He said, "I heard the sound of you in the garden, and I was afraid, because I was naked; and I hid myself."

11. He said, "Who told you that you were naked? Have you eaten from the tree of which I commanded you not to eat?"

12. The man said, "The woman whom you gave to be with me, she gave me fruit from the tree, and I ate."

13. Then the LORD God said to the woman, "What is this that you have done?" The woman said, "The serpent tricked me, and I ate."

14. The LORD God said to the serpent, "Because you have done this, cursed are you among all animals and among all wild creatures; upon your belly you shall go, and dust you shall eat all the days of your life.

15. I will put enmity between you and the woman, and between your offspring and hers; he will strike your head, and you will strike his heel."

16. To the woman he said, "I will greatly increase your pangs in childbearing; in pain you shall bring forth children, yet your desire shall be for your husband, and he shall rule over you."

17. And to the man he said, "Because you have listened to the voice of your wife, and have eaten of the tree about which I commanded you, 'You shall not eat of it,' cursed is the ground because of you; in toil you shall eat of it all the days of your life;

18. thorns and thistles it shall bring forth for you; and you shall eat the plants of the field.

19. By the sweat of your face you shall eat bread until you return to the ground, for out of it you were taken; you are dust, and to dust you shall return."

20. The man named his wife Eve, because she was the mother of all living.

21. And the LORD God made garments of skins for the man and for his wife, and clothed them.

22. Then the LORD God said, "See, the man has become like one of us, knowing good and evil; and now, he might reach out his hand and take also from the tree of life, and eat, and live forever"

23. therefore the LORD God sent him out from the garden of Eden, to cultivate the ground from which he was taken.

24. So He drove the man out; and at the east of the garden of Eden He stationed the cherubim and the flaming sword which turned every direction to guard the way to the tree of life.

First of all, nowhere do the texts say explicitly that all human beings are to die because Adam and his partner sinned. In fact, nowhere in the Old Testament is this stated. Genesis 2:16–17 says "The LORD God commanded the man, saying, "From any tree of the garden you may eat freely; but from the tree of the knowledge of good and evil you shall not eat, for in the day that you eat from it you will surely die." Here, the word death is not defined. And in Genesis 3, Adam ate from the tree of the knowledge of good and evil and was told that he would return to the ground because out of the ground he was taken. Therefore, the readers infer from the story that Adam was to die because he disobeyed.

However, if Adam's death was a part of the punishment and, as a result, all people die, how do we interpret the eventual death of all other living creatures? Do they, too, die due to sin of Adam? If so, where is the justification? Did the first animal of each kind in the Garden of Eden disobey God? Do lions die because the first lion disobeyed God? Even if Adam did not sin, could a human being not be killed by another or by accident? Going back to Scripture, if human beings are immortal, what happens to God's initial blessing for increasing and multiplication (Genesis 1:28): "God blessed them; and God said to them, "Be fruitful and multiply, and fill the earth..."" The world is now experiencing the problems of overpopulation: food and water shortage, waste, air pollution, and so on. Does not God's initial blessing imply the limited life span of the human beings on earth? God knows that when the earth becomes filled with human beings because they don't die, they must stop being fruitful and multiplying. Therefore, for this blessing to be a blessing, the created human beings must be mortal beings.

Even when we read the texts without any training, we cannot deduce from them the fact that all human beings die because of Adam's sin. We might say that Adam was to die because he disobeyed God. Yet even that statement is ambiguous because when we read Genesis 3, it seems that death is a natural consequence, not a punishment.[6] As a result of punishment for Adam's sin, God says (verse 19), "By the sweat of your face you shall eat bread until you return to the ground, for out of it you were taken; you are dust, and to dust you shall return." It is not clear whether the second clause of the verse (until you return to the ground, for out of it you were taken; you are dust, and to dust you shall return) is a part of the punishment or not. The first clause of the verse clearly belongs to punishment: "By the sweat of your face you shall eat bread." However, "until you return to the ground" seems to assist the first clause by limiting the effective time of punishment to this earthly life. If death were a part of punishment, the word "until" עַד should not be used. The writer of the text could have used a conjunction such as "By the sweat of your face you shall eat bread and you shall return to the ground." In the second clause, "for out of it you were taken; you are dust, and to dust you shall return" seems to simply clarify and reinforce the reason why man would return to the ground. And the word "return" שׁוּב supports the notion that death is not a part of punishment, but the natural consequence.

Clearly these texts should not be interpreted literally. When interpreted literally, several other problems occur. For instance, Eve (or maybe women) and the snake (or maybe the species of snakes)[7] would not die because death was not a part of the punishment to them. Only Adam (or maybe men) is to die because only Adam was bound to the covenant in Genesis 2 and 3. Furthermore we all know that snakes do not eat the dust and not all women are subject to the punishment given to Eve and not all men are farmers. The text asks justice for its interpretation.

If the texts should not be interpreted literally, how can we interpret them?

The Hebrew of Genesis is fifth-century BC Hebrew, so we know that the final redaction and editing happened then. However, these particular texts were written much earlier in Palestine, sometime after the Exodus from the Egypt (possibly tenth-century BC), by someone or a group who knew the Law very well and were trying to give some answers (which are not necessarily true) to the basic and fundamental life questions from the viewpoint of their culture, worldview, religion, and tradition.

First, about the location of composition

The word "east," found several times in Genesis (2:8, 11:2, 16:12, 25:6, 29:1), when used as a geographical direction implies a standard point of direction: "east from a particular viewpoint."

Let us have a close look at the texts:

2:8 The LORD God planted a garden toward the east, in Eden; and there He placed the man whom He had formed.

11:2 It came about as they journeyed east, that they found a plain in the land of Shinar and settled there.

16: 12 "He will be a wild donkey of a man, His hand will be against everyone, And everyone's hand will be against him; And he will live to the east of all his brothers."

25: 6 but to the sons of his concubines, Abraham gave gifts while he was still living, and sent them away from his son Isaac eastward, to the land of the east.

29: 1 Then Jacob went on his journey, and came to the land of the sons of the east.

Here the texts suggest that the place from which east is viewed is Palestine. When Mesopotamia and east of the Jordan were viewed from Palestine, the stories make sense. And thereby we can positively assume that Genesis was written in Palestine.

Second, about the time of composition

If a proper noun was used in describing a primeval event, the story was actually written after that proper noun was well established in a given community. We can find several proper nouns in Genesis 2: 11–14:

11. The name of the first is Pishon; it flows around the whole land of Havilah, where there is gold.
12. The gold of that land is good; the bdellium and the onyx stone are there.
13. The name of the second river is Gihon; it flows around the whole land of Cush.
14. The name of the third river is Tigris; it flows east of Assyria And the fourth river is the Euphrates.

In describing the area of Eden, there are seven proper nouns: Pishon, Havilah, Gihon, Cush, Tigris, Assyria, and Euphrates. The writer seems to have had some specialized knowledge about the land of Havilah; therefore, we can safely assume that this text was written at least after the nation Assyria and two rivers, Tigris and Euphrates, were known to the people of the region.

The most significant expression that makes the readers assume a possible composition date for the texts is "To this day." This expression is found in Genesis 19: 37–38; 26:33; 32:32; 35:19–20; 47:26.

19: 37–38 The firstborn bore a son, and called his name Moab; he is the father of the Moabites to this day. As for the younger, she also bore a son, and called his name Ben-ammi; he is the father of the sons of Ammon to this dy.

These verses are the last part of the story of Sodom. The text itself proves that this story was written at least after the nations Moab and Ammon were established and well known to the Israelites.

26: 33 So he called it Shibah; therefore the name of the city is Beersheba to this day.

Here at least after the city Beersheba was known to the Israelites, this story of Isaac was written in Palestine.

32: 32 Therefore, to this day the sons of Israel do not eat the sinew of the hip which is on the socket of the thigh, because he touched the socket of Jacob's thigh in the sinew of the hip.

This well known story of Jacob was probably written after the nation Israel was settled and its customs institutionalized in tenth-century BC.

35: 19–20 So Rachel died and was buried on the way to Ephrath (that is, Bethlehem). Jacob set up a pillar over her grave; that is the pillar of Rachel's grave to this day.

This story of Rachel's death was written or redacted sometime after Bethlehem was known to the Israelites in Palestine.

47: 26 Joseph made it a statute concerning the land of Egypt valid to this day, that Pharaoh should have the fifth; only the land of the priests did not become Pharaoh's.

We can recognize that this story regarding Joseph was written after the life of Joseph, at least sometime after the Exodus.

In addition, the name for God in Exodus present a clue of a possible date of Genesis. According to Exodus 3:13–15; 6:2–3, the name Yahweh was first known to Moses.[8] Since the name Yahweh was used in Genesis accounts (the LORD [Yahweh] God in Genesis 2 and 3), we can conservatively conclude that Genesis was written sometime after the Exodus.

Therefore, on the basis of Genesis itself, we can comfortably conclude that Genesis was written in Palestine at least some time after the Exodus, most likely sometime after the Davidic Dynasty was institutionalized.

Third, about the intended answers
Answers to questions regarding the nation (In comparison with Eden and the Promised Land)

In this case, Eden represents the Promised Land, and Adam and Eve represent the people of God who were given the Law. The snake might be interpreted as a force that made Israel sin against God. Hosea 6:7 supports this viewpoint: "But like Adam they have transgressed the covenant; There they have dealt treacherously against Me."

The questions this story may have been written to address include:
To whom does the Promised Land belong?
An intended answer might be that it belongs to God because God made Eden and had the authority to evict the people in it.

Why did God promise or give the Promised Land, Canaan, to us?
An intended answer might be that God wanted his people to keep the Law and obey God and to cultivate the given fertile land.

Why were we evicted from the Promised Land?
Framed in the context of the Babylonian Captivity, this might be a natural question. Considering the actual immediate penalty of disobedience was eviction from Eden, an intended answer might be "because we disobeyed God and broke the Law." In this case, death in 2:17 should be interpreted as the death of the nation, destruction of Israel/Judea, eviction from the Promised Land, or the Babylonian Captivity.[9] To see the collective notion of "life" and "death," we need to refer to Deuteronomy 30:

1. "So it shall be when all of these things have come upon you, the blessing and the curse which I have set before you, and you call them to mind in all nations where the LORD your God has banished you,

2. and you return to the LORD your God and obey Him with all your heart and soul according to all that I command you today, you and your sons,

3. then the LORD your God will restore you from captivity, and have compassion on you, and will gather you again from all the peoples where the LORD your God has scattered you.

4. "If your outcasts are at the ends of the earth, from there the LORD your God will gather you, and from there He will bring you back.

5. "The LORD your God will bring you into the land which your fathers possessed, and you shall possess it; and He will prosper you and multiply you more than your fathers

6. "Moreover the LORD your God will circumcise your heart and the heart of your descendants, to love the LORD your God with all your heart and with all your soul, so that you may live

7. "The LORD your God will inflict all these curses on your enemies and on those who hate you, who persecuted you.

8. "And you shall again obey the LORD, and observe all His commandments which I command you today.

9. "Then the LORD your God will prosper you abundantly in all the work of your hand, in the offspring of your body and in the offspring of your cattle and in the produce of your ground, for the LORD will again rejoice over you for good, just as He rejoiced over your fathers;

10. if you obey the LORD your God to keep His commandments and His statutes which are written in this book of the law, if you turn to the LORD your God with all your heart and soul.

11. "For this commandment which I command you today is not too difficult for you, nor is it out of reach.

12. "It is not in heaven, that you should say, 'Who will go up to heaven for us to get it for us and make us hear it, that we may observe it?'

13. "Nor is it beyond the sea, that you should say, 'Who will cross the sea for us to get it for us and make us hear it, that we may observe it?'

14. "But the word is very near you, in your mouth and in your heart, that you may observe it.

15. "See, I have set before you today life and prosperity, and death and adversity;

16. in that I command you today to love the LORD your God, to walk in His ways and to keep His commandments and His statutes and His judgments, that you may live and multiply, and that the LORD your God may bless you in the land where you are entering to possess it.

17. "But if your heart turns away and you will not obey, but are drawn away and worship other gods and serve them,

18. I declare to you today that you shall surely perish. You will not prolong your days in the land where you are crossing the Jordan to enter and possess it.

19. "I call heaven and earth to witness against you today, that I have set before you life and death, the blessing and the curse. So choose life in order that you may live, you and your descendants,

20. by loving the LORD your God, by obeying His voice, and by holding fast to Him; for this is your life and the length of your days, that you may live in the land which the LORD swore to your fathers, to Abraham, Isaac, and Jacob, to give them."

In verses 14 and 19, "life" and "death" unequivocally mean "prosperity of the nation" and "adversity of the nation." If the texts (Genesis 2 and 3) were written in tenth-century BC and redacted in fifth-century BC by an individual or a group who knew the Law well, "death" in 2:17 could, in fact, mean "the end of the nation" or "eviction from the land"; the story of their nation reflected in the story of Eden.

Answers to questions regarding individuals

Why are there male and female in human society?
Because when a male was created first, he felt lonely and needed a partner.

How could a living being get a name?
Because the first man called.

Why does a man leave his father's house to live with his wife?
We can assume that at a time this particular culture was popular in ancient Israel since, in a patriarchal society, usually it is a woman who leaves one's father's house. An intended answer might be that first woman came out of first man.

How does a human being know right and wrong?
Because the first couple did wrong.

Why does a snake crawl on its abdomen on the ground?
Because a snake seduced the first woman and made her sin.

Why does a woman abhor a snake?
Because a snake seduced the first woman and made her sin.

Why does a husband rule over a wife?
Because the first wife made her husband sin.

Why does a woman suffer when she delivers?
Because the first wife sinned and made her husband sin.

Why does a man have to labor in the field?
We can assume that when the text was written, an agricultural society was pretty well established which means the text was written sometime after the nation of Israel was institutionalized and stabilized for agriculture. An intended answer might be "because the first man sinned and thus was evicted from the fertile land."

Why does a human being feel ashamed when naked and needs to wear clothes?
Because the first couple sinned against God and had knowledge regarding human sexuality.

Why does a human being die?

We can assume two possible answers intended by a writer(s), though as I have shown above, these intended answers are not necessarily true. First, a human being dies because the first human being disobeyed God. Second, a human being dies because the first human being was made out of the ground. So, death is natural.

Here none of the answers is objectively or scientifically factual. The writer(s) of the texts simply tried to give answers from their socio-political-cultural-religious perspectives. Is it possible for the reader to accept some answers as true and reject others? In other words, if someone insists that an answer to the question, "Why does a human being die?" is that the first human being disobeyed God is true, must he or she accept all other answers intended by the writer(s) of the texts? At the very least we might say that when Eden was compared to the Promised Land, and the history of Israel/Judea was reflected in the story of Eden, the answers intended for the nation might have been true to them.

For better understanding, we need to study the literary background of the texts of Genesis 2 and 3. The texts in Genesis belong to a larger category of the Pentateuch. Contrary to the traditional view that Moses was the author, modern biblical scholars are generally in agreement that the Pentateuch is in reality a composite work, the product of many hands over a long period of time. Since nobody can know exactly what happened in the process of composition, it is generally understood that it should be judged solely by how well it does its work. The "documentary hypothesis," as a working hypothesis introduced by Julius Wellhausen in its classic form, has proved to be a master key that has opened many interpretive doors and, with each success, the hypothesis has generated more options, more ways of coming to the text.[10]

Wellhausen did not recognize the pre-literary tradition and insisted that the stories of Genesis were generally reflections of life and religion in the period of the Monarchy, which he erroneously projected backward into pre-Mosaic times.[11] Hermann Gunkel, building on Wellhausen's work, saw that the narratives of Genesis were a prose form of earlier poetic traditions.[12] Gunkel designated Genesis as legend rather than history. One of the significant differences between legend and history is that legend is originally oral tradition, while history is usually considered to be recorded in written form. Legends are not lies. They convey a certain fact or truth of life; they are a particular form of poetry. No one calls poetry a lie. Therefore, legends are as much true as poetry and require the readers' recognition to be understood properly. The important point will be the poetic tone of the narratives. History, which claims to inform us of what actually happened, is in its very nature prose; legend is by nature poetry, it aims to please, elevate, inspire, and move. Those who would do justice to such narratives should have some aesthetic faculty to realize what the story is and what it purports to be.[13] In fact, poetic narrative is much better than prose as a medium of religious ideology.[14]

Another distinguishing feature of legend vs. history is each's distinct sphere of interest. History tends to focus on significant public occurrences; legend deals with things that interest the common people, with personal or private matters. Historians do not report minor incidents, while popular legend delights in such details.[15]

The manner in which narratives speak of God is one of the surest means of determining whether they are historical or legendary. Consider the speeches of God in Genesis: God speaks in all respects as one person does to another. We are able to comprehend this as the naïve conception of the human community of old. This argument for the manner of God's speech is immensely strengthened when we compare the narratives considered to be legendary with those identified as strict Israelite history. The particular person-like manner of God's speech in Genesis is not found throughout the Old Testament, but only in certain definite portions of Genesis.[16]

However, Gunkel failed to recognize that much legend is transmitted orally and perceived as history, just as much of history can be seen as a more sophisticated form of legend.[17] These Genesis narratives had already existed for decades, even centuries, before being written down, and they existed, not as legend known and handed on by only a few people, but rather as an element integral to the life, thought, culture, and religious faith of the people of Israel and their forebears. This is the real sense and significance of the terms legend or tradition history or myth, that dominates Genesis research today.[18] We now know that the legends of Genesis had been handed down with extraordinary fidelity for many centuries before they were written down as history, usually in abbreviated form, around the tenth century BC.[19]

In terms of myth, Genesis is divided into two parts:

1. The origin of the world and of the progenitors of the human race, the stories down to the tower of Babel; their locality being remote and their sphere of interest, the whole world.
2. The patriarchs of Israel: Abraham, Isaac, and Jacob, and Jacob's sons, the locality and the sphere of interest being Canaan and adjacent lands.[20]

Likewise, in terms of subject matter, Genesis also breaks into two distinctive and unequal parts: The first contains chapters 1–11; it is restricted to what has come to be known as Primeval History; the second part, chapters 12–50, takes up the Story of the Patriarchs.[21]

Genesis chapters 2 and 3 fall in the Primeval History part. Primeval History is broadly conceived as a preface, a prelude to the particular story with which the rest of the Pentateuch is concerned. Primeval History seeks to give a universal setting for what is to be the early history of one particular people, Israel.[22] The prominence of the action of God in Primitive History indicates a decidedly more "mythical" character than the Story of the Patriarchs.

Christians need to recognize the significance of myths because many myths attempt to answer questions from the perspective of their own time and culture.[24] The texts (Genesis 2 and 3) should be interpreted as myth, not as something that actually happened (history). However, the texts still try to give some answers to some questions and can convey some important theological meanings from the perspective of its author(s). The theological meaning might be that there is a high order all human beings must observe, and when they fail, there must be consequences.

The first eleven chapters of Genesis are the product of a long process of growth, in which the two stages of composition are recognized—both oral tradition and written activity. For the oral tradition, by the explicit references to places in Primeval History, such as the Tigris and Euphrates Rivers and Nimrod's lands and cities, Babylon, Ur, and Haran, we see that Mesopotamia is designated explicitly as the place of origin. Therefore, Primeval History should be interpreted on the basis of its orientation toward Mesopotamia.[25] For the written activity, some scholars believe that Genesis 1–11 is a composite of two written works, the J (Yahwist) source and the P (priestly) source, composed in Palestine. J and P are not authors in our sense of the word, but are primarily collectors who fashioned the traditional materials into a single work, a cohesive Primeval History. They worked not only as collectors, but also as authors and theologians.[26]

Claus Westermann presents this outline of the Primeval History, Genesis 1–11:

1:1–2:4a (P) Creation of the World and Humanity
2:4b–3: 24 (J) Creation of Humanity
4:1–16 (J) Cain and Abel
4: 17–26 (J) Genealogy of Cain's Descendants
5:1–32 (P) Genealogy from Adam to Noah
6:1–4 (J) The Sons of the Gods and the Giants
6:5–9:17 (JP) The Flood
9:18–27 (JP) Noah and His Sons
10:1–32 (JP) The Table of Nations
11:1–9 (J) The Tower of Babel
11:10–26 (P) Genealogy of Shem[27]

According to this presentation, the story of Eden is the work of J. Gunkel recognized J as a school instead of as a single compiler or editor.[28] However,

Ephraim Avigdor Speiser believed that J was a single author because the use of Yahweh remained constant as the hallmark of the document.[29] He highly praises J as a master of art:

J's style is clear and direct, but its simplicity is that of consummate art. J's world, in diametric contrast to P's, is emphatically earth-centered. And his earth is peopled with actors so natural and candid that even their relations with Yahweh are reduced to human scale, so that God himself becomes anthropomorphic. What is truly distinctive about this writer (J) is his inclusive style, his economy and boldness of presentation, his insight into human nature, and the recognition that a higher order and purpose may lie behind seemingly incomprehensible human events. [30]

Speiser thought that a work with such distinctive personal traits could stem only from a single, individual author.

Regarding the date of J, the prevailing tendency today is to put J in the tenth century BC, or about a hundred years earlier.[31] Scholars believe that some sort of political influence is an antecedent presumption to the writing of J.[32] Gale A. Yee expounds on this presumption in terms of the sociopolitical context of the early Israelite monarchy. In the tenth century BC, Solomon undermined tribal organization and kin-group loyalties by cutting across tribal boundaries and forming them into twelve administrative districts, thus redirecting them to the centralized government in Jerusalem.[33] In the interest of the monarchy, according to Yee, the Yahwist (J), through literature, tried to resolve the sociopolitical contradiction of Israel reflected in the regression to a tributary model economic system. Israel had rejected the tributary system two hundred years earlier when it became a tribal confederacy. Genesis 2–3 explains that the current relationship between the king and his people, the tributary economy, has its theological origin in the relationship between the divine and the human at the primordial beginning. Regarding sexuality and gender in the story, Yee argues that, to legitimize royal interests and to justify the current lower status of the peasant in the tributary economy, the story shifts the point of conflict from the public arena of class relations between men to the more private domain of household relations between men and women.[34]

This study clearly states a few principles for interpreting the texts. First, it confirms that the texts cannot be interpreted literally because they are the elaborated poetic prose which had been influenced by Mesopotamian myths and redacted by a Jewish writer from the perspective of monotheism and national ideologies. Second, by this very reasoning the texts should not be interpreted dogmatically. Third, the proper interpretation requires a sense of aesthetics because of the literary genre of the text: poetry, legend, and myth.

These hermeneutical principles provide greater opportunity to come to the text with logic and reason. The real question involved in Primeval History is not whether a statement is true or false, but what it meant to those whose story was being told.[35]

Westermann thought that Genesis chapter 3 was once an independent narrative and later related to chapter 2 by means of traditions regarding the immortality of human beings.[36] Whereas chapter 2 presents the positive aspects of human community, chapter 3 presents its negative aspects. The message of the text, in this case, might be that there is no ideal human community.[37] Speiser agreed with Westermann in terms of the theme of chapter 3. However, he narrowed down the human community to the nation of Israel. He asserted that J built his work around a central theme, which is the record of a central spiritual experience of a nation, the unfaithfulness of Israel. Since a nation is made up of individuals, J had traced the nation's ancestors all the way back in time.

J made use of traditions that had originated in Mesopotamia as he treated Primeval History in Genesis. The motifs in chapter 3—sexual awareness, wisdom, and searching for immortality—are familiar ones to which a variety of ancient sources attend. All three motifs are found jointly in a single passage of the Gilgamesh epic.[38] The essential story of the epic revolves around the relationship between Gilgamesh, a king who has become distracted and disheartened by his rule, and a friend, Enkidu, who is half-wild and who undertakes dangerous quests with Gilgamesh. Much of the epic focuses on Gilgamesh's thoughts of loss following Enkidu's death. In the epic, Enkidu was effectively tempted by the prostitute, only to be repudiated by the world of nature: "But he now had wisdom, broader understanding, 'You are wise Enkidu, you are like a god.'" The prostitute marks his new status by improvising some clothing for him.[39] The epic is often credited by historians as being one of the first literary works with high emphasis on immortality.[40] In the end of the epic, Gilgamesh's search for immortality[41] is favored with a concession: He is permitted to take back with him a magic plant that offers the bread of rejuvenation, but not the boon of immortality. But he soon is robbed of it by a serpent.[42]

Mesopotamia provides another possible tradition for the text: the tale of Adapa.[43] Like "Adam," its cognate in Hebrew, the Akkadian word "Adapa" means "man." Adapa was the first of the seven sages of Eridu, who lived before the flood. These sages talked with the gods, performed their rites, and helped them bring order and civilization to mankind. The story of Adapa begins by saying that Ea (Adapa's god, Enki) disclosed "the broad design of the land" to Adapa, giving him wisdom, but not "eternal life."[44] Even though we have various Mesopotamian traditions for Genesis, the specific source and the precise channel of transmission remain uncertain. In addition, we, as interpreters, cannot know how J himself interpreted the text. Nevertheless, it would be irrational to dismiss as mere coincidence, as some interpreters have done, the significant amount and detail of correspondence between the biblical texts and Mesopotamian traditions.[45]

Summary

Paul tried to utilize Genesis 2 and 3 to make a point that everyone needs Jesus to be saved from sin and death. His argument assumed that everyone dies because of Adam's sin. However, since the notion of evangelism (personal decision to accept Jesus) contradicted that assumption, his effort to present Jesus as the second Adam failed. This failure of logic paradoxically detaches the natural death of human beings from the Sin of Adam. Since we cannot find any legitimate basis for Original Sin and Total Depravity from Paul's use of Genesis 2 and 3, we examined the texts themselves to see if there is any exegetical indication that can elicit Original Sin and Total Depravity. The exegetical study confirms some facts regarding those texts. Genesis 2 and 3 cannot be interpreted literally since the texts were myth, tradition, or legend history strongly related to Mesopotamian traditions. What those texts meant to its contemporary audience should be a major concern of interpretation. Death in the texts should be understood based upon Deuteronomy 30 which shares the same context of land, law, and expulsion and was written by someone or a group who knew the Law well. Death in Genesis 2:16–17, when understood based upon Deuteronomy 30:1, 15, 18, 19, is seen as the curse on and adversity for the nation, expulsion from the Promised Land, the end of the nation, or the Babylonian captivity. Death in Genesis 3:19 should be understood as the natural death of the living being.

For Paul, utilizing Genesis 2 and 3, death of the human beings, becomes the major concern in relation to the saving power of Jesus Christ.

In talking about death, we need to consider four kinds of death: the death of a nation by divine judgment, the natural death (extinction) of a nation, the death of a human being by judgment, and the natural death of the human beings. In the Bible, the death of a nation and the death of a human being by judgment are certainly related to sin. When the nation Israel/Judea was judged by God as a sinful nation, God destroyed them through conquest by Assyria and Babylon, the death of a nation. When an individual committed a crime against the laws and was judged to death, his or her death should be considered as a result of a sin. For example, Exodus 31:15 says "'For six days work may be done, but on the seventh day there is a Sabbath of complete rest, holy to the LORD; whoever does any work on the Sabbath day shall surely be put to death." If anyone violated this Sabbath law and was judged to death by God or the legitimate authority, it might be said that he or she died because of a sin. Therefore, death resulting from sin must mean judged death, not natural death.

Paul believes that Jesus died for the sin of His people through his execution at the hand of Rome. Following the relationship of sin and death presented above, if Jesus died by a natural cause or an accident, his death would have nothing to do with sin. Therefore, when it is said that Jesus died for the sin of His people, his death must be a judged death for those who, otherwise, would be judged to death by God. Since he died for His people, all members of His kingdom must be beneficiaries of His death. In this context, the death of the nation is the best analogy for the redemptive death of Jesus because not all individual Christians are judged to death by God.[46] With logic and reason, it should be said that Jesus was judged to death for the sin of His nation—the Christian Church, which, through his sacrifice was preserved eternally from the destruction judged by God. Unlike the death of a nation or a human being by judgment, the natural death of a nation and that of human beings cannot be considered the result of the sin committed or the sin transmitted from Adam of Genesis 2 and 3. Sometimes a nation is naturally dissolved. We cannot say that all destructed or dissolved nations were judged by God. Likewise, the natural death of the human being has nothing to do with sin. It is simply the final chapter of life. When someone dies at the age of one hundred, we hardly say that he or she died because of a sin. Also, death does not always convey a negative notion. We know that a few people wish for death because to them the quality of human life means more than life itself. And we should remember that the long life of an individual human being is considered as a blessing in the Old Testament, even in the Messianic passages like Isaiah 65:17–25. This text does not describe a natural death as a curse or a result of a sin and likewise does not promise an immortal human life as a promised blessing:

17. "For behold, I create new heavens and a new earth; And the former things will not be remembered or come to mind.

18. "But be glad and rejoice forever in what I create; For behold, I create Jerusalem for rejoicing And her people for gladness.

19. "I will also rejoice in Jerusalem and be glad in My people; And there will no longer be heard in her the voice of weeping and the sound of crying.

20. "No longer will there be in it an infant who lives but a few days, or an old man who does not live out his days; For the youth will die at the age of one hundred And the one who does not reach the age of one hundred will be thought accursed.

21. "They will build houses and inhabit them; They will also plant vineyards and eat their fruit.

22. "They will not build and another inhabit, They will not plant and another eat; For as the lifetime of a tree, so will be the days of My people, And My chosen ones will wear out the work of their hands.

23. "They will not labor in vain, or bear children for calamity; For they are the offspring of those blessed by the LORD, And their descendants with them.

24. "It will also come to pass that before they call, I will answer; and while they are still speaking, I will hear.

25. "The wolf and the lamb will graze together, and the lion will eat straw like the ox; and dust will be the serpent's food They will do no evil or harm in all My holy mountain," says the LORD.

Genesis 2 and 3 might be interpreted in connection with the death of the nation but they do not explain a cause of the unavoidable natural death of the human being. All human beings do not die because of the sin of Adam. On the contrary, in the process of universalizing Christianity, because all human beings die, all human beings became sinners.

Paul used not only the Genesis accounts, but also natural law and general revelation to expand the sin of Judea to include the entire world (the sin of the world). I will examine the difference between natural law and Jewish Law to prove the incompatibility of both and the illogicality of utilizing general revelation. I argue, therefore, that the sin of Judea should not be expanded to the sin of the world or to include all human society.

B. Utilizing Natural Law and General Revelation

Criticism on Utilizing Natural Law:
Romans 2:11–15

A sin can be defined as breaking or violating a given law of a particular society, whether that law is a written or unwritten one. When someone is called a sinner, therefore, there must be a process to determine whether he or she is guilty according to a law. The Jewish Law was the revealed and written law, bound to Jewish society through a special covenant between God, as the legislator and judge, and the Jewish people, as the observers with particular interest in covenantal punishment. When a Jew was called a sinner, therefore, he or she was guilty according to judgment of God or the judicial authority of the Jewish society. By contrast, natural law means the law believed to be naturally implanted into all human beings, an unwritten law in its nature with no binding written covenant between the legislative body and the humans. According to natural law, it is virtually impossible to call someone a sinner because judgment is arbitrary and ambiguous because there are no objective criteria upon which to base judgment. Positive law means a human-made law based upon the universal human conscience (probably natural law) and a particular situation or circumstances of a given society. There are, in general, legislative and judicial bodies authorized by a society which judges a citizen of that society accordingly. In this sense, if God as the Law-giver is not considered, Jewish law can be called a positive law.

The point I want to make in this section is this: Even though all Jewish people are judged as sinners because they fall short of adhering to Jewish Law, it does not follow that all human beings are sinners according to natural law. Each law has its own domain of jurisdiction and (written or unwritten) criteria for judgment. Especially when covenantal punishment is concerned, these laws and, accordingly, sinners, must be distinguished from one another, because covenantal punishment as a part of the Jewish Law is only related to the sinners who break or violate Jewish Law, not natural law. However, by assuming that all Jews are sinners because they cannot observe Jewish Law perfectly, Paul infers that all human beings are sinners, too, because they cannot observe the natural law perfectly and, therefore, are subject to divine judgment. All human beings may fail in their adherence to natural law, or their conscience, but they do not break or violate the Jewish Law. In other words, they cannot be subject to the divine judgment imposed upon the Jews because they were never part of the covenant with God. Through Paul's utilizing of natural law, the sin of Judea became the sin of the world and therefore, by becoming the sinners of the world, all human beings became subject to the final destruction.

I will try to prove incompatibility of both laws and, show accordingly, that sinners according to natural law are different from sinners according to Jewish Law. I hope to prove thereby that the sin of the world is different from the sin of Judea and is immune to covenantal punishment.
Let us read the relevant text:

Romans 2:11–15
11. For there is no partiality with God.
12. For all who have sinned without the Law will also perish without the Law, and all who have sinned under the Law will be judged by the Law;
13. for it is not the hearers of the Law who are just before God, but the doers of the Law will be justified.
14. For when Gentiles who do not have the Law do instinctively the things of the Law, these, not having the Law, are a law to themselves,
15. in that they show the work of the Law written in their hearts, their conscience bearing witness and their thoughts alternately accusing or else defending them

In the text, Paul does not say explicitly that the Jewish Law and natural law are the same; however, he assumes that God is the legislator and judge for both laws (verses 11 and 12). Verse 12a is complemented by verses 14 and 15; therefore, both the Jews and the Gentiles have the law. According to verse 13 and presumed by the immediate context 3:9, 20, 23, it is implied that all Jews are sinners because they cannot practice the Jewish Law perfectly and all Gentiles are sinners, too, because they cannot practice their conscience (natural law) perfectly. The implication for the Jews is reinforced by his following observation on the Jews (Romans 2:17–29) and the implication for the Gentiles is reinforced by his previous observation on the Gentiles (or Greeks) (Romans 1:18–32). And all together support Paul's conclusion that all human beings are under sin (Romans 3:9) and have sinned (Romans 3:23).

The structure of Paul's argument to understand all human beings as sinners is analyzed as follows:

Conclusive statement:	**"All have sinned"**	**(3:23)**
Supporting proofs:	People under the Law	(3:19–20)
	Quoted the O.T. Psalm 14 or 53	(3:10–18)
Sub-conclusion	**"All under sin"**	**(3:9)**
Supporting proofs:	Paul's observation on Jews	(2:17–29)
	Justice of God	(2:1–16)
	Paul's observation on Gentiles (or Greeks)[47]	(1:18–32)

Paul states his sub-conclusion, that all are under sin, in the following verses: that the Gentiles (or Greeks) are sinners (Rom.1:18–32); that both the Jews and the Gentiles are sinners by the justice of God which employs natural law (Rom. 2:1–16); and that Jews are sinners (Rom. 2:17–29).

The text belongs to the section "Justice of God" Since all supporting proofs are used to elicit Paul's conclusion that all human beings are sinners, "Justice of God" including the notion of the natural law implies that all Jews and Gentiles must be the sinners because God is God of justice. By this argument in the text, Jewish Law is implicitly identified with natural law. Visualization of this identification will be helpful:

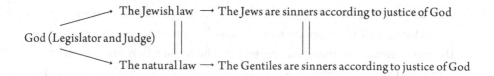

By implicitly identifying Jewish Law with natural law, the sin of Judea became the sin of the world. This identification is reinforced in this text:

Romans 3:29–30

29. Or is God the God of Jews only? Is He not the God of Gentiles also? Yes, of Gentiles also,

30. since indeed God who will justify the circumcised by faith and the uncircumcised through faith is one.

Here, Jews and Gentiles are co-mingled implicitly using God as the common denominator, because, according to Paul, God is of both the Jews and the Gentiles. Historically and spiritually, however, the Jews are distinguished from the Gentiles through the covenantal entity; likewise, Jewish Law is distinct from natural law. To understand how this implied linkage is incorrect, and that the sin of the Jews and the Gentiles are incompatible, and, therefore, the covenantal judgment cannot be applied to the world, we need to first understand the incompatibility of the two laws.

The initial question regarding the text is this: Is the proposition of verse 2:12 true? Is the premise dividing the human beings into two groups, one without the law and the other with the law, or the Gentiles and the Jews, reasonable? Can the law and conscience, or natural law, be compared? Since all human beings are naturally bound to conscience, with law added on to a certain society or group of the people, conscience and law should be complementary, not comparable. Those who have the law also have conscience. It would be irrational to say that the law given to the Jews eliminated or replaced their consciences. Those who have the law should be judged by both the law and conscience. Verse 2:12 reveals, therefore, the incompatibility of the propositions.

Second, as stated above, Jewish Law was bound by the special covenant between God, as legislator and judge, and the Jewish people, as the observers. Natural law has no such expressed relationship between God and humankind. Exodus chapter 19 to 24 states the details of the covenant; let us read verses 24:1–10:

1. Then He said to Moses, "Come up to the LORD, you and Aaron, Nadab and Abihu and seventy of the elders of Israel, and you shall worship at a distance.
2. "Moses alone, however, shall come near to the LORD, but they shall not come near, nor shall the people come up with him."
3. Then Moses came and recounted to the people all the words of the LORD and all the ordinances; and all the people answered with one voice and said, "All the words which the LORD has spoken we will do!"
4. Moses wrote down all the words of the LORD. Then he arose early in the morning, and built an altar at the foot of the mountain with twelve pillars for the twelve tribes of Israel.
5. He sent young men of the sons of Israel, and they offered burnt offerings and sacrificed young bulls as peace offerings to the LORD.
6. Moses took half of the blood and put it in basins, and the other half of the blood he sprinkled on the altar.
7. Then he took the book of the covenant and read it in the hearing of the people; and they said, "All that the LORD has spoken we will do, and we will be obedient!"
8. So Moses took the blood and sprinkled it on the people, and said, "Behold the blood of the covenant, which the LORD has made with you in accordance with all these words."
9. Then Moses went up with Aaron, Nadab and Abihu, and seventy of the elders of Israel,
10. and they saw the God of Israel; and under His feet there appeared to be a pavement of sapphire, as clear as the sky itself.

Even though, as Paul implies, we assume God as the legislator and judge of natural law, when did God summon all human beings or representatives of the humans and made such a covenant between them? Also, even though we assume that there is a law implanted on the hearts of every human being, how do we know that these laws, natural law or consciences, are identical for all people, as are the laws stated in the book of the covenant (verse 7)? Without any proof of the covenant between God and all human beings, and with a lack of objective criteria for judgment, the natural law should not be compared or identified with Jewish Law.

Third, the nature of each law is different. The core of the Jewish Law is doubtlessly the Ten Commandments (Exodus chapter 20). Let us think about the forth commandment to see how Jewish Law differs from natural law. Exodus 20: 8–11 says:

"Remember the Sabbath day, to keep it holy. Six days you shall labor and do all your work, but the seventh day is a Sabbath of the LORD your God; in it you shall not do any work, you or your son or your daughter, your male or your female servant or your cattle or your sojourner who stays with you. For in six days the LORD made the heavens and the earth, the sea and all that is in them, and rested on the seventh day; therefore, the LORD blessed the Sabbath day and made it holy."

Does natural law teach the human beings about the law of Sabbath? Does anyone's conscience say anything about observing Sabbath? If anyone breaks or violates the law of Sabbath, is he or she considered a sinner? We know of no nation besides Israel or Judea which was condemned by God or a prophet for breaking the Sabbath. Even to the people of Israel, this law was unique and bound to the covenant.

Let us think about the time before and after the covenant to clarify the nature of the Jewish law requiring the specially designed sacrifice for forgiveness and redemption. Could the people of Israel break the forth commandment before the covenant was made? Of course, they could not break it and be punished, because there was no law regarding the Sabbath before the covenant with God at Mount Sinai. However, after the covenant, the punishment for violating the law of Sabbath was severe. Exodus 31:15 says: "For six days work may be done, but on the seventh day there is a Sabbath of complete rest, holy to the LORD; whoever does any work on the Sabbath day shall surely be put to death." Even though there is no biblical account to support this thesis, doubtless Israel did not keep Sabbath in Egypt. As Egyptian slaves, they could not even dream of such a day of rest. They might work every day, yet, nobody was stoned due to breaking the Sabbath. The law regarding the Sabbath was apparently constituted and executed after the covenant was made.

How about the third commandment? Exodus 20:7 says: "You shall not take the name of the LORD your God in vain, for the LORD will not leave him unpunished who takes His name in vain." Does natural law teach the name of God? Was there any nation besides Israel or Judea condemned by God or a prophet because she broke the third commandment? Even in the Bible, God revealed the name Yahweh first to Moses (Exodus 3:13–15; 6:3). How could the people of Israel break the third commandment when they did not know the name of God?

Unlike the third and fourth commandments, the fifth commandment, "You shall not murder," (Exodus 20:13) seems to fit with natural law. Was or is there a human society or culture that does not count murder as a sin? A murder has been considered a sin or crime in any ordered society or culture because otherwise society could not continue. Certainly, murder had been considered a sin to the people of Israel even before the covenant was made. The fifth through tenth commandments seem to fit into natural law because they are applicable to any human society that requires order, while the first to forth commandments seem unique as the Jewish Law because they relate particularly to the relationship between God and the people of Israel.

The inevitable conclusion must be that natural law and the Jewish Law are not the same; however, a certain scope of each law overlaps. The following diagram visualizes distinction between both laws:

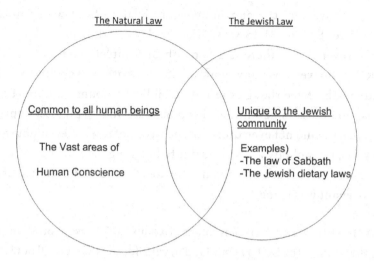

The Natural Law — The Jewish Law

Common to all human beings

The Vast areas of

Human Conscience

Unique to the Jewish community

Examples)
-The law of Sabbath
-The Jewish dietary laws

The overlapped area would be the fifth through tenth commandments and some general ethical laws which could be attributed to the human conscience.

As a conclusion, Jewish Law and natural law should not be confused as the same thing. However, through Paul's utilizing natural law in conjunction with the notion of justice, Jewish Law was identified with natural law implicitly and, as a result, the sin of Judea was expanded to the sin of the world.

Further, even though Paul did not utilize the Roman law for his argument and the Jews described the Gentiles as "the people without the law" (Romans 2:14; Acts 2:23 (ἄνομος)), Roman law existed as a positive, or man-made, law.

Was not Jesus crucified according to the Roman law? Paul himself was rescued from the Jewish accusation by appealing to the Roman law: Paul said, "I am standing before Caesar's tribunal, where I ought to be tried. I have done no wrong to the Jews, as you also very well know. If, then, I am a wrongdoer and have committed anything worthy of death, I do not refuse to die; but if none of those things is true of which these men accuse me, no one can hand me over to them. I appeal to Caesar" (Acts

25:10–11). The trials of Jesus and Paul described in the New Testament reveal that there was conflict between Jewish Law and the Roman law: From the perspective of the Jews, Jesus and Paul deserved to die according to the Jewish Law; however, from the perspective of Roman law, Jesus and Paul were sinless. From Paul's perspective, the Gentiles were those under Greek culture and Roman rule. Therefore, we should acknowledge that Paul's Gentiles, even though they were described as Greeks, were bound to the Roman laws. In fact, Jewish Law was a revealed law and Roman law was a positive law. In Paul's time, not only Romans, but Chinese, Indians, Persians, and German tribes had a positive law with its own unique scope of legal jurisdiction. But a positive law, bound to a particular period of a society and requiring socially and culturally defined justice, should be distinguished from Jewish Law which was bound to the special Covenant. So that even though all Jews were sinners according to Jewish Law and therefore subject to divine judgment, people of a given society, while subject to their own laws, are not sinners subject to divine judgment.

In Paul's time, therefore, Jewish Law and the Roman law should be distinguished, just as Jewish Law is distinguished from natural law. Similarly, a certain scope of the Roman law overlapped Jewish Law, as seen in the following diagram:

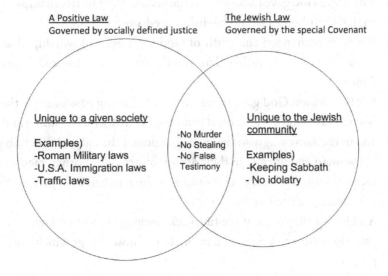

A Positive Law
Governed by socially defined justice

The Jewish Law
Governed by the special Covenant

Unique to a given society

Examples)
-Roman Military laws
-U.S.A. Immigration laws
-Traffic laws

-No Murder
-No Stealing
-No False
Testimony

Unique to the Jewish community

Examples)
-Keeping Sabbath
- No idolatry

Criticism on Utilizing General Revelation: Romans 1:18–32

Along with natural law, Paul utilizes general revelation to elicit his conclusion that all human beings are sinners. Let us look at the relevant text:

Romans 1:18–32

18. For the wrath of God is revealed from heaven against all ungodliness and unrighteousness of men who suppress the truth in unrighteousness,

19. because that which is known about God is evident within them; for God made it evident to them.

20. For since the creation of the world His invisible attributes, His eternal power and divine nature, have been clearly seen, being understood through what has been made, so that they are without excuse.

21. For even though they knew God, they did not honor Him as God or give thanks, but they became futile in their speculations, and their foolish heart was darkened.

22. Professing to be wise, they became fools,

23. and exchanged the glory of the incorruptible God for an image in the form of corruptible man and of birds and four-footed animals and crawling creatures.

24. Therefore God gave them over in the lusts of their hearts to impurity, so that their bodies would be dishonored among them.

25. For they exchanged the truth of God for a lie, and worshiped and served the creature rather than the Creator, who is blessed forever. Amen.

26. For this reason God gave them over to degrading passions; for their women exchanged the natural function for that which is unnatural,

27. and in the same way also the men abandoned the natural function of the woman and burned in their desire toward one another, men with men committing indecent acts and receiving in their own persons the due penalty of their error.

28. And just as they did not see fit to acknowledge God any longer, God gave them over to a depraved mind, to do those things which are not proper,

29. being filled with all unrighteousness, wickedness, greed, evil; full of envy, murder, strife, deceit, malice; they are gossips,

30. slanderers, haters of God, insolent, arrogant, boastful, inventors of evil, disobedient to parents,

31. without understanding, untrustworthy, unloving, unmerciful;

32. and although they know the ordinance of God, that those who practice such things are worthy of death, they not only do the same, but also give hearty approval to those who practice them.

The text is Paul's observation of the Gentiles (or Greeks) which he used as a supporting proof to his conclusion that all human beings are sinners. The basis of his observation is "general revelation," that God reveals the existence and universal aspects of God by means of general or encompassing ways such as nature or history, as opposed to specific and direct words or actions, referred to as "special revelation."

The problem is not general revelation itself but rather Paul's assumption that the Gentiles had it: that which is known about God is evident within them (verse 19); so that they are without excuse (verse 20) for they knew God (verse 21) and they know the ordinance of God (verse 32). Is this assumption true?

Just as in the case of natural law, the initial question is this: If this assumption is true, why did God reveal God's self and give the Law to the people of Israel? Weren't the people of Israel human beings? Were they not able to know of God through general revelation like the Gentiles? Why did God reveal God's self to Abraham and Moses? Why did God give the Ten Commandments to the people of Israel at Mount Sinai?

Further, the Old Testament testifies that even those who had special revelation forgot and sinned against God so that God had to send prophets to remind them of things which had been given through special revelation. If so, what would be the basis of this assumption that the Gentiles must know of God through general revelation?

Finally, why did or does the gospel have to be preached? Why do the people need to know of God and the kingdom of God through Jesus? Paul could simply remind the Gentiles of the things known through general revelation and encourage them to live up to the laws they already had on their hearts.

I receive general revelation because I know of God through Jesus and the Bible. Paul's experience of general revelation is manifested in the Old Testament, Jesus, and his direct spiritual experiences. We might say that Socrates, Plato, and Aristotle knew of God through general revelation. It will involve complicated philosophical arguments to know the existence and nature of God through general revelation because there are things that oppose the existence and goodness of God such as evil, pains, disorder, and chaos, along with things that support it. Even though it is clear to me, I cannot say that you must know because I know.

Paul's assumption regarding general revelation—that the Gentiles know the existence of God as well as God's invisible attributes and His eternal power and divine nature—is illogical. Therefore, his assumption cannot be the basis for the wrath of God toward the Gentiles (verses 18 and 19). However, through Paul's interpretation of general revelation, the Gentiles became sinners and, as a result, the sin of Judea was expanded to the win of the world.

Along with utilizing Genesis chapter 2 & 3 (Original Sin), natural law, and the general revelation, the sin of Judea became the sin of the world through Paul's use of universal expressions ("all" and "world").

C. Adopting the Universal Expressions: "World" and "All"

In the New Testament, often, the world of Judea is expressed simply as "world." And all people of Judea, simply "everyone." John 12:19 presents a good example: "So the Pharisees said to one another, 'You see that you are not doing any good; look, the world has gone after Him'"? Just before this, John 12:12–13 says, "On the next day the large crowd who had come to the feast, when they heard that Jesus was coming to Jerusalem, took the branches of the palm trees and went out to meet Him, and began to shout, 'Hosanna! Blessed is he who comes in the name of the Lord, even the King of Israel.'" Is the large crowd who greeted Jesus in Jerusalem on the Palm Sunday "the world"? No. Here "the world" must be restricted to "the Jewish world."

This kind of universal expression is found many times in the Old Testament. There, the world often means the world of the writer's vicinity, Palestine or Mesopotamia or the Middle East. I would like to present some examples. Genesis 41:56–57 says, "When the famine was spread over all the face of the earth (כָל־פְּנֵי הָאָרֶץ), then Joseph opened all the storehouses, and sold to the Egyptians; and the famine was severe in the land of Egypt. The people of all the earth (וְכָל־הָאָרֶץ) came to Egypt to buy grain from Joseph, because the famine was severe in all the earth." Even though we don't have any written report about the famine that the family of Jacob experienced, it would be exceedingly unreasonable to believe that all earth actually experienced the same severe famine and the people of all the earth actually came to Egypt to buy grain from Joseph. I don't think the Chinese, the Mongolians, the Germanic people, the Native Americans came to Egypt to buy grain. Isn't this a rhetorical expression used to make a point about the seriousness and significance of the event? It is reasonable to believe the famine was limited to the vicinity of Egypt. 1 Chronicles 29:30 says "Now the acts of King David, from first to last, are written in the chronicles of Samuel the seer, in the chronicles of Nathan the prophet, and in the chronicles of Gad the seer, with all his reign, his power, and the circumstances which came on him, on Israel, and on all the kingdoms of the lands (כָּל־מַמְלְכוֹת הָאֲרָצוֹת). Here, "all the kingdoms of the lands" should mean the near nations of ancient Israel. Jeremiah 50:23 says, "How the hammer of the whole earth (כָּל־הָאָרֶץ) has been cut off and broken! How Babylon has become an object of horror among the nations!" Here again, "the whole earth" should mean the nations which were conquered by the Babylonian empire.

Of course some universal expressions related to Creation should be understood literally; such as in Psalm 57:5 "Be exalted above the heavens, O God; Let Your glory be above all the earth (הָאָרֶץ כָּל־)"; in Psalm 89:11 "The heavens are Yours, the earth also is Yours; The world and all (וּמְלֹאָהּ לְתֵב) it contains, You have founded them."

Even though universal expressions sometimes literally meant the world and all of its inhabitants; the world and all people therein were in God's mind; and the New Testament and its proclamation, certainly, were aimed for the world, universal expressions applied to Judea or Church should be interpreted rhetorically. The readers of the Bible should distinguish one from the other in order to understand the meaning of a text correctly. I think, however, failing to distinguish between rhetorical universal expressions and literal universal expressions has been a cause of ambiguity and equivocalness in Christian theology.

Writers of the New Testament, by means of adopting universal expressions, intentionally or unintentionally caused Judea to become synonymous with the world. Universal expressions played a significant role in all steps of universalizing Christianity: making the sin of the Judea the sin of the world, the Judgment on Judea the Judgment on the world, and the only savior of Judea the only savior of the world. Here, let us first consider how these universal expressions played a significant role in making the sin of Judea the sin of the world.[48]

John 1:29 says: "The next day he saw Jesus coming to him and said, 'Behold, the Lamb of God who takes away the sin of the world (κόσμου)!'" Here "world" should be interpreted rhetorically as Judea or the people of God; the author utilized this universal expression to emphasize the wholeness of their nation.

Again Matthew 1:21 clarifies the domain of Jesus's redemption: "She will bear a Son; and you shall call His name Jesus, for He will save His people from their sins." Jesus came to Judea to save His people from their sins as the Promised Messiah, as the Lamb of the Passover.

Who are His people? During his ministry, when he called the Twelve Disciples, the Jews who believed and followed would be identified as His people. Later when the Good News was preached to the Gentiles, Christians, the people of Church, would be identified as His people. John's term "Lamb of God" confines the domain of Jesus's redemption to the Jews. Called either the Lamb of the Passover or the Scapegoat of Yom Kipper[49], the Lamb or Goat was killed for the people of God. John the Baptist's audience were Jews who had the context for redemption. Therefore John 1:29 could be rewritten this way: "The next day he saw Jesus coming to him and said, 'Behold, the Lamb of God who takes away the sin of Judea.'" Confusion might have arisen because it seems that the term "world" was used elsewhere in the same chapter to denote the literal world:

9. There was the true Light which, coming into the world (κόσμῳ), enlightens every (πάντα) man.
10. He was in the world, and the world was made through Him, and the world did not know Him.
11. He came to His own, and those who were His own did not receive Him.
12. But as many as received Him, to them He gave the right to become children of God, even to those who believe in His name,
13. who were born, not of blood nor of the will of the flesh nor of the will of man, but of God.

The term "world" in verse 9 and 10 sounds as if it means the literal world and every human being in it. However, the scope of the world and every man are redefined in verses 11 to 13.
Let us analyze the text:

	Domain	People
9.	coming into the world	every man
10.	was in the world	the world (did not know Him)
	the world (was made through Him)	
11.	came to His own	those who were His own

12.   as many as received Him
                                 children of God
                                 those who believe in his name
13.   who were born
                                 not of blood
                                 nor of the will of the flesh
                                 nor of the will of man
                                 but of God

The world in verse 9 seems like the literal world. That notion is reinforced, "the world was made through Him," in verse 10. However, that notion is immediately challenged by the following phase "the world did not know Him." The world that did not know Jesus was the Jewish world, not the whole world in a literal sense. The other world besides the Jewish world never had a chance to know Jesus. Also, Isaiah 43:1 and 15 declare that God is the creator of the nation Israel: "But now, thus says the LORD, your Creator, O Jacob, And He who formed you, O Israel, 'Do not fear, for I have redeemed you; I have called you by name; you are Mine!'" and "I am the LORD, your Holy One, The Creator of Israel, your King." Isaiah 41:20 even declares that the restored new Israel would be the creation of God: "That they may see and recognize, And consider and gain insight as well, That the hand of the LORD has done this, And the Holy One of Israel has created it." Creation does not always mean the universe and nature. It means a nation, too. Therefore, even though the world in "the world was made through Him" in verse 10 is interpreted as the nation Judea, nothing is wrong. Since Jesus was already identified with God as the Word in verses 1 to 3[50], not only Jesus created the Universe, the whole world, but also created the nation Israel/Judea. This narrowed notion of the world becomes clearer in verse 11: "He came to His own, and those who were His own did not receive Him." The world becomes His own nation, Judea, and the people of the world become His own people, the Jews. In verses 12 and 13, His own nation and people are replaced by the Church and Christians.

In this context, the text can be paraphrased in this way:

9. There was the true Light which, coming into Judea, enlightens every Jew.
10. He was in Judea, and Judea was made through Him, and the Jews did not know Him.
11. He came to His own nation, and those Jews who were His own did not receive Him.
12. But as many as received Him, to them He gave the right to become children of God, even to those who believe in His name,
13. who were born, not of blood nor of the will of the flesh nor of the will of man, but of God.

Therefore, it is useful and vindicated to rewrite John 1:29: "The next day he saw Jesus coming to him and said, 'Behold, the Lamb of God who takes away the sin of Judea.'"

However, as stated in John 1:12–13, the door to become children of God is open widely through Jesus. In this sense, it can be said that Jesus came to the earth for the sin of the world; but not to take away the sin of the whole world because only the sin of those who believe would be taken away. The critical step must be considered: a person needs first to believe in Jesus and accordingly accept His kingship. Once he or she is claimed as His own, a member of His nation, he or she will benefit from the atonement and redemption in the collective sense. The Lamb of God does not take away the sin of the world without discerning His own.

Let us look at the famous verse beloved by all Christians: John 3:16 "For God so loved the world, that He gave His only begotten Son, that whoever believes in Him shall not perish, but have eternal life."

This verse does not say anything about the sin of the world explicitly. However, the "that" clauses imply the sin of the world: Because the world is under sin, God gave His only begotten Son out of God's love for the world. Initially God's love for the world was the reason God planned to set up the holy kingdom on this earth. However, doesn't the Old Testament exclusively express God's love toward Israel, Jerusalem, and His people? Hosea 11:1 says "When Israel was a youth I loved him, and out of Egypt I called My son." It is important to note the connection between love and God's son, Israel, and that "son" is identified as Jesus in Matthew 2:15. Further, we need to consider Isaiah chapters 40 to 66. Isn't that ardent hope of God for the restored Israel in those chapters "love"? Didn't God so love Judea, Jerusalem, and His people, that "He gave His only begotten Son, that whoever believes in Him shall not perish, but have eternal life? Who were waiting for the promised Messiah? The Jews. To them, when the Messiah they were longing for turned out to be the only begotten Son of God, wasn't that the full expression of God's love?

Let us read some passages from the Old Testament to have a sense regarding God's love toward His people:

Deuteronomy 4:37
"Because He loved your fathers, therefore He chose their descendants after them And He personally brought you from Egypt by His great power,

Deuteronomy 7:8
but because the LORD loved you and kept the oath which He swore to your forefathers, the LORD brought you out by a mighty hand and redeemed you from the house of slavery, from the hand of Pharaoh king of Egypt.

Deuteronomy 10:15
"Yet on your fathers did the LORD set His affection to love them, and He chose their descendants after them, even you above all peoples, as it is this day.

Deuteronomy 23: 5
"Nevertheless, the LORD your God was not willing to listen to Balaam, but the LORD your God turned the curse into a blessing for you because the LORD your God loves you.

Deuteronomy 33:3
"Indeed, He loves the people; All Your holy ones are in Your hand, And they followed in Your steps; Everyone receives of Your words.

Jeremiah 31:20
"Is Ephraim My dear son? Is he a delightful child? Indeed, as often as I have spoken against him, I certainly still remember him; Therefore, My heart yearns for him; I will surely have mercy on him," declares the LORD.

Ezekiel 16:8
"Then I passed by you and saw you, and behold, you were at the time for love; so, I spread My skirt over you and covered your nakedness. I also swore to you and entered into a covenant with you so that you became Mine," declares the Lord GOD.

Zephaniah 3:17
"The LORD your God is in your midst, A victorious warrior He will exult over you with joy, He will be quiet in His love, He will rejoice over you with shouts of joy.

1 King 10:9
"Blessed be the LORD your God who delighted in you to set you on the throne of Israel; because the LORD loved Israel forever, therefore He made you king, to do justice and righteousness."

2 Chronicle 9:8
"Blessed be the LORD your God who delighted in you, setting you on His throne as king for the LORD your God; because your God loved Israel establishing them forever, therefore He made you king over them, to do justice and righteousness."

Psalm 47: 4
He chooses our inheritance for us, the glory of Jacob whom He loves. Selah.

Malachi 1: 2

"I have loved you," says the LORD But you say, "How have You loved us?" "Was not Esau Jacob's brother?" declares the LORD "Yet I have loved Jacob;"

When we consider the context of the verse, the argument becomes clearer. Let us read John 3:10–22:

10. Jesus answered and said to him, "Are you the teacher of Israel and do not understand these things?
11. "Truly, truly, I say to you, we speak of what we know and testify of what we have seen, and you do not accept our testimony.
12. "If I told you earthly things and you do not believe, how will you believe if I tell you heavenly things?
13. "No one has ascended into heaven, but He who descended from heaven: the Son of Man.
14. "As Moses lifted up the serpent in the wilderness, even so must the Son of Man be lifted up;
15. so that whoever believes will in Him have eternal life.
16. "For God so loved the world (κόσμον), that He gave His only begotten Son, that whoever believes in Him shall not perish, but have eternal life.
17. "For God did not send the Son into the world to judge the world, but that the world might be saved through Him.
18. "He who believes in Him is not judged; he who does not believe has been judged already, because he has not believed in the name of the only begotten Son of God.
19. "This is the judgment, that the Light has come into the world, and men loved the darkness rather than the Light, for their deeds were evil.
20. "For everyone who does evil hates the Light, and does not come to the Light for fear that his deeds will be exposed.
21. "But he who practices the truth comes to the Light, so that his deeds may be manifested as having been wrought in God."

22. After these things Jesus and His disciples came into the land of Judea,
and there He was spending time with them and baptizing.

In the text, Jesus was having a conversation with Nicodemus. Who was
Nicodemus? John 3:1 says that he was a man of the Pharisees and a ruler
of the Jews.[51] Jesus identifies him as the teacher of Israel. Therefore, the
most fundamental information about Nicodemus is that he knew very
well about Jewish Law and tradition. Not just knowledge, we can fairly
say that he has devoted his whole life to preserve and promote Jewish
Law and tradition. Let us hear what Jesus said from the perspective of
Nicodemus. When Nicodemus heard the word "world" from Jesus, he
would have interpreted that word as "Judea." Jesus himself limits the scope
of the conversation to the tradition of the Jews: Verse 11. "Truly, truly, I
say to you, we speak of what we know and testify of what we have seen,
and you do not accept our testimony." Here "we" at least includes Jesus
and His disciples and may include the Jews. Either way, Jesus speaks in the
Jewish tradition. Also, Jesus compares His death with the lifted serpent:
Verse 14. "As Moses lifted up the serpent in the wilderness, even so must
the Son of Man be lifted up." Who were saved by looking up to the lifted
serpent?[52] In Deuteronomy 21:8–9, some people of Israel who looked up
to the serpent were saved. In this context, "whoever believes" in verses
15 and 16 should be initially applied to the people of God. To Jesus and
Nicodemus, "any Jew who believes in Jesus" was "whoever believes." Since
at the time the book of John was written[53], the gospel had already spread
out to the Gentiles, we don't know if the author adopted these universal
expressions intentionally to include the Gentiles. However, the context
of the conversation clearly confines the scope of "world" to "the Jewish
world." Further, for verse 18 to be true, it is necessary that the identity
of Jesus should have been known to all people to make "judgment" the
just judgment. Who knew Jesus and cared about His identity? The Jews.
This judgment should not be applied to Chinese or Japanese who did not
even know Jesus and thereby did not have any option to believe or not to
believe. Verse 19 makes this argument even clearer: "This is the judgment,
that the Light has come into the world, and men loved the darkness rather
than the Light, for their deeds were evil." The judgment is based upon the

decision to believe or not to believe. Therefore, those who are judged must
have an option to make a decision. And since the Light has come into the
world, the judgment is confined within the world. Since the world should
be the place that has known Jesus and can make a decision to believe or
not to believe, the world must be the Jewish world which has known about
Jesus and His claim of identity. Verse 22 makes this argument even more
transparent. In verse 19, Jesus says, "the Light has come into the world,"
and in verse 22, "After these things Jesus and His disciples came into the
land of Judea." In this context, the world is clearly the land of Judea.

Therefore, just like John 1:9–13, we can paraphrase the text in this way:

10. Jesus answered and said to him, "Are you the teacher of Israel and do
    not understand these things?
11. "Truly, truly, I say to you, we speak of what we know and testify of
    what we have seen, and you do not accept our testimony.
12. "If I told you earthly things and you do not believe, how will you
    believe if I tell you heavenly things?
13. "No one has ascended into heaven, but He who descended from
    heaven: the Son of Man.
14. "As Moses lifted up the serpent in the wilderness, even so must the
    Son of Man be lifted up;
15. so that whoever believes, will in Him have eternal life.
16. "For God so loved Judea (or can be Israel), that He gave His only
    begotten Son, that whoever believes in Him shall not perish, but have
    eternal life.
17. "For God did not send the Son into Judea, to judge Judea, but that
    Judea might be saved through Him.
18. "He who believes in Him is not judged; he who does not believe has
    been judged already, because he has not believed in the name of the
    only begotten Son of God.
19. "This is the judgment, that the Light has come into Judea, and men
    loved the darkness rather than the Light, for their deeds were evil.
20. "For everyone who does evil hates the Light, and does not come to the
    Light for fear that his deeds will be exposed.

21. "But he who practices the truth comes to the Light, so that his deeds may be manifested as having been wrought in God."
22. After these things Jesus and His disciples came into the land of Judea, and there He was spending time with them and baptizing.

Again, in verse 16, "whoever believes" would include the Gentiles since the door to be the children of God was open to the world through Jesus. However, this would happen later, after the Pentecost. In this text, when the conversation relating to the world and judgment, the world should be interpreted as Judea or Israel. And then "whoever believes" in the verse should initially mean "any Jew who believes" and secondarily might be expanded to "any human being" in the world.

In the paraphrased text, the conversation between Jesus and Nicodemus makes more sense and the third party in the conversation ("whoever" in vv. 15–16, "he" in v. 18; 21, "men" in v. 19, "everyone" in v. 20) has a better chance of being identified.

Therefore, the rewritten John 3:16 (For God so loved Judea (Israel), that He gave His only begotten Son, that whoever believes in Him shall not perish, but have eternal life) is vindicated, and the sin of Judea, rather than the sin of the world, is implied.[54]

By adopting universal expressions, the Gospel of John made a significant contribution toward universalizing Christianity: Reinterpreting the sin of Judea to be the sin of the world.

Let us look at some passages in Romans which contain more universal expressions.

Romans 3: 9–26
9. What then? Are we better than they? Not at all; for we have already charged that both Jews and Greeks are all (πάντας) under (ὑπό) sin;
10. as it is written, "THERE IS NONE RIGHTEOUS, NOT EVEN ONE;

11. THERE IS NONE WHO UNDERSTANDS, THERE IS NONE WHO SEEKS FOR GOD;

12. ALL (πάντες) HAVE TURNED ASIDE, TOGETHER THEY HAVE BECOME USELESS; THERE IS NONE WHO DOES GOOD, THERE IS NOT EVEN ONE."

13. "THEIR THROAT IS AN OPEN GRAVE, WITH THEIR TONGUES THEY KEEP DECEIVING," "THE POISON OF ASPS IS UNDER THEIR LIPS";

14. "WHOSE MOUTH IS FULL OF CURSING AND BITTERNESS";

15. THEIR FEET ARE SWIFT TO SHED BLOOD,

16. DESTRUCTION AND MISERY ARE IN THEIR PATHS,

17. AND THE PATH OF PEACE THEY HAVE NOT KNOWN."

18. "THERE IS NO FEAR OF GOD BEFORE THEIR EYES."

19. Now we know that whatever the Law says, it speaks to those who are under the Law, so that every (πᾶν) mouth may be closed and all the world (πᾶς ὁ κόσμος) may become accountable to God;

20. because by the works of the Law no flesh will be justified in His sight; for through the Law comes the knowledge of sin.

21. But now apart from the Law the righteousness of God has been manifested, being witnessed by the Law and the Prophets,

22. even the righteousness of God through faith in Jesus Christ for all those who believe; for there is no distinction;

23. for all (πάντες) have sinned and fall short of the glory of God,

24. being justified as a gift by His grace through the redemption which is in Christ Jesus;

25. whom God displayed publicly as a propitiation in His blood through faith This was to demonstrate His righteousness, because in the forbearance of God He passed over the sins previously committed;

26. for the demonstration, I say, of His righteousness at the present time, so that He would be just and the justifier of the one who has faith in Jesus.

We find Romans chapter 3 full of universal expressions: "all under sin" (verse 9); "none righteous, not even one" (verse 10); "none who understands, none who seeks for God" (verse 11); "all have turned," "none who does good, not even one" (verse 12); "every mouth," "all the world" (verse 19); "all have sinned and fall short of the glory of God" (verse 23). Note that "none" or "not even one" are negative universal expressions having the same effect as "all" or "every."

My task is to demonstrate how the sin of Judea became the sin of the world through Paul's use of universal expressions. For the task, I will examine the validity and meaning of "all" in verse 23 since this verse explicitly says that all have sinned: πάντες γὰρ ἥμαρτον.

Some preliminary information is needed to understand Romans better. In Romans, Paul divides the human race into three groups: Jews, Greeks (or Gentiles), and Christians.[55] And when he uses the word "we," sometimes he is identifying himself with Jews, sometimes with Christians, sometimes with both. Also, when Paul speaks of sin, his main concern is with the sin of the non-Christians (Jews or Greeks) even though the Old Testament and Jesus are concerned with the sin of "the people of God", and from the perspective of the New Testament, that means the sin of the Christians. To compare "all have sinned" in verse 23 with the redemptive work of Jesus Christ, verse 9 plays a significant role as a medium or sub-conclusion: "both Jews and Greeks are all under sin." Since Paul divides the human race into three groups, if all the people of two groups (Jews and Greeks) are under sin, essentially the world is situated under sin because Christians would be in the saved group. Therefore verse 9 implies that the world is under sin. Here, the sin of Judea is not expanded to the world implicitly. Instead, more explicitly, Paul says that, from the viewpoint of Christians, the other groups (Jews and Greeks) are under sin and, therefore, the world excluding Christians is under sin. Let us look again at the structure of Paul's argument presented in the previous section (B):

Conclusive statement:	**"All have sinned"**	(3:23)
Supporting proofs:	People under the Law	(3:19–20)
	Quoted the O.T. Psalm 14 or 53	(3:10–18)
Sub-conclusion	"All under sin"	(3:9)
Supporting proofs:	Paul's observation on Jews	(2:17–29)
	Justice of God	(2:1–16)
	Paul's observation on Gentiles (or Greeks)	(1:18–32)

I will study each section to demonstrate that "all" in 3:23 cannot mean literally "all people of the world," but instead possibly "the people of Judea" in the collective sense as a group of the people.

To draw the sub-conclusion, Paul basically utilizes three proofs: his observation on Greeks, the Justice of God as a general principle, and his observation on Jews.

First, when we read Paul's observation on Greeks (1:18–32), we can find that Paul is, in fact, talking about a particular group of the Greeks (or Gentiles):

Romans 1:18–32
18. For the wrath of God is revealed from heaven against
      all ungodliness and unrighteousness of men who suppress
      the truth in unrighteousness,
19. because that which is known about God is evident within them; for
   God made it evident to them.
20. For since the creation of the world His invisible attributes, His eternal
   power and divine nature, have been clearly seen, being understood
   through what has been made, so that they are without excuse.
21. For even though they knew God,
      they did not honor Him as God or give thanks, but they
      became futile in their speculations, and their foolish heart
      was darkened.

22.   Professing to be wise, they became fools,

23.   and exchanged the glory of the incorruptible God for an
                 image in the form of corruptible man and of birds and four-
                 footed animals and crawling creatures.

24. Therefore God gave them
                 over in the lusts of their hearts to impurity, so that their
                 bodies would be dishonored among them.

25.   For they exchanged the truth of God for a lie, and worshiped
                 and served the creature rather than the Creator,
who is blessed forever. Amen.

26. For this reason God gave them
                 over to degrading passions; for their women exchanged the
                 natural function for that which is unnatural,

27.   and in the same way also the men abandoned the natural
                 function of the woman and burned in their desire toward
                 one another, men with men committing indecent acts and
                 receiving in their own persons the due penalty of their error.

28. And just as they did not see fit to acknowledge God any longer, God
    gave them
                 over to a depraved mind, to do those things which are not
                 proper,

29.   being filled with all unrighteousness, wickedness, greed,
                 evil; full of envy, murder, strife, deceit, malice; they are
                 gossips,

30.   slanderers, haters of God, insolent, arrogant, boastful,
                 inventors of evil, disobedient to parents,

31.   without understanding, untrustworthy, unloving,
                 unmerciful;

32. and although they know the ordinance of God, that those who practice
    such things are worthy of death,
                 they not only do the same, but also give hearty approval to
                 those who practice them.

Can we apply this passage to all the Gentiles, those who are neither
Christian nor Jew? Verse 18 says, "For the wrath of God is revealed from

heaven against all ungodliness and unrighteousness of men who suppress the truth in unrighteousness." Did all Gentiles suppress "the truth in unrighteousness"? Here, Paul is actually talking about a specific group of people, not even all Greeks, but a certain group of Greeks. We know that not all Greeks were involved in homosexual activity (verses 26–27); neither were all Greeks filled with all unrighteousness, wickedness, greed, evil; full of envy, murder, strife, deceit, malice; and were gossips, slanderers, haters of God, insolent, arrogant, boastful, inventors of evil, disobedient to parents, without understanding, untrustworthy, unloving, unmerciful (verses 29–31). In fact, his observation on "Gentiles" is about a particular group of Gentiles "who suppress the truth in unrighteousness."

It is not difficult to find some righteous Gentiles. Cornelius should be considered as righteous: Acts 10:1–2 "Now there was a man at Caesarea named Cornelius, a centurion of what was called the Italian cohort, a devout man and one who feared God with all his household, and gave many alms to the Jewish people and prayed to God continually." How about the centurion who came to Jesus for his servant and was praised by Jesus in Matthew 8:5–13? How about another centurion who praised God and verified the innocence of Jesus at the cross in Luke 23:46: "Now when the centurion saw what had happened, he began praising God, saying, 'Certainly this man was innocent.'" On Palm Sunday, there were some Greeks who came to Jerusalem to observe the Passover and they even wanted to meet with Jesus in John 12:20–21: "Now there were some Greeks among those who were going up to worship at the feast; these then came to Philip, who was from Bethsaida of Galilee, and began to ask him, saying, 'Sir, we wish to see Jesus.'" Also, according to Acts 13:16; 26, there were several Gentiles (God-fearers) even in the Synagogue of Pisidian Antioch:

14. But going on from Perga, they arrived at Pisidian Antioch, and on the Sabbath day they went into the synagogue and sat down
16. Paul stood up, and motioning with his hand said, "Men of Israel, and you who fear God, listen:

26. Brethren, sons of Abraham's family, and those among you who fear God, to us the message of this salvation has been sent.

After his generalization about the Gentiles, Paul presents the Justice of God (2: 1–16) as a proof or basis to elicit the sub-conclusion, "all under sin" (3:9) and the conclusive sentence "all have sinned" (3:23).

Romans 2:1–16

1. Therefore you have no excuse, everyone of you who passes judgment, for in that which you judge another, you condemn yourself; for you who judge practice the same things.
2. And we know that the judgment of God rightly falls upon those who practice such things.
3. But do you suppose this, O man, when you pass judgment on those who practice such things and do the same yourself, that you will escape the judgment of God?
4. Or do you think lightly of the riches of His kindness and tolerance and patience, not knowing that the kindness of God leads you to repentance?
5. But because of your stubbornness and unrepentant heart you are storing up wrath for yourself in the day of wrath and revelation of the righteous judgment of God,
6. who WILL RENDER TO EACH PERSON ACCORDING TO HIS DEEDS:
7. to those who by perseverance in doing good seek for glory and honor and immortality, eternal life;
8. but to those who are selfishly ambitious and do not obey the truth, but obey unrighteousness, wrath and indignation.
9. There will be tribulation and distress for every soul of man who does evil, of the Jew first and also of the Greek,
10. but glory and honor and peace to everyone who does good, to the Jew first and also to the Greek.
11. For there is no partiality with God.

12. For all who have sinned without the Law will also perish without the Law, and all who have sinned under the Law will be judged by the Law;

13. for it is not the hearers of the Law who are just before God, but the doers of the Law will be justified.

14. For when Gentiles who do not have the Law do instinctively the things of the Law, these, not having the Law, are a law to themselves,

15. in that they show the work of the Law written in their hearts, their conscience bearing witness and their thoughts alternately accusing or else defending them,

16. on the day when, according to my gospel, God will judge the secrets of men through Christ Jesus.

As he expounds upon it, Paul's concept of the Justice of God sounds logical and persuasive. However, the concept of the Justice of God is incompatible with Paul's conclusions that "all under sin" and "all have sinned." This incompatibility extends to "all death" where Paul cites Genesis Chapter 5: "Therefore, just as through one man sin entered into the world, and death through sin, and so death spread to all men, because all sinned" (verse 12). How can one speak of the Justice of God in this regard? It is not ours to say. God alone can and does decide who is righteous and who is not; therefore, statements like "some" under sin or "some" have sinned would be more appropriate, rather than the more expansive "all."

We can conclude from the text that some people are assumed to be "not under sin"; having "not sinned." As Paul himself states, the Justice of God means "rendering to each person according to his deeds" (verse 6) with "no partiality" (verse 11). Paul himself paraphrases well the meaning in the following verses (7–10) and recognizes those who, by perseverance in doing good, seek for glory and honor and immortality; eternal life (verse 7); to everyone who does good (verse 10). Also, he makes it clear that not only Christians are judged as "good" through the redemptive work of Jesus, but some Jews and Greeks (verses 9–10). If Paul truly believes what he states, he should avoid the universal expressions "all" for sin which opposes the concept of divine justice. For the Justice of God to work, each person will be called accordingly and then judged by God.

Of course, we know that nobody is perfect. In addition to those who willfully do wrong, some people don't have the mental faculty to make ethical or moral decisions, to discern right from wrong. Others make mistakes which can cause pain, suffering, and even death. Therefore, it is erroneous to conclude that "all under sin" or "all have sinned." If "all under sin" and "all have sinned" are true based on "nobody is absolutely perfect," you could just as easily turn it around to say "all under good" and "all have done good" because nobody is absolutely imperfect. It is God alone who judges and redeems. Therefore, Paul's insertion of "the Justice of God" in chapter 2 ironically opposes his own assertions that "all under sin" and "all have sinned" and, later, in Chapter 5, the notion of Original Sin and Total Depravity in relationship with natural death.

After presenting his argument for the Justice of God, Paul offers his observation on Jews (2:17–29) as a proof to elicit the sub-conclusion "all under sin": "What then? Are we better than they? Not at all; for we have already charged that both Jews and Greeks are all (πάντας) under (ὑπό) sin" (3:9) and his conclusive phrase "all have sinned" (3:23).

Romans 2:17–29
17. But if you bear the name "Jew" and rely upon the Law and boast in God,
18. and know His will and approve the things that are essential, being instructed out of the Law,
19. and are confident that you yourself are a guide to the blind, a light to those who are in darkness,
20. a corrector of the foolish, a teacher of the immature, having in the Law the embodiment of knowledge and of the truth,
21. you, therefore, who teach another, do you not teach yourself? You who preach that one shall not steal, do you steal?
22. You who say that one should not commit adultery, do you commit adultery? You who abhor idols, do you rob temples?

23. You who boast in the Law, through your breaking the Law, do you dishonor God?

24. For "THE NAME OF GOD IS BLASPHEMED AMONG THE GENTILES BECAUSE OF YOU," just as it is written.

25. For indeed circumcision is of value if you practice the Law; but if you are a transgressor of the Law, your circumcision has become uncircumcision.

26. So if the uncircumcised man keeps the requirements of the Law, will not his uncircumcision be regarded as circumcision?

27. And he who is physically uncircumcised, if he keeps the Law, will he not judge you who though having the letter of the Law and circumcision are a transgressor of the Law?

28. For he is not a Jew who is one outwardly, nor is circumcision that which is outward in the flesh.

29. But he is a Jew who is one inwardly; and circumcision is that which is of the heart, by the Spirit, not by the letter; and his praise is not from men, but from God.

Just as in the case with the Greeks, Paul is talking about a particular group of the Jews. Certainly not all Jews stole, committed adultery, robbed the temple, and dishonored God (verses 21–23). Not all Jews were hypocrites and transgressors.

As in the case with the Greeks, even in the New Testament, we can find righteous Jews. The father of Jesus, Joseph, was certainly "righteous," Matthew 1:9: "And Joseph her husband, being a righteous man and not wanting to disgrace her, planned to send her away secretly." The parents of John the Baptist (father Zacharias and mother Elizabeth) were called "righteous," Luke 1:6: "They were both righteous in the sight of God, walking blamelessly in all the commandments and requirements of the Lord." Simeon who greeted Jesus at the Temple eight days after his birth was also called "righteous," Luke 2:25: "And there was a man in Jerusalem whose name was Simeon; and this man was righteous and devout, looking for the consolation of Israel; and the Holy Spirit was upon him."

Nathanael, even before he knew Jesus, should be considered as "righteous," John 1:47: "Jesus saw Nathanael coming to Him, and said of him, "Behold, an Israelite indeed, in whom there is no deceit!"

How about Nicodemus who came to Jesus by night? How about the born-blind who opened his eyes at Siloam? How about those women who followed and wept over Jesus at the cross? Weren't they righteous?

After presenting his observation on Greeks, the Justice of God, and his observation on Jews, Paul states his sub-conclusion in 3:9: "What then? Are we better than they? Not at all; for we have already charged that both Jews and Greeks are all (πάντας) under (ὑπό) sin."
In verse 9b, Paul identifies himself with Christians to make this assertion: "for we have already charged that both Jews and Greeks are all under sin." However, this charge has no basis. First, Paul's proofs are weak. He has been talking about some, not all, Greeks and Jews. He sampled some sinful people and used them to make generalized statements in verse 9b. Therefore "already" in verse 9b cannot be true. Also, the Justice of God does not support this charge but rather defies it. Second, the statement itself has some problems. In verse 9b, it is Paul himself, not "we," in fact, who is trying to charge that both Jews and Greeks are all under sin. If the subject "we" includes Paul and the readers (Christians in Rome)[56], it would not be possible for Paul to know whether the readers would agree with him or not. Since the logical problem happened in his generalization, even the hypothetical subject "we" should not be justified.

Even though the charge has no base, the readers may not see the problem because the expression "all under sin" is ambiguous and equivocal. Since Paul does not say here that "all are sinners or have sinned," but "all under sin" and the Greek word ὑπό means "under the influence of something," the statement can be interpreted using context as "all have sinned" or else "all under influence of sin" if we take a more literal meaning. However, since the statement (3:9) is used as a sub-conclusion to lead the argument to the conclusive statement "all have sinned" (3:23), I would argue it should be contextually understood as "all have sinned."

After the charge in 3:9, Paul presents more proofs to support it and lead the argument to the conclusive statement in 3:23. Let us look at 3:10–18:

10. as it is written, "THERE IS NONE RIGHTEOUS, NOT EVEN ONE;
11. THERE IS NONE WHO UNDERSTANDS, THERE IS NONE WHO SEEKS FOR GOD;
12. ALL (πάντες) HAVE TURNED ASIDE, TOGETHER THEY HAVE BECOME USELESS; THERE IS NONE WHO DOES GOOD, THERE IS NOT EVEN ONE.
13. THEIR THROAT IS AN OPEN GRAVE, WITH THEIR TONGUES THEY KEEP DECEIVING, THE POISON OF ASPS IS UNDER THEIR LIPS;
14. WHOSE MOUTH IS FULL OF CURSING AND BITTERNESS;
15. THEIR FEET ARE SWIFT TO SHED BLOOD,
16. DESTRUCTION AND MISERY ARE IN THEIR PATHS,
17. AND THE PATH OF PEACE THEY HAVE NOT KNOWN."
18. "THERE IS NO FEAR OF GOD BEFORE THEIR EYES."

To load biblical authority on his argument, Paul quotes passages from Psalm 14 or 53. In verses 10 to 12, we can see the repeated universal expressions: "None," "not even one," and "all." These verses sound as if they are about the total depravity of humankind. However, in the following verses, 13 through 18, the word "their" cannot be applied to the whole of humankind. In fact, Psalm 14 and 53 describe the condition of the fool or the oppressor of the Israel, not the whole of humankind:

Psalm 14:1–7
1. The fool has said in his heart, "There is no God." They are corrupt, they have committed abominable deeds; There is no one who does good.
2. The LORD has looked down from heaven upon the sons of men To see if there are any who understand, Who seek after God.
3. They have all turned aside, together they have become corrupt; There is no one who does good, not even one.
4. Do all the workers of wickedness not know, Who eat up my people as they eat bread, And do not call upon the Lord?

5. There they are in great dread, For God is with the righteous generation.
6. You would put to shame the counsel of the afflicted, But the LORD is his refuge.
7. Oh, that the salvation of Israel would come out of Zion! When the LORD restores His captive people, Jacob will rejoice, Israel will be glad.

Psalm 53:1–6

1. The fool has said in his heart, "There is no God," They are corrupt, and have committed abominable injustice; There is no one who does good.
2. God has looked down from heaven upon the sons of men To see if there is anyone who understands, Who seeks after God.
3. Every one of them has turned aside; together they have become corrupt; There is no one who does good, not even one.
4. Have the workers of wickedness no knowledge, Who eat up My people as though they ate bread And have not called upon God?
5. There they were in great fear where no fear had been; For God scattered the bones of him who encamped against you; You put them to shame, because God had rejected them.
6. Oh, that the salvation of Israel would come out of Zion! When God restores His captive people, Let Jacob rejoice, let Israel be glad

In these texts, two groups of the people are identified. The first group contains "the fool," "they," "the sons of men," "everyone of them," and "all the workers of wickedness." The second group comprises "my people," "the righteous generation," "Israel," "his captive people," and "Jacob." It is clear that the verses quoted by Paul in Romans 3:10–18 are actually the description of the condition of the oppressor or enemy of Israel, not the whole of humankind. Therefore, this quotation from the Old Testament, in fact, does not support the charge in 3:9 (all under sin) and fails to lead the argument to the conclusive statement in 3:23 (all have sinned).

After quoting from the Old Testament, Paul presents one more argument to reach his conclusive statement in 3:23. Here Paul is explicitly talking about the sin of Judea, that is, the sin of the people who are under the Law:

3:19–20

19. Now we know that whatever the Law says, it speaks to those who are under the Law, so that every (πᾶν) mouth may be closed and all the world (πᾶς ὁ κόσμος) may become accountable to God;

20. because by the works of the Law no flesh will be justified in His sight; for through the Law comes the knowledge of sin.

In this text, three universal expressions are adopted: "every month," "all the world," and "no flesh." However, the text itself doubtlessly means that "every mouth" means "every mouth of those who are under the Law" and "all the world" means "all of those who are under the Law" and "no flesh" means "no flesh of those who are under the Law" because whatever the Law says, it speaks to those who are under the Law, not to those who are not under the Law. Therefore, in fact, this proof does not support Paul's conclusive statement: "for all (πάντες) have sinned and fall short of the glory of God" 3:23. The only way to connect this argument to the conclusive statement might be to interpret the conclusive statement (3:23) in this way: "for all who are under the Law have sinned and fallen short of the glory of God." Since this interpretation contrasts the sin of Judea with the redemption of Jesus, confining the redemptive work of Jesus to the Church, and contrasting the sin of Judea with the sin of the Church, it makes much better sense. However, ironically, this interpretation will negate Paul's overall argument that the world is under sin and thus Jesus is the only way to salvation.

Paul's conclusive statement "for all (πάντες) have sinned and fall short of the glory of God" (3:23) is re-emphasized in 5:12 in relation to the Genesis account: "Therefore, just as through one man sin entered into the world, and death through sin, and so death spread to all men, because all sinned" (5:12). Here clearly "all sinned" does not mean "all those who are under the Law," but rather "all human beings." However, the validity of this re-emphasizing statement has been already examined in the previous section: Paul changed the universal expression "all" to "many."

By utilizing or adopting universal expressions, Paul tries to make all humans beings sinners except the Christians. However, the proofs and arguments he presents have no base or are illogical. Paul presents the sin of a group of Greeks, inserts the notion of the Justice of God, presents the sin of a group of Jews and then proclaims "all under sin" on the basis of these proofs. And then he quotes from Psalm 14 or 53 which has nothing to do with the sin of the world but rather with the sin of the oppressors of Israel. He then states that all under the Law (the Jews) are accountable and concludes "for all (πάντες) have sinned and fall short of the glory of God" (3:23) in comparison with the redemptive work of Jesus (3:24–26). And this conclusive statement Is re-emphasized in 5:12.

Therefore, through Paul's universal expressions, the sin of a group of Gentiles and the sin of a group of Jews became generalized to be the sin of the world. Since my concern is with Judea and the sin of Judea, understood in collective sense, I can conclude that the sin of Judea (a group of the Jews) became the sin of the world by Paul's use of universal expressions.

Conclusion: Chapter I. The Sin of Judea Became the Sin of the World
What the Prophets condemned was the sin of the Kingdom of God. What Jesus condemned was the sin of Judea. What Jesus died for was the sin of His people who belong to His new Kingdom, whether they were the Jews or the Gentiles. Therefore, when the redemptive sacrifice of Jesus Christ is considered, the sin of Judea and the sin of the Church as the Kingdom of God should be compared with each other (this will be discussed in detail in Chapter 2). However, in the New Testament writings, instead of comparing Judea to the Church, what initially was meant for a Judean audience was projected to and heard by the entire world and thus the sin of Judea got translated into the sin of the world through three methods:

1. Utilizing the Original Sin (Genesis 2 & 3) that deduces Total Depravity
2. Utilizing Natural Law and General Revelation
3. Adopting the universal expressions "world" and "all"

Before I move to the next presentation, I want to recognize three problems involved in expanding the sin of Judea to the sin of the world.

First, the disciples proclaimed the world and the individuals in it to be "sinful" without any basis. As I have already shown, Paul's claims are based upon either generalization or an absence of logic. His arguments, rather than being based upon reason, logic, and a description of what happened, are based upon his need to justify his personal conviction that the world is under sin and Jesus is the only path to salvation. Whereas, the Gospels, unlike Paul's writings, mostly adopted all-encompassing expressions without clearly defining their scope.

Second, the phrase "sin of the nation" (Israel or Judea), certainly does not mean that every single member of Judea, every Jew, is without exception a sinner. The sin of the nation should be understood collectively. When the majority of the nation, or the representatives of the nation, are sinners, the nation might be called sinful in a collective sense. In this sense, Israel and Judea were called sinful and judged by God. However, when the sin of Judea became the sin of the world, it was made so based upon the idea that every single human being is a sinner without exception.

Third, the world was never in a covenant relationship with God, yet it was condemned as if it were. When did God summon the totality of mankind and give it the Law? If the argument is that God gave the Law to Adam (and through Adam all humankind), there is no reason for God to appear at Mount Sinai. If it is argued that God gave conscience as the Law to every human being, likewise, why did God give the Law to His people? As far as sin is related to redemptive sacrifice, that sin must be the sin of the Covenant community and understood collectively. The sin of the world which never had a Covenant with God was related to the redemptive sacrifice of Jesus, as if it had the Covenant with God.

Once the sin of the Judea became understood as the sin of the world, the judgment on Judea began to be thought of as the judgment on the world.

CHAPTER 2
The Judgment on Judea Became the Judgment on the World: The End of Judea Became the End of the World

The judgment on Judea should have been compared to the judgment on the Church. Because of the sin of Judea, Judea would be judged collectively by God, which would lead to the end of the nation by the Second Coming of the Messiah. On the other hand, because of the redemptive work of Jesus, the Church would not be judged by God despite its collective sin, that is, the salvation of the Church and the establishment of the Eternal Kingdom of God brought about by the Second Coming of the Messiah. Instead of comparing Judea to the Church, however, the end of the Judea was preached and expanded to the non-Jewish world as the end of the world.

In the Old Testament, the sin of Israel/Judea and the destruction of both nations by divine intervention were the main theme of the prophets, particularly focusing on the destruction of Jerusalem and the temple. Likewise, in the New Testament, what Jesus condemned was the sin of the Judea and what Jesus warned of was the destruction of Judea, Jerusalem, and the temple. However, when the gospel left Palestinian soil, it carried that condemnation outward, warning of the end of the world.

In this section, I will try to prove that Christian eschatology is in fact already fulfilled, because the eschaton about which the disciples preached was actually the eschaton on Judea. What Jesus said in the Gospels about the Judgment, the End, Salvation and the Second Coming actually refers to the end of Judea and the destruction of Jerusalem, events which took place in AD 70. Through historical accounts from Josephus and Eusebius, I will prove that the eschatological statements found in the Gospels are actually about the AD 70 event, and then I will try to prove that the eschatological statements in the Epistles are actually allusions to those events as well, however, applied to outside of Judea and non-Jewish Christians as the eschaton of the world. And then I will argue that the eschaton in the Revelation is mainly about the end of the Roman Empire which persecuted the Christian Church; further, I will argue that the end of the world described in 20:7–15 that entails vision of the new world was, in fact, a distorted allusion of the already happened AD 70 event that was preached about and believed by the Christian Church to be the end of the world.

Therefore, in the New Testament, I find three eschatons: in the Gospels, in the Epistles, and in the Revelation. All three are closely interwoven with the AD 70 event. Also, the End, the Judgment, and Salvation are closely related to the Second Coming of the Messiah, as foretold in the New Testament because those events are executed by the returned Messiah. Therefore, when I say the eschatological statements, it will include all four: The End, the Judgment, Salvation, and the Second Coming.

Preliminary Knowledge

To move forward, we need to know what happened in AD 70 when Jerusalem was totally destroyed by the Roman armies led by Titus.

The historical accounts were well recorded by the Jewish historian Josephus who was actually involved in the Jewish revolt against the Roman Empire and was therefore an eye-witness to the end of Jerusalem and all of Judea. The relevant accounts to our subject were recorded in his book,

The Wars of the Jews (Book 5, 6, and 7 chapter 1). Chapter 10 of Book 5 and chapters 3 and 5 of Book 6 are particularly important to the subject and were well summarized by a Christian historian Eusebius in his book, Ecclesiastical History, Book 3, in the following chapters:

Chapter 5: The last siege of the Jews after Christ
Chapter 6: The famine which oppressed the Jews
Chapter 7: The prediction of Christ
Chapter 8: The signs that preceded the war

It is important to read Eusebius' summarized accounts (following) prior to examining the relevant texts in order to understand the argument I present.[57]

The following are direct quotations from the book.

Chapter 5. The Last Siege of the Jews after Christ

1. After Nero had held the power thirteen years and Galba and Otho had ruled a year and six months, Vespasian, who had become distinguished in the campaigns against the Jews, was proclaimed sovereign in Judea and received the title of Emperor from the armies there. Setting out immediately, therefore, for Rome, he entrusted the conduct of the war against the Jews to his son Titus.
2. For the Jews after the ascension of our Savior, in addition to their crime against him, had been devising as many plots as they could against his apostles. First Stephen was stoned to death by them, and after him James, the son of Zebedee and the brother of John, was beheaded, and finally James, the first that had obtained the episcopal seat in Jerusalem after the ascension of our Savior, died in the manner already described. But the rest of the apostles, who had been incessantly plotted against with a view to their destruction, and had been driven out of the land of Judea, went unto all nations to preach the Gospel, relying upon the power of Christ, who had said to them, "Go ye and make disciples of all the nations in my name."

3.   But the people of the church in Jerusalem had been commanded by a
     revelation, vouchsafed to approved men there before the war, to leave
     the city and to dwell in a certain town of Perea called Pella. And when
     those that believed in Christ had come thither from Jerusalem, then,
     as if the royal city of the Jews and the whole land of Judea were entirely
     destitute of holy men, the judgment of God at length overtook those
     who had committed such outrages against Christ and his apostles, and
     totally destroyed that generation of impious men.

4.   But the number of calamities which everywhere fell upon the nation at
     that time; the extreme misfortunes to which the inhabitants of Judea
     were especially subjected, the thousands of men, as well as women and
     children, that perished by the sword, by famine, and by other forms of
     death innumerable,—all these things, as well as the many great sieges
     which were carried on against the cities of the Judea, and; excessive
     sufferings endured by those that fled to Jerusalem itself, as to a city of
     perfect safety, and finally the general course of the whole war, as well
     as its particular occurrences in detail, and how at last the abomination
     of desolation, proclaimed by the prophets, stood in the very temple of
     God, so celebrated of old, the temple which was now awaiting its total
     and final destruction by fire,—all these things any one that wishes
     may find accurately described in the history written by Josephus.

5.   But it is necessary to state that this writer records that the multitude of
     those who were assembled from all Judea at the time of the Passover,
     to the number of three million souls, were shut up in Jerusalem "as in
     a prison," to use his own words.

6.   For it was right that in the very days in which they had inflicted
     suffering upon the Savior and the Benefactor of all, the Christ of
     God, that in those days, shut up "as in a prison," they should meet with
     destruction at the hands of divine justice.

7.   But passing by the particular calamities which they suffered from the
     attempts made upon them by the sword and by other means, I think it
     necessary to relate only the misfortunes which the famine caused, that
     those who read this work may have some means of knowing that God

was not long in executing vengeance upon them for their wickedness against the Christ of God.

Chapter 6. The Famine which oppressed them

1. Taking the fifth book of the History of Josephus again in our hands, let us go through the tragedy of events which then occurred.
2. "For the wealthy," he says, "it was equally dangerous to remain. For under pretense that they were going to desert men were put to death for their wealth. The madness of the seditions increased with the famine and both the miseries were inflamed more and more day by day.
3. Nowhere was food to be seen; but, bursting into the houses men searched them thoroughly, and whenever they found anything to eat they tormented the owners on the ground that they had denied that they had anything; but if they found nothing, they tortured them on the ground that they had more carefully concealed it.
4. The proof of their having or not having food was found in the bodies of the poor wretches. Those of them who were still in good condition they assumed were well supplied with food, while those who were already wasted away they passed by, for it seemed absurd to slay those who were on the point of perishing for want.
5. Many, indeed, secretly sold their possessions for one measure of wheat, if they belonged to the wealthier class, of barley if they were poorer. Then shutting themselves up in the innermost parts of their houses, some ate the grain uncooked on account of their terrible want, while others baked it according as necessity and fear dictated.
6. Nowhere were tables set, but, snatching the yet uncooked food from the fire, they tore it in pieces. Wretched was the fare, and a lamentable spectacle it was to see the more powerful secure an abundance while the weaker mourned.
7. Of all evils, indeed, famine is the worst, and it destroys nothing so effectively as shame. For that which under other circumstances is worthy of respect, in the midst of famine is despised. Thus women snatched the food from the very mouths of their husbands and

children, from their fathers, and what was most pitiable of all, mothers from their babes. And while their dearest ones were wasting away in their arms, they were not ashamed to take away from them the last drops that supported life.

8. And even while they were eating thus they did not remain undiscovered. But everywhere the rioters appeared, to rob them even of these portions of food. For whenever they saw a house shut up, they regarded it as a sign that those inside were taking food. And immediately bursting open the doors they rushed in and seized what they were eating, almost forcing it out of their very throats.

9. Old men who clung to their food were beaten, and if the women concealed it in their hands, their hair was torn for so doing. There was pity neither for gray hairs nor for infants, but, taking up the babes that clung to their morsels of food, they dashed them to the ground. But to those that anticipated their entrance and swallowed what they were about to seize, they were still more cruel, just as if they had been wronged by them.

10. And they devised the most terrible modes of torture to discover food, stopping up the privy passages of the poor wretches with bitter herbs, and piercing their seats with sharp rods. And men suffered things horrible even to hear of, for the sake of compelling them to confess to the possession of one loaf of bread, or in order that they might be made to disclose a single drachm of barley which they had concealed. But the tormentors themselves did not suffer hunger.

11. Their conduct might indeed have seemed less barbarous if they had been driven to it by necessity; but they did it for the sake of exercising their madness and of providing sustenance for themselves for days to come.

12. And when any one crept out of the city by night as far as the outposts of the Romans to collect wild herbs and grass, they went to meet him; and when he thought he had already escaped the enemy, they seized what he had brought with him, and even though oftentimes the man would entreat them, and, calling upon the most awful name of God, adjure them to give him a portion of what he had obtained at the risk

of his life, they would give him nothing back. Indeed, it was fortunate if the one that was plundered was not also slain."

13. To this account Josephus, after relating other things, adds the following: "The possibility of going out of the city being brought to an end, all hope of safety for the Jews was cut off. And the famine increased and devoured the people by houses and families. And the rooms were filled with dead women and children, the lanes of the city with the corpses of old men.

14. Children and youths, swollen with the famine, wandered about the market-places like shadows, and fell down wherever the death agony overtook them. The sick were not strong enough to bury even their own relatives, and those who had the strength hesitated because of the multitude of the dead and the uncertainty as to their own fate. Many, indeed, died while they were burying others, and many betook themselves to their graves before death came upon them.

15. There was neither weeping nor lamentation under these misfortunes; but the famine stifled the natural affections. Those that were dying a lingering death looked with dry eyes upon those that had gone to their rest before them. Deep silence and death-laden night encircled the city.

16. But the robbers were more terrible than these miseries; for they broke open the houses, which were now mere sepulchres, robbed the dead and stripped the covering from their bodies, and went away with a laugh. They tried the points of their swords in the dead bodies, and some that were lying on the ground still alive they thrust through in order to test their weapons. But those that prayed that they would use their right hand and their sword upon them, they contemptuously left to be destroyed by the famine. Every one of these died with eyes fixed upon the temple; and they left the seditious alive.

17. These at first gave orders that the dead should be buried out of the public treasury, for they could not endure the stench. But afterward, when they were not able to do this, they threw the bodies from the walls into the trenches.

18. And as Titus went around and saw the trenches filled with the dead, and the thick blood oozing out of the putrid bodies, he groaned aloud, and, raising his hands, called God to witness that this was not his doing."

19. After speaking of some other things, Josephus proceeds as follows: "I cannot hesitate to declare what my feelings compel me to. I suppose, if the Romans had longer delayed in coming against these guilty wretches, the city would have been swallowed up by a chasm, or overwhelmed with a flood, or struck with such thunderbolts as destroyed Sodom. For it had brought forth a generation of men much more godless than were those that suffered such punishment. By their madness indeed was the whole people brought to destruction."

20. And in the sixth book he writes as follows: "Of those that perished by famine in the city the number was countless, and the miseries they underwent unspeakable. For if so much as the shadow of food appeared in any house, there was war, and the dearest friends engaged in hand-to-hand conflict with one another, and snatched from each other the most wretched supports of life.

21. Nor would they believe that even the dying were without food; but the robbers would search them while they were expiring, lest anyone should feign death while concealing food in his bosom. With mouths gaping for want of food, they stumbled and staggered along like mad dogs, and beat the doors as if they were drunk, and in their impotence they would rush into the same houses twice or thrice in one hour.

22. Necessity compelled them to eat anything they could find, and they gathered and devoured things that were not fit even for the filthiest of irrational beasts. Finally they did not abstain even from their girdles and shoes, and they stripped the hides off their shields and devoured them. Some used even wisps of old hay for food, and others gathered stubble and sold the smallest weight of it for four Attic drachma.

23. "But why should I speak of the shamelessness which was displayed during the famine toward inanimate things? For I am going to relate a fact such as is recorded neither by Greeks nor Barbarians; horrible to relate, incredible to hear. And indeed I should gladly have omitted this

calamity, that I might not seem to posterity to be a teller of fabulous tales, if I had not innumerable witnesses to it in my own age. And besides, I should render my country poor service if I suppressed the account of the sufferings which she endured.

24. "There was a certain woman named Mary that dwelt beyond Jordan, whose father was Eleazer, of the village of Bathezor (which signifies the house of hyssop). She was distinguished for her family and her wealth, and had fled with the rest of the multitude to Jerusalem and was shut up there with them during the siege.

25. The tyrants had robbed her of the rest of the property which she had brought with her into the city from Perea. And the remnants of her possessions and whatever food was to be seen the guards rushed in daily and snatched away from her. This made the woman terribly angry, and by her frequent reproaches and imprecations she aroused the anger of the rapacious villains against herself.

26. But no one either through anger or pity would slay her; and she grew weary of finding food for others to eat. The search, too, was already become everywhere difficult, and the famine was piercing her bowels and marrow, and resentment was raging more violently than famine. Taking, therefore, anger and necessity as her counsellors, she proceeded to do a most unnatural thing.

27. Seizing her child, a boy which was sucking at her breast, she said, Oh, wretched child, in war, in famine, in sedition, for what do I preserve thee? Slaves among the Romans we shall be even if we are allowed to live by them. But even slavery is anticipated by the famine, and the rioters are more cruel than both. Come, be food for me, a fury for these rioters, and a bye-word to the world, for this is all that is wanting to complete the calamities of the Jews.

28. And when she had said this she slew her son; and having roasted him, she ate one half herself, and covering up the remainder, she kept it. Very soon the rioters appeared on the scene, and, smelling the nefarious odor, they threatened to slay her immediately unless she should show them what she had prepared. She replied that she had

saved an excellent portion for them, and with that she uncovered the remains of the child.

29. They were immediately seized with horror and amazement and stood transfixed at the sight. But she said This is my own son, and the deed is mine. Eat for I too have eaten. Be not more merciful than a woman, nor more compassionate than a mother. But if you are too pious and shrink from my sacrifice, I have already eaten of it; let the rest also remain for me.

30. At these words the men went out trembling, in this one case being affrighted; yet with difficulty did they yield that food to the mother. Forthwith the whole city was filled with the awful crime, and as all pictured the terrible deed before their own eyes, they trembled as if they had done it themselves.

31. Those that were suffering from the famine now longed for death; and blessed were they that had died before hearing and seeing miseries like these."

32. Such was the reward which the Jews received for their wickedness and impiety, against the Christ of God.

Chapter 7. The Predictions of Christ

1. It is fitting to add to these accounts the true prediction of our Savior in which he foretold these very events.

2. His words are as follows: "Woe unto them that are with child, and to them that give suck in those days! But pray ye that your flight be not in the winter, neither on the Sabbath day. For there shall be great tribulation, such as was not since the beginning of the world to this time, no, nor ever shall be." (Matthew 24: 19–21).

3. The historian, reckoning the whole number of the slain, says that eleven hundred thousand persons perished by famine and sword, and that the rest of the rioters and robbers, being betrayed by each other after the taking of the city, were slain. But the tallest of the youths and those that were distinguished for beauty were preserved for the triumph. Of the rest of the multitude, those that were over seventeen years of age were sent as prisoners to labor in the works of Egypt, while

still more were scattered through the provinces to meet their death in the theaters by the sword and by beasts. Those under seventeen years of age were carried away to be sold as slaves, and of these alone the number reached ninety thousand.

4. These things took place in this manner in the second year of the reign of Vespasian (AD 70), in accordance with the prophecies of our Lord and Savior Jesus Christ, who by divine power saw them beforehand as if they were already present, and wept and mourned according to the statement of the holy evangelists, who give the very words which he uttered, when, as if addressing Jerusalem herself, he said:

5. "If thou hadst known, even thou, in this day, the things which belong unto thy peace! But now they are hid from thine eyes. For the days shall come upon thee, that thine enemies shall cast a rampart about thee, and compass thee round, and keep thee in on every side, and shall lay thee and thy children even with the ground." (Luke 19: 42–44).

6. And then, as if speaking concerning the people, he says, "For there shall be great distress in the land, and wrath upon this people. And they shall fall by the edge of the sword and shall be led away captive into all nations. And Jerusalem shall be trodden down of the Gentiles, until the times of the Gentiles be fulfilled." (Luke 21: 23b–24). And again: "When ye shall see Jerusalem compassed with armies, then know that the desolation thereof is nigh." (Luke 21:20).

7. If anyone compares the words of our Saviour with the other accounts of the historian concerning the whole war, how can one fail to wonder, and to admit that the foreknowledge and the prophecy of our Savior were truly divine and marvelously strange.

8. Concerning those calamities, then, that befell the whole Jewish nation after the Savior's passion and after the words which the multitude of the Jews uttered, when they begged the release of the robber and murderer, but besought that the Prince of Life should be taken from their midst, it is not necessary to add anything to the account of the historian.

9. It is appropriate, however, to observe that those events signal the graciousness of that all-good Providence which held back the

destruction of Judea for a full forty years, during which time many of the apostles and disciples, as well as James were still alive and dwelling in Jerusalem itself. During such time Divine Providence furnished signs warning those guilty of crime against the Christ of the things which would happen to them if they did not repent.

10. Since these matters have been thought worthy of mention by the historian already cited, we cannot do better than to recount them for the benefit of the readers of this work.

Chapter 8. The Signs which preceded the War

1. Taking, then, the work of this author, read what he records in the sixth book of his History. His words are as follows: "Thus were the miserable people won over at this time by the impostors and false prophets; but they did not heed nor give credit to the visions and signs that foretold the approaching desolation. On the contrary, as if struck by lightning, and as if possessing neither eyes nor understanding, they slighted the proclamations of God.

2. At one time a star, in form like a sword, stood over the city, and a comet, which lasted for a whole year; and again before the revolt and before the disturbances that led to the war, when the people were gathered for the feast of unleavened bread, on the eighth of the month Xanthicus, at the ninth hour of the night, so great a light shone about the altar and the temple that it seemed to be bright day; and this continued for half an hour. This seemed to the unskillful a good sign, but was interpreted by the sacred scribes as portending those events which very soon took place.

3. And at the same feast a cow, led by the high priest to be sacrificed, brought forth a lamb in the midst of the temple.

4. And the eastern gate of the inner temple, which was of bronze and very massive, and which at evening was closed with difficulty by twenty men, and rested upon iron-bound beams, and had bars sunk deep in the ground, was seen at the sixth hour of the night to open of itself.

5. And not many days after the feast, on the twenty-first of the month Artemisium, a certain marvelous vision was seen which passes belief.

The prodigy might seem fabulous were it not related by those who saw it, and were not the calamities which followed deserving of such signs. For before the setting of the sun chariots and armed troops were seen throughout the whole region in mid-air, wheeling through the clouds and encircling the cities.

6. And at the feast which is called Pentecost, when the priests entered the temple at night, as was their custom, to perform the services, they said that at first they perceived a movement and a noise, and afterward a voice as of a great multitude, saying, 'Let us go hence.'

7. But what follows is still more terrible; for a certain Jesus, the son of Ananias, a common countryman, four years before the war, when the city was particularly prosperous and peaceful, came to the feast, at which it was customary for all to make tents at the temple to the honor of God, and suddenly began to cry out: 'A voice from the east, a voice from the west, a voice from the four winds, a voice against Jerusalem and the temple, a voice against bridegrooms and brides, a voice against all the people.' Day and night he went through all the alleys crying thus.

8. But certain of the more distinguished citizens, vexed at the ominous cry, seized the man and beat him with many stripes. But without uttering a word in his own behalf, or saying anything in particular to those that were present, he continued to cry out in the same words as before.

9. And the rulers, thinking, as was true, that the man was moved by a higher power, brought him before the Roman governor. And then, though he was scourged to the bone, he neither made supplication nor shed tears, but, changing his voice to the most lamentable tone possible, he answered each stroke with the words, 'Woe, woe unto Jerusalem.'"

10. The same historian records another fact still more wonderful than this. He says that a certain oracle was found in their sacred writings which declared that at that time a certain person should go forth from their country to rule the world. He himself understood that this was fulfilled in Vespasian.

11. But Vespasian did not rule the whole world, but only that part of
    it which was subject to the Romans. With better right could it be
    applied to Christ; to whom it was said by the Father, "Ask of me, and
    I will give thee the heathen for thine inheritance, and the ends of the
    earth for thy possession." At that very time, indeed, the voice of his
    holy apostles "went throughout all the earth, and their words to the
    end of the world."

I will quote some additional passages from Josephus for better
understanding:

Book 5 Chapter 1 fourth paragraph

And now there were three treacherous factions in the city, the one parted
from the other. Eleazar and his party, that kept the sacred first-fruits,
came against John in their cups. Those that were with John plundered
the populace, and went out with zeal against Simon. This Simon had his
supply of provisions from the city, in opposition to the seditious. When,
therefore, John was assaulted on both sides, he made his men turn about,
throwing his darts upon those citizens that came up against him, from the
cloisters he had in his possession, while he opposed those that attacked
him from the temple by his engines of war. And if at any time he was freed
from those that were above him, which happened frequently, from their
being drunk and tired, he sallied out with a great number upon Simon and
his party; and this he did always in such parts of the city as he could come
at, till he set on fire those houses that were full of corn, and of all other
provisions. The same thing was done by Simon, when, upon the other's
retreat, he attacked the city also; as if they had, on purpose, done it to serve
the Romans, by destroying what the city had laid up against the siege, and
by thus cutting off the nerves of their own power. Accordingly, it so came
to pass, that all the places that were about the temple were burnt down,
and were become an intermediate desert space, ready for fighting on both
sides of it; and that almost all that corn was burnt, which would have been
sufficient for a siege of many years. So they were taken by the means of the

famine, which it was impossible they should have been, unless they had thus prepared the way for it by this procedure.

Book 5 Chapter 1 fifth paragraph

Nay, John abused the sacred materials, and employed them in the construction of his engines of war; for the people and the priests had formerly determined to support the temple, and raise the holy house twenty cubits higher; for king Agrippa had at a very great expense, and with very great pains, brought thither such materials as were proper for that purpose, being pieces of timber very well worth seeing, both for their straightness and their largeness; but the war coming on, and interrupting the work, John had them cut, and prepared for the building him towers, he finding them long enough to oppose from them those his adversaries that thought him from the temple that was above him. He also had them brought and erected behind the inner court over against the west end of the cloisters, where alone he could erect them; whereas the other sides of that court had so many steps as would not let them come nigh enough the cloisters.

Book 5 Chapter 1 sixth paragraph

Thus did John hope to be too hard for his enemies by these engines constructed by his impiety; but God himself demonstrated that his pains would prove of no use to him, by bringing the Romans upon him, before he had reared any of his towers; for Titus, when he had gotten together part of his forces about him, and had ordered the rest to meet him at Jerusalem, marched out of Cesarea. He had with him those three legions that had accompanied his father when he laid Judea waste, together with that twelfth legion which had been formerly beaten with Cestius; which legion, as it was otherwise remarkable for its valor, so did it march on now with greater alacrity to avenge themselves on the Jews, as remembering what they had formerly suffered from them. Of these legions he ordered the fifth to meet him, by going through Emmaus, and the tenth to go up by Jericho; he also moved himself, together with the rest; besides whom, marched those auxiliaries that came from the kings, being now more in number than before, together with a considerable number that came to his assistance from Syria. Those also that had been selected out of these four legions, and sent with Mucianus to Italy, had their places filled up out of these soldiers that came out of Egypt with Titus; who were two thousand men, chosen out of the armies at Alexandria. There followed him also three thousand drawn from those that guarded the river Euphrates; as also there came Tiberius Alexander, who was a friend of his, most valuable, both for his good-will to him, and for his prudence. He had formerly been governor of Alexandria, but was now thought worthy to be general of the army [under Titus]. The reason of this was, that he had been the first who encouraged Vespasian very lately to accept this his new dominion, and joined himself to him with great fidelity, when things were uncertain, and fortune had not yet declared for him. He also followed Titus as a counselor, very useful to him in this war, both by his age and skill in such affairs.

Book 5 Chapter 10 fifth paragraph

It is therefore impossible to go distinctly over every instance of these men's iniquity. I shall therefore speak my mind here at once briefly: That neither did any other city ever suffer such miseries, nor did any age ever breed a generation more fruitful in wickedness than this was, from the beginning of the world.

Book 5 Chapter 12 first paragraph

TITUS THOUGHT FIT TO ENCOMPASS THE CITY ROUND WITH A WALL; AFTER WHICH THE FAMINE CONSUMED THE PEOPLE BY WHOLE HOUSES AND FAMILIES TOGETHER.

1. AND now did Titus consult with his commanders what was to be done. Those that were of the warmest tempers thought he should bring the whole army against the city and storm the wall; for that hitherto no more than a part of their army had fought with the Jews; but that in case

the entire army was to come at once, they would not be able to sustain their attacks, but would be overwhelmed by their darts. But of those that were for a more cautious management, some were for raising their banks again; and others advised to let the banks alone, but to lie still before the city, to guard against the coming out of the Jews, and against their carrying provisions into the city, and so to leave the enemy to the famine, and this without direct fighting with them; for that despair was not to be conquered, especially as to those who are desirous to die by the sword, while a more terrible misery than that is reserved for them. However, Titus did not think it fit for so great an army to lie entirely idle, and that yet it was in vain to fight with those that would be destroyed one by another; he also showed them how impracticable it was to cast up any more banks, for want of materials, and to guard against the Jews coming out still more impracticable; as also, that to encompass the whole city round with his army was not very easy, by reason of its magnitude, and the difficulty of the situation, and on other accounts dangerous, upon the sallies the Jews might make out of the city. For although they might guard the known passages out of the place, yet would they, when they found themselves under the greatest distress, contrive secret passages out, as being well acquainted with all such places; and if any provisions were carried in by stealth, the siege would thereby be longer delayed. He also owned that he was afraid that the length of time thus to be spent would diminish the glory of his success; for though it be true that length of time will perfect everything, yet that to do what we do in a little time is still necessary to the gaining reputation. That therefore his opinion was, that if they aimed at quickness joined with security, they must build a wall round about the whole city; which was, he thought, the only way to prevent the Jews from coming out any way, and that then they would either entirely despair of saving the city, and so would surrender it up to him, or be still the more easily conquered when the famine had further weakened them; for that besides this wall, he would not lie entirely at rest afterward, but would take care then to have banks raised again, when those that would oppose them were become weaker. But that if anyone should think such a work to be too great, and not to be finished without much difficulty, he ought to consider that it is not fit for Romans to undertake any small work, and that none but God himself could with ease accomplish any great thing whatsoever.

Book 6 Chapter 5 second paragraph

A false prophet was the occasion of these people's destruction, who had made a public proclamation in the city that very day, that God commanded them to get upon the temple, and that there they should receive miraculous signs of their deliverance. Now there was then a great number of false prophets suborned by the tyrants to impose on the people, who denounced this to them, that they should wait for deliverance from God; and this was in order to keep them from deserting, and that they might be buoyed up above fear and care by such hopes. Now a man that is in adversity does easily comply with such promises; for when such a seducer makes him believe that he shall be delivered from those miseries which oppress him, then it is that the patient is full of hopes of such his deliverance.

Book 6 Chapter 9 fourth paragraph

Many also of those that had been put in prison by the tyrants were now brought out; for they did not leave off their barbarous cruelty at the very last: yet did God avenge himself upon them both, in a manner agreeable to justice. As for John, he wanted food, together with his brethren, in these caverns, and begged that the Romans would now give him their right hand for his security, which he had often proudly rejected before; but for Simon, he struggled hard with the distress he was in, till he was forced to surrender himself, as we shall relate hereafter; so he was reserved for the triumph, and to be then slain; as was John condemned to perpetual imprisonment. And now the Romans set fire to the extreme parts of the city, and burnt them down, and entirely demolished its walls.

Book 7 Chapter 1 first paragraph

Now as soon as the army had no more people to slay or to plunder, because there remained none to be the objects of their fury, (for they would not have spared any, had there remained any other work to be done,) Caesar gave orders that they should now demolish the entire city and temple, but should leave as many of the towers standing as were of the greatest eminency; that is, Phasaelus, and Hippicus, and Mariamne; and so much of the wall as enclosed the city on the west side. This wall was spared, in order to afford a camp for such as were to lie in garrison, as were the towers also spared, in order to demonstrate to posterity what kind of city it was, and how well fortified, which the Roman valor had subdued; but for all the rest of the wall, it was so thoroughly laid even with the ground by those that dug it up to the foundation, that there was left nothing to make those that came thither believe it had ever been inhabited. This was the end which Jerusalem came to by the madness of those that were for innovations; a city otherwise of great magnificence, and of mighty fame among all mankind.

I will compare the accounts of Josephus to the biblical accounts and refer to how Eusebius interpreted those. In this section of the study, the readers should notice that the universal expressions, used similarly to the case of "sin," play a significant role in universalizing Christianity.

A. The Eschaton in the Gospels

Let us read the major relevant texts: Matthew 24:1–51, Mark 13:1–37, and Luke 21:5–36.

Matthew 24:1–51

1. Jesus came out from the temple and was going away when His disciples came up to point out the temple buildings to Him.
2. And He said to them, "Do you not see all these things? Truly I say to you, not one stone here will be left upon another, which will not be torn down."
3. As He was sitting on the Mount of Olives, the disciples came to Him privately, saying, "Tell us, when will these things happen, and what will be the sign of Your coming (παρουσίας), and of the end (συντελείας) of the age (αἰῶνος)?"

4. And Jesus answered and said to them, "See to it that no one misleads you.

5. "For many will come in my name, saying, 'I am the Christ,' and will mislead many.

6. "You will be hearing of wars and rumors of wars. See that you are not frightened, for those things must take place, but that is not yet the end.

7. "For nation will rise against nation, and kingdom against kingdom, and in various places there will be famines and earthquakes.

8. "But all these things are merely the beginning of birth pangs.

9. "Then they will deliver you to tribulation, and will kill you, and you will be hated by all nations because of My name.

10. "At that time many will fall away and will betray one another and hate one another.

11. "Many false prophets will arise and will mislead many.

12. "Because lawlessness is increased, most people's love will grow cold.

13. "But the one who endures to the end, he will be saved.

14. "This gospel of the kingdom shall be preached in the whole world as a testimony to all the nations, and then the end will come.

15. "Therefore when you see the abomination of desolation which was spoken of through Daniel the prophet, standing in the holy place (let the reader understand),

16. then those who are in Judea must flee to the mountains.

17. "Whoever is on the housetop must not go down to get the things out that are in his house.

18. "Whoever is in the field must not turn back to get his cloak.

19. "But woe to those who are pregnant and to those who are nursing babies in those days!

20. "But pray that your flight will not be in the winter, or on a Sabbath.

21. "For then there will be a great tribulation, such as has not occurred since the beginning of the world until now, nor ever will.

22. "Unless those days had been cut short, no life would have been saved; but for the sake of the elect those days will be cut short.

23. "Then if anyone says to you, 'Behold, here is the Christ,' or 'There He is,' do not believe him.

24. "For false Christs and false prophets will arise and will show great signs and wonders, so as to mislead, if possible, even the elect.

25. "Behold, I have told you in advance.

26. "So if they say to you, 'Behold, He is in the wilderness,' do not go out, or, 'Behold, He is in the inner rooms,' do not believe them.

27. "For just as the lightning comes from the east and flashes even to the west, so will the coming of the Son of Man be.

28. "Wherever the corpse is, there the vultures will gather.

29. "But immediately after the tribulation of those days the sun will be darkened, and the moon will not give its light, and the stars will fall from the sky, and the powers of the heavens will be shaken.

30. "And then the sign of the Son of Man will appear in the sky, and then all the tribes of the earth will mourn, and they will see the son of man coming on the clouds of the sky with power and great glory.

31. "And He will send forth His angels with a great trumpet and they will gather together His elect from the four winds, from one end of the sky to the other.

32. "Now learn the parable from the fig tree: when its branch has already become tender and puts forth its leaves, you know that summer is near;

33. so, you too, when you see all these things, recognize that He is near, right at the door.

34. "Truly I say to you, this generation will not pass away until all these things take place.

35. "Heaven and earth will pass away, but my words will not pass away.

36. "But of that day and hour no one knows, not even the angels of heaven, nor the Son, but the Father alone.

37. "For the coming of the Son of Man will be just like the days of Noah.

38. "For as in those days before the flood they were eating and drinking, marrying and giving in marriage, until the day that Noah entered the ark,

39. and they did not understand until the flood came and took them all away; so will the coming of the Son of Man be.

40. "Then there will be two men in the field; one will be taken and one will be left.

41. "Two women will be grinding at the mill; one will be taken and one will be left.

42. "Therefore be on the alert, for you do not know which day your Lord is coming.

43. "But be sure of this, that if the head of the house had known at what time of the night the thief was coming, he would have been on the alert and would not have allowed his house to be broken into.

44. "For this reason you also must be ready; for the Son of Man is coming at an hour when you do not think He will.

45. "Who then is the faithful and sensible slave whom his master put in charge of his household to give them their food at the proper time?

46. "Blessed is that slave whom his master finds so doing when he comes.

47. "Truly I say to you that he will put him in charge of all his possessions.

48. "But if that evil slave says in his heart, 'My master is not coming for a long time,'

49. and begins to beat his fellow slaves and eat and drink with drunkards;

50. the master of that slave will come on a day when he does not expect him and at an hour which he does not know,

51. and will cut him in pieces and assign him a place with the hypocrites; in that place there will be weeping and gnashing of teeth.

Mark 13:1–37

1. As He was going out of the temple, one of His disciples said to Him, "Teacher, behold what wonderful stones and what wonderful buildings!"

2. And Jesus said to him, "Do you see these great buildings? Not one stone will be left upon another which will not be torn down."

3. As He was sitting on the Mount of Olives opposite the temple, Peter and James and John and Andrew were questioning Him privately,

4. "Tell us, when will these things be, and what will be the sign when all these things are going to be fulfilled?"

5. And Jesus began to say to them, "See to it that no one misleads you.

6. "Many will come in my name, saying, 'I am He!' and will mislead many.

7. "When you hear of wars and rumors of wars, do not be frightened; those things must take place; but that is not yet the end.

8. "For nation will rise up against nation, and kingdom against kingdom; there will be earthquakes in various places; there will also be famines. These things are merely the beginning of birth pangs.

9. "But be on your guard; for they will deliver you to the courts, and you will be flogged in the synagogues, and you will stand before governors and kings for my sake, as a testimony to them.

10. "The gospel must first be preached to all the nations.

11. "When they arrest you and hand you over, do not worry beforehand about what you are to say, but say whatever is given you in that hour; for it is not you who speak, but it is the Holy Spirit.

12. "Brother will betray brother to death, and a father his child; and children will rise up against parents and have them put to death.

13. "You will be hated by all because of my name, but the one who endures to the end, he will be saved.

14. "But when you see the abomination of desolation standing where it should not be (let the reader understand), then those who are in Judea must flee to the mountains.

15. "The one who is on the housetop must not go down, or go in to get anything out of his house;

16. and the one who is in the field must not turn back to get his coat.

17. "But woe to those who are pregnant and to those who are nursing babies in those days!

18. "But pray that it may not happen in the winter.

19. "For those days will be a time of tribulation such as has not occurred since the beginning of the creation which God created until now, and never will.

20. "Unless the Lord had shortened those days, no life would have been saved; but for the sake of the elect, whom He chose, He shortened the days.

21. "And then if anyone says to you, 'Behold, here is the Christ'; or, 'Behold, He is there'; do not believe him;

22. for false Christs and false prophets will arise, and will show signs and wonders, in order to lead astray, if possible, the elect.

23. "But take heed; behold, I have told you everything in advance.

24. "But in those days, after that tribulation, the sun will be darkened and the moon will not give its light,

25. And the stars will be falling from heaven, and the powers that are in the heavens will be shaken.

26. "Then they will see the Son of Man coming in clouds with great power and glory.

27. "And then He will send forth the angels, and will gather together His elect from the four winds, from the farthest end of the earth to the farthest end of heaven.

28. "Now learn the parable from the fig tree: when its branch has already become tender and puts forth its leaves, you know that summer is near.

29. "Even so, you too, when you see these things happening, recognize that He is near, right at the door.

30. "Truly I say to you, this generation will not pass away until all these things take place.

31. "Heaven and earth will pass away, but my words will not pass away.

32. "But of that day or hour no one knows, not even the angels in heaven, nor the Son, but the Father alone.

33. "Take heed, keep on the alert; for you do not know when the appointed time will come.

34. "It is like a man away on a journey, who upon leaving his house and putting his slaves in charge, assigning to each one his task, also commanded the doorkeeper to stay on the alert.

35. "Therefore, be on the alert--for you do not know when the master of the house is coming, whether in the evening, at midnight, or when the rooster crows, or in the morning--

36. in case he should come suddenly and find you asleep.

37. "What I say to you I say to all, 'Be on the alert!'"

Luke 21:5–36

5. And while some were talking about the temple, that it was adorned with beautiful stones and votive gifts, He said,

6. "As for these things which you are looking at, the days will come in which there will not be left one stone upon another which will not be torn down."

7. They questioned Him, saying, "Teacher, when therefore will these things happen? And what will be the sign when these things are about to take place?"

8. And He said, "See to it that you are not misled; for many will come in My name, saying, 'I am He,' and, 'The time is near ' Do not go after them.

9. "When you hear of wars and disturbances, do not be terrified; for these things must take place first, but the end does not follow immediately."

10. Then He continued by saying to them, "Nation will rise against nation and kingdom against kingdom,

11. and there will be great earthquakes, and in various places plagues and famines; and there will be terrors and great signs from heaven.

12. "But before all these things, they will lay their hands on you and will persecute you, delivering you to the synagogues and prisons, bringing you before kings and governors for My name's sake.

13. "It will lead to an opportunity for your testimony.

14. "So make up your minds not to prepare beforehand to defend yourselves;

15. for I will give you utterance and wisdom which none of your opponents will be able to resist or refute.

16. "But you will be betrayed even by parents and brothers and relatives and friends, and they will put some of you to death,

17. and you will be hated by all because of My name.

18. "Yet not a hair of your head will perish.

19. "By your endurance you will gain your lives.

20. "But when you see Jerusalem surrounded by armies, then recognize that her desolation is near.

21. "Then those who are in Judea must flee to the mountains, and those who are in the midst of the city must leave, and those who are in the country must not enter the city;

22. because these are days of vengeance, so that all things which are written will be fulfilled.

23. "Woe to those who are pregnant and to those who are nursing babies in those days; for there will be great distress upon the land and wrath to this people;

24. and they will fall by the edge of the sword, and will be led captive into all the nations; and Jerusalem will be trampled under foot by the Gentiles until the times of the Gentiles are fulfilled.

25. "There will be signs in sun and moon and stars, and on the earth dismay among nations, in perplexity at the roaring of the sea and the waves,

26. men fainting from fear and the expectation of the things which are coming upon the world; for the powers of the heavens will be shaken.

27. "Then they will see the son of man coming in a cloud with power and great glory.

28. "But when these things begin to take place, straighten up and lift up your heads, because your redemption is drawing near."

29. Then He told them a parable: "Behold the fig tree and all the trees;

30. as soon as they put forth leaves, you see it and know for yourselves that summer is now near.

31. "So you also, when you see these things happening, recognize that the kingdom of God is near.

32. "Truly I say to you, this generation will not pass away until all things take place.

33. "Heaven and earth will pass away, but My words will not pass away.

34. "Be on guard, so that your hearts will not be weighted down with dissipation and drunkenness and the worries of life, and that day will not come on you suddenly like a trap;

35. for it will come upon all those who dwell on the face of all the earth.

36. "But keep on the alert at all times, praying that you may have strength to escape all these things that are about to take place, and to stand before the Son of Man."

Since several universal expressions are adopted in the texts, we easily assume that the texts are describing the eschaton, or end of the whole world.

Consider these universal expressions:

Matthew 13: 38
and the field is the world; and as for the good seed, these are the sons of the kingdom; and the tares are the sons of the evil one;

Matthew 24:3, 9, 22, 29, 30–31
3. As He was sitting on the Mount of Olives, the disciples came to Him privately, saying, "Tell us, when will these things happen, and what will be the sign of Your coming, and of the end of the age?"
9. "Then they will deliver you to tribulation, and will kill you, and you will be hated by all nations because of My name.
22. "Unless those days had been cut short, no life would have been saved; but for the sake of the elect those days will be cut short.
29. "But immediately after the tribulation of those days the sun will be darkened, and the moon will not give its light, and the stars will fall from the sky, and the powers of the heavens will be shaken.
30. "And then the sign of the Son of Man will appear in the sky, and then all the tribes of the earth will mourn, and they will see the son of man coming on the clouds of the sky with power and great glory.
31. "And He will send forth His angels with a great trumpet and they will gather together His elect from the four winds, from one end of the sky to the other.

Matthew 25:31–33
31. "But when the Son of Man comes in His glory, and all the angels with Him, then He will sit on His glorious throne.

32. "<u>All the nations</u> will be gathered before Him; and He will separate them from one another, as the shepherd separates the sheep from the goats;

33. and He will put the sheep on His right, and the goats on the left.

Mark 13:13, 27

13. "You will be hated by <u>all</u> because of my name, but the one who endures to the end, he will be saved.

27. "And then He will send forth the angels, and will gather together His elect from the four winds, from the farthest end of the earth to the farthest end of heaven.

Luke 21:17, 26, 35

17. and you will be hated by <u>all</u> because of My name.

26. men fainting from fear and the expectation of the things which are coming upon <u>the world</u>; for the powers of the heavens will be shaken.

35. for it will come upon all those who dwell on the face of <u>all the earth</u>.

Because of these universal expressions the readers might be confused about the scope of the event. Just like in the case of "sin," however, the writer intentionally or unintentionally adopted rhetorical universal expressions, but the scope of the event is clearly confined to the temple, Jerusalem, Judea, and the Jewish people in the texts.

In this discourse with the disciples, the place under discussion is the temple in Jerusalem. The explicit places and people are found in these verses:

Matthew 24:16
then those who are in <u>Judea</u> must flee to the mountains.

Mark 13:3, 14

3.   As He was sitting on the <u>Mount of Olives opposite the temple</u>, Peter and James and John and Andrew were questioning Him privately,

14. "But when you see the abomination of desolation standing where it should not be (let the reader understand), then those who are in Judea must flee to the mountains.

Luke 21:20–24

20. "But when you see Jerusalem surrounded by armies, then recognize that her desolation is near.
21. "Then those who are in Judea must flee to the mountains, and those who are in the midst of the city must leave, and those who are in the country must not enter the city;
23. "Woe to those who are pregnant and to those who are nursing babies in those days; for there will be great distress upon the land and wrath to this people;
24. and they will fall by the edge of the sword, and will be led captive into all the nations; and Jerusalem will be trampled under foot by the Gentiles until the times of the Gentiles are fulfilled.

As for the time, some Gospel verses limit it to within one generation, or forty years. If Jesus said these sayings around AD 30 that fits well since the destruction happened in AD 70.

Matthew 23:35–36

35. so that upon you may fall the guilt of all the righteous blood shed on earth, from the blood of righteous Abel to the blood of Zechariah, the son of Berechiah, whom you murdered between the temple and the altar.
36. Truly I say to you, all these things will come upon this generation.

Matthew 24:34

Truly I say to you, this generation will not pass away until all these things take place.

Mark 13:30

Truly I say to you, this generation will not pass away until all these things take place.

Luke 11:50–51

50. so that the blood of all the prophets, shed since the foundation of the world, may be charged against <u>this generation,</u>

51. from the blood of Abel to the blood of Zechariah, who was killed between the altar and the house of God; yes, I tell you, it shall be charged against <u>this generation.</u>'

Luke 21:32

"Truly I say to you,<u> this generation</u> will not pass away until all things take place.

The Gospels clarify the time as an imminent happening, even saying that some of the disciples who were listening to Jesus would witness the judgment and the Second Coming:

Matthew 10:23

"But whenever they persecute you in one city, flee to the next; for truly I say to you, <u>you will not finish going through the cities of Israel until the Son of Man comes.</u>"

Matthew 16:27–28

27. "For the Son of Man is going to come in the glory of His Father with His angels, and will then repay every man (holistic expression) according to his deeds.

28. "Truly I say to you, there are <u>some of those who are standing here</u> who will not taste death until they see the Son of Man coming in His kingdom."

Mark 9:1

And Jesus was saying to them, "Truly I say to you, there are <u>some of those who are standing here</u> who will not taste death until they see the kingdom of God after it has come with power."

Luke 9:27

"But I say to you truthfully, there are <u>some of those standing here</u> who will not taste death until they see the kingdom of God."

Therefore, the texts themselves prove that the eschatological statements in the Gospels refer to the AD 70 event. It does not matter whether the texts were written before or after AD 70; I will not spend space to discern the date of the texts. Even if the texts were written after AD 70, they still have value as a prophecy of Jesus. The important thing is to know whether the texts are talking about the end of Judea in Ad 70 or the end of the world. Once we are confident that the eschatological statements in the Gospels—which include language about the judgment, the end, and the Second Coming—are about the end of the Judea rather than the end of the world, we are forced to reexamine Christian eschatology as it has heretofore been understood.

When we compare the biblical accounts with the accounts from Josephus and Eusebius, the facts become clearer.

Not one stone

Matthew 24:2

And He said to them, "Do you not see all these things? Truly I say to you, not one stone here will be left upon another, which will not be torn down."

Mark 13:2

And Jesus said to him, "Do you see these great buildings? Not one stone will be left upon another which will not be torn down."

Luke 21:6

"As for these things which you are looking at, the days will come in which there will not be left one stone upon another which will not be torn down."

Josephus: Book 6 Chapter 9 the last verse of fourth paragraph

And now the <u>Romans set fire to the extreme parts of the city, and burnt them down, and entirely demolished its walls.</u>

Josephus: Book 7 Chapter 1 first paragraph

Now as soon as the army had no more people to slay or to plunder, because there remained none to be the objects of their fury, (for they would not have spared any, had there remained any other work to be done,) <u>Caesar gave orders that they should now demolish the entire city and temple, but should leave as many of the towers standing as were of the greatest eminency</u>; that is, Phasaelus, and Hippicus, and Mariamne; and so much of the wall as enclosed the city on the west side. This wall was spared, in order to afford a camp for such as were to lie in garrison, as were the towers also spared, in order to demonstrate to posterity what kind of city it was, and how well fortified, which the Roman valor had subdued; <u>but for all the rest of the wall, it was so thoroughly laid even with the ground by those that dug it up to the foundation, that there was left nothing</u> to make those that came thither believe it had ever been inhabited. This was the end which Jerusalem came to by the madness of those that were for innovations; a city otherwise of great magnificence, and of mighty fame among all mankind.

False prophets

Matthew 24:5, 24

5. "For many will come in My name, saying, 'I am the Christ,' and will mislead many.
11. Many false prophets will arise and will mislead many.
24. For false Christs and false prophets will arise and will show great signs and wonders, so as to mislead, if possible, even the elect.

Mark 13:22

for false Christs and false prophets will arise, and will show signs and wonders, in order to lead astray, if possible, the elect.

Luke 21:8

And He said, "See to it that you are not misled; for many will come in My name, saying, 'I am He,' and, 'The time is near ' Do not go after them.

Josephus: Book 6 Chapter 5 second paragraph

A false prophet was the occasion of these people's destruction, who had made a public proclamation in the city that very day, that God commanded them to get upon the temple, and that there they should receive miraculous signs of their deliverance. Now there was then a great number of false prophets suborned by the tyrants to impose on the people, who denounced this to them, that they should wait for deliverance from God; and this was in order to keep them from deserting, and that they might be buoyed up above fear and care by such hopes. Now a man that is in adversity does easily comply with such promises; for when such a seducer makes him believe that he shall be delivered from those miseries which oppress him, then it is that the patient is full of hopes of such his deliverance.

Flight from Judea and Jerusalem

Matthew 24:16–18

16. then those who are in Judea must flee to the mountains.

17. "Whoever is on the housetop must not go down to get the things out that are in his house.

18. "Whoever is in the field must not turn back to get his cloak."

Mark 13:14–16

14. "But when you see the abomination of desolation standing where it should not be (let the reader understand), then those who are in Judea must flee to the mountains.

15. "The one who is on the housetop must not go down, or go in to get anything out of his house;

16. and the one who is in the field must not turn back to get his coat.

Luke 21:20–21

20. "But when you see Jerusalem surrounded by armies, then recognize that her desolation is near.

21. "Then those who are in Judea must flee to the mountains, and those who are in the midst of the city must leave, and those who are in the country must not enter the city;

Eusebius: Chapter 5 fourth paragraph

But the number of calamities which everywhere fell upon the nation at that time; the extreme misfortunes to which the inhabitants of Judea were especially subjected, the thousands of men, as well as women and children, that perished by the sword, by famine, and by other forms of death innumerable,—all these things, as well as the many great sieges which were carried on against the cities of the Judea, and excessive sufferings endured by those that fled to Jerusalem itself, as to a city of perfect safety, and finally the general course of the whole war, as well as its particular occurrences in detail, and how at last the abomination of desolation, proclaimed by the prophets, stood in the very temple of God, so celebrated of old, the temple which was now awaiting its total and final destruction by fire,—all these things any one that wishes may find accurately described in the history written by Josephus.

Eusebius: Chapter 5 fifth paragraph

But it is necessary to state that this writer records that the multitude of those who were assembled from all Judea at the time of the Passover, to the number of three million souls, were shut up in Jerusalem "as in a prison," to use his own words.

Eusebius: Chapter 6 thirteenth paragraph 13

To this account Josephus, after relating other things, adds the following: "The possibility of going out of the city being brought to an end, all hope of safety for the Jews was cut off. And the famine increased and devoured the people by houses and families. And the rooms were filled with dead women and children, the lanes of the city with the corpses of old men.

Winter or Sabbath

Matthew 24:20

"But pray that your flight will not be in the winter, or on a Sabbath.

Mark 13:18

"But pray that it may not happen in the winter.

Eusebius: Chapter 5 fifth paragraph

But it is necessary to state that this writer records that the multitude of those who were assembled from all Judea <u>at the time of the Passover</u>, to the number of three million souls, were shut up in Jerusalem "as in a prison," to use his own words.

Army and war

Matthew 22:1–7

1. Jesus spoke to them again in parables, saying,
2. "The kingdom of heaven may be compared to a king who gave a wedding feast for his son.
3. "And he sent out his slaves to call those who had been invited to the wedding feast, and they were unwilling to come.
4. "Again he sent out other slaves saying, 'Tell those who have been invited, "Behold, I have prepared my dinner; my oxen and my fattened livestock are all butchered and everything is ready; come to the wedding feast."'
5. "But they paid no attention and went their way, one to his own farm, another to his business,
6. and the rest seized his slaves and mistreated them and killed them.
7. "But the king was enraged, and he sent his armies and destroyed those murderers and set their city on fire.

Matthew 24:6

"You will be hearing of wars and rumors of wars. See that you are not frightened, for those things must take place, but that is not yet the end.

Luke 19:41–44

41. When He approached Jerusalem, He saw the city and wept over it,
42. saying, "If you had known in this day, even you, the things which make for peace! But now they have been hidden from your eyes.
43. "For the days will come upon you when your enemies will throw up a barricade against you, and surround you and hem you in on every side,

44. and they will level you to the ground and your children within you, and they will not leave in you one stone upon another, because you did not recognize the time of your visitation."

Luke 21:9, 20

19. "When you hear of wars and disturbances, do not be terrified; for these things must take place first, but the end does not follow immediately."
20. "But when you see Jerusalem surrounded by armies, then recognize that her desolation is near.

Eusebius: Chapter 5 first paragraph

After Nero had held the power thirteen years and Galba and Otho had ruled a year and six months, Vespasian, who had become distinguished in the campaigns against the Jews, was proclaimed sovereign in Judea and received the title of Emperor from the armies there. Setting out immediately, therefore, for Rome, he entrusted the <u>conduct of the war against the Jews</u> to his son Titus.

Josephus: Book 5 Chapter 1 sixth paragraph

For Titus, when he had gotten together part of his forces about him, and had ordered the rest to meet him at Jerusalem, marched out of Cesarea. He had with him those three legions that had accompanied his father <u>when he laid Judea waste</u>, together with that twelfth legion which had been formerly beaten with Cestius; which legion, as it was otherwise remarkable for its valor, so did it march on now with greater alacrity to avenge themselves on the Jews, as remembering what they had formerly suffered from them. Of these legions he ordered the fifth to meet him, by going through Emmaus, and the tenth to go up by Jericho; he also moved himself, together with the rest; besides whom, marched those auxiliaries that came from the kings, being now more in number than before, together with a considerable number that came to his assistance from Syria. Those also that had been selected out of these four legions, and sent with Mucianus to Italy, had their places filled up out of these soldiers that came out of Egypt with Titus; who were two thousand men, chosen out of the armies at Alexandria. There followed him also three thousand drawn from those that guarded the river Euphrates.

Josephus: Book 5 Chapter 12 first paragraph

TITUS THOUGHT FIT TO ENCOMPASS THE CITY ROUND WITH A WALL; AFTER WHICH THE FAMINE CONSUMED THE PEOPLE BY WHOLE HOUSES AND FAMILIES TOGETHER.

1.   AND now did Titus consult with his commanders what was to be done. Those that were of the warmest tempers thought he should bring the whole army against the city and storm the wall; for that hitherto no more than a part of their army had fought with the Jews; but that in case the entire army was to come at once, they would not be able to sustain their attacks, but would be overwhelmed by their darts. But of those that were for a more cautious management, some were for raising their banks again; and others advised to let the banks alone, but to lie still before the city, to guard against the coming out of the Jews, and against their carrying provisions into the city, and so to leave the enemy to the famine, and this without direct fighting with them; for that despair was not to be conquered, especially as to those who are desirous to die by the sword, while a more terrible misery than that is reserved for them (and the following accounts).

Famine and woe
Matthew 24:19
"But woe to those who are pregnant and to those who are nursing babies in those days!

Mark 13:8, 17
8.   "For nation will rise up against nation, and kingdom against kingdom; there will be earthquakes in various places; there will also be famines. These things are merely the beginning of birth pangs.

17. "But woe to those who are pregnant and to those who are nursing babies in those days!

Luke 21:11, 23

11. and there will be great earthquakes, and in various places plagues and famines; and there will be terrors and great signs from heaven.

23. "Woe to those who are pregnant and to those who are nursing babies in those days; for there will be great distress upon the land and wrath to this people

Luke 23:27–30

27. And following Him was a large crowd of the people, and of women who were mourning and lamenting Him.

28. But Jesus turning to them said, "Daughters of Jerusalem, stop weeping for Me, but weep for yourselves and for your children.

29. "For behold, the days are coming when they will say, 'Blessed are the barren, and the wombs that never bore, and the breasts that never nursed.'

30. "Then they will begin to say to the mountains, 'fall on us,' and to the hills, 'cover us.'"

Josephus: Book 5 Chapter 1 fourth paragraph

And now there were three treacherous factions in the city, the one parted from the other. Eleazar and his party, that kept the sacred first-fruits, came against John in their cups. Those that were with John plundered the populace, and went out with zeal against Simon. This Simon had his supply of provisions from the city, in opposition to the seditious. When, therefore, John was assaulted on both sides, he made his men turn about, throwing his darts upon those citizens that came up against him, from the cloisters he had in his possession, while he opposed those that attacked him from the temple by his engines of war. And if at any time he was freed from those that were above him, which happened frequently, from their being drunk and tired, he sallied out with a great number upon Simon and his party; and this he did always in such parts of the city as he could come at, till he set on fire those houses that were full of corn, and of all other provisions. The same thing was done by Simon, when, upon the other's retreat, he attacked the city also; as if they had, on purpose, done it to serve the Romans, by destroying what the city had laid up against the siege, and by thus cutting off the nerves of their own power. Accordingly, it so came to pass, that all the places that were about the temple were burnt down, and were become an intermediate desert space, ready for fighting on both sides of it; and that almost all that corn was burnt, which would have been sufficient for a siege of many years. <u>So they were taken by the means of the famine</u>, which it was impossible they should have been, unless they had thus prepared the way for it by this procedure.

Eusebius: Chapter 6. The Famine which oppressed them

7. Of all evils, indeed, famine is the worst, and it destroys nothing so effectively as shame. For that which under other circumstances is worthy of respect, in the midst of famine is despised. <u>Thus women snatched the food from the very mouths of their husbands and children, from their fathers, and what was most pitiable of all, mothers from their babes. And while their dearest ones were wasting away in their arms, they were not ashamed to take away from them the last drops that supported life.</u>

9. Old men who clung to their food were beaten, and if the women concealed it in their hands, their hair was torn for so doing. There was pity neither for gray hairs nor for infants, but, taking up the babes that clung to their morsels of food, they dashed them to the ground. But to those that anticipated their entrance and swallowed what they were about to seize, they were still more cruel, just as if they had been wronged by them.

13. To this account Josephus, after relating other things, adds the following: "<u>The possibility of going out of the city being brought to an end, all hope of safety for the Jews was cut off. And the famine increased and devoured the people by houses and families. And the rooms were filled with dead women and children, the lanes of the city with the corpses of old men.</u>

14. Children and youths, swollen with the famine, wandered about the market-places like shadows, and fell down wherever the death agony overtook them. The sick were not strong enough to bury even their own relatives, and those who had the strength hesitated because of the multitude of the dead and the uncertainty as to their own fate. Many, indeed, died while they were burying others, and many betook themselves to their graves before death came upon them.

24. "There was a certain woman named Mary that dwelt beyond Jordan, whose father was Eleazer, of the village of Bathezor (which signifies the house of hyssop). She was distinguished for her family and her wealth, and had fled with the rest of the multitude to Jerusalem and was shut up there with them during the siege. (The whole story of Mary)

Intensity of tribulation

Matthew 10:15

"Truly I say to you, it will be more tolerable for the land of Sodom and Gomorrah in the day of judgment than for that city.

Matthew 24:21–22

21. "For then there will be a great tribulation, such as has not occurred since the beginning of the world until now, nor ever will.

22. "Unless those days had been cut short, no life would have been saved; but for the sake of the elect those days will be cut short.

Mark 13:19, 20

19. "For those days will be a time of tribulation such as has not occurred since the beginning of the creation which God created until now, and never will.

20. "Unless the Lord had shortened those days, no life would have been saved; but for the sake of the elect, whom He chose, He shortened the days."

Josephus: Book 5 Chapter 10 fifth paragraph

It is therefore impossible to go distinctly over every instance of these men's iniquity. I shall therefore speak my mind here at once briefly: <u>That neither did any other city ever suffer such miseries, nor did any age ever breed a generation more fruitful in wickedness than this was, from the beginning of the world.</u>

Eusebius: Chapter 6 nineteenth paragraph

After speaking of some other things, Josephus proceeds as follows: "I cannot hesitate to declare what my feelings compel me to. I suppose, if the Romans had longer delayed in coming against these guilty wretches, the city would have been swallowed up by a chasm, or overwhelmed with a flood, or struck with such thunderbolts as destroyed Sodom. For it had brought forth a generation of men much more godless than were those that suffered such punishment. By their madness indeed was the whole people brought to destruction."

The abomination of desolation
Matthew 24:15
"Therefore, when you see the abomination of desolation which was spoken of through Daniel the prophet, standing in the holy place (let the reader understand),"

Mark 13:14
"But when you see the abomination of desolation standing where it should not be (let the reader understand), then those who are in Judea must flee to the mountains."

Josephus: Book 5 Chapter 1 fifth paragraph

Nay, John abused the sacred materials, and employed them in the construction of his engines of war; for the people and the priests had formerly determined to support the temple, and raise the holy house twenty cubits higher; for king Agrippa had at a very great expense, and with very great pains, brought thither such materials as were proper for that purpose, being pieces of timber very well worth seeing, both for their straightness and their largeness; but the war coming on, and interrupting the work, John had them cut, and prepared for the building him towers, he finding them long enough to oppose from them those his adversaries that thought him from the temple that was above him. He also had them brought and erected behind the inner court over against the west end of the cloisters, where alone he could erect them; whereas the other sides of that court had so many steps as would not let them come nigh enough the cloisters.

Death, sword, and captivity
Matthew 24:28
"Wherever the corpse is, there the vultures will gather."

Luke 21:24
and they will fall by the edge of the sword, and will be led captive into all the nations; and Jerusalem will be trampled under foot by the Gentiles until the times of the Gentiles are fulfilled.

Eusebius: Chapter 7 third paragraph

The historian, reckoning the whole number of the slain, says that <u>eleven hundred thousand persons perished by famine and sword, and that the rest of the rioters and robbers, being betrayed by each other after the taking of the city, were slain.</u> But the tallest of the youths and those that were distinguished for beauty were preserved for the triumph. Of the rest of the multitude, those that were over seventeen years of age were sent as prisoners to labor in the works of Egypt, while still more were scattered through the provinces to meet their death in the theaters by the sword and by beasts. Those under seventeen years of age were carried away to be sold as slaves, and of these alone the number reached ninety thousand.

Signs and the Second Coming
Matthew 10:23
"But whenever they persecute you in one city, flee to the next; for truly I say to you, you will not finish going through the cities of Israel until the Son of Man comes."

Matthew 16:27–28
27. "For the Son of Man is going to come in the glory of His Father with His angels, and will then repay every man (holistic expression) according to his deeds.
28. "Truly I say to you, there are some of those who are standing here who will not taste death until they see the Son of Man coming in His kingdom."

Matthew 24:29–31
29. "But immediately after the tribulation of those days the sun will be darkened, and the moon will not give its light, and the stars will fall from the sky, and the powers of the heavens will be shaken.
30. "And then the sign of the Son of Man will appear in the sky, and then all the tribes of the earth [note universal expression] will mourn, and they will see the Son of Man coming on the clouds of the sky with power and great glory.
31. "And He will send forth His angels with a great trumpet and they will gather together His elect from the four winds, from one end of the sky to the other.

Mark 9:1
And Jesus was saying to them, "Truly I say to you, there are some of those who are standing here who will not taste death until they see the kingdom of God after it has come with power."

Mark 13:24–27
24. "But in those days, after that tribulation, the sun will be darkened and the moon will not give its light,

25. And the stars will be falling from heaven, and the powers that are in the heavens will be shaken.

26. "Then they will see the Son of Man coming in clouds with great power and glory.

27. "And then He will send forth the angels, and will gather together His elect from the four winds, from the farthest end of the earth to the farthest end of heaven."

Luke 9:27

"But I say to you truthfully, there are some of those standing here who will not taste death until they see the kingdom of God."

Luke 21:11, 25–27

11. and there will be great earthquakes, and in various places plagues and famines; and there will be terrors and great signs from heaven.

25. "There will be signs in sun and moon and stars, and on the earth dismay among nations, in perplexity at the roaring of the sea and the waves,

26. men fainting from fear and the expectation of the things which are coming upon the world (universal express); for the powers of the heavens will be shaken.

27. "Then they will see the son of man coming in a cloud with power and great glory."

Acts 1: 6–11 should be understood in this context as a saying of Jesus himself.

6. So when they had come together, they were asking Him, saying, "Lord, is it at this time You are restoring the kingdom to Israel?"

7. He said to them, "It is not for you to know times or epochs which the Father has fixed by His own authority;

8. but you will receive power when the Holy Spirit has come upon you; and you shall be My witnesses both in Jerusalem, and in all Judea and Samaria, and even to the remotest part of the earth."

9. And after He had said these things, He was lifted up while they were looking on, and a cloud received Him out of their sight.

10. And as they were gazing intently into the sky while He was going, behold, two men in white clothing stood beside them.

11. They also said, "Men of Galilee, why do you stand looking into the sky? This Jesus, who has been taken up from you into heaven, will come in just the same way as you have watched Him go into heaven."

Since Josephus was a devout Jew, not a Christian, and his main concern was to leave the historical accounts of the end of his beloved country, he did not leave any record or explanation related to the Second Coming of Christ. However, the following historical story (especially verses 7 through 9) strongly implies that Jesus was seriously involved in that event. This account might provide an objective proof of the Second Coming of Jesus Christ in AD 70.

Eusebius: Chapter 8. The Signs which preceded the War

The whole chapter is worth reading again.

1. Taking, then, the work of this author, read what he records in the sixth book of his History. His words are as follows: "Thus were the miserable people won over at this time by the impostors and false prophets; but they did not heed nor give credit to the visions and signs that foretold the approaching desolation. On the contrary, as if struck by lightning, and as if possessing neither eyes nor understanding, they slighted the proclamations of God.

2. At one time a star, in form like a sword, stood over the city, and a comet, which lasted for a whole year; and again before the revolt and before the disturbances that led to the war, when the people were gathered for the feast of unleavened bread, on the eighth of the month Xanthicus, at the ninth hour of the night, so great a light shone about the altar and the temple that it seemed to be bright day; and this continued for half an hour. This seemed to the unskillful a good sign, but was interpreted by the sacred scribes as portending those events which very soon took place.

3. And at the same feast a cow, led by the high priest to be sacrificed, brought forth a lamb in the midst of the temple.

4. And the eastern gate of the inner temple, which was of bronze and very massive, and which at evening was closed with difficulty by twenty men, and rested upon iron-bound beams, and had bars sunk deep in the ground, was seen at the sixth hour of the night to open of itself.

5. And not many days after the feast, on the twenty-first of the month Artemisium, a certain marvelous vision was seen which passes belief. The prodigy might seem fabulous were it not related by those who saw it, and were not the calamities which followed deserving of such signs. For before the setting of the sun chariots and armed troops were seen throughout the whole region in mid-air, wheeling through the clouds and encircling the cities.

6. And at the feast which is called Pentecost, when the priests entered the temple at night, as was their custom, to perform the services, they said that at first they perceived a movement and a noise, and afterward a voice as of a great multitude, saying, "Let us go hence."

7. But what follows is still more terrible; for a certain Jesus, the son of Ananias, a common countryman, four years before the war[58], when the city was particularly prosperous and peaceful, came to the feast, at which it was customary for all to make tents at the temple to the honor of God, and suddenly began to cry out: A voice from the east, a voice from the west, a voice from the four winds, a voice against Jerusalem and the temple, a voice against bridegrooms and brides, a voice against all the people.' Day and night he went through all the alleys crying thus.

8. But certain of the more distinguished citizens, vexed at the ominous cry, seized the man and beat him with many stripes. But without uttering a word in his own behalf, or saying anything in particular to those that were present, he continued to cry out in the same words as before.

9. And the rulers, thinking, as was true, that the man was moved by a higher power, brought him before the Roman governor. And then, though he was scourged to the bone, he neither made supplication

nor shed tears, but, changing his voice to the most lamentable tone possible, he answered each stroke with the words, 'Woe, woe unto Jerusalem.'"

10. The same historian records another fact still more wonderful than this. He says that a certain oracle was found in their sacred writings which declared that at that time a certain person should go forth from their country to rule the world. He himself understood that this was fulfilled in Vespasian.

11. But Vespasian did not rule the whole world, but only that part of it which was subject to the Romans. With better right could it be applied to Christ; to whom it was said by the Father, "Ask of me, and I will give thee the heathen for thine inheritance, and the ends of the earth for thy possession." At that very time, indeed, the voice of his holy apostles "went throughout all the earth, and their words to the end of the world."

Salvation
Matthew 24:13
"But the one who endures to the end, he will be saved

Mark 13:13
"You will be hated by all because of my name, but the one who endures to the end, he will be saved."

Luke 21:19–28
19. "By your endurance you will gain your lives."
28. "But when these things begin to take place, straighten up and lift up your heads, because your redemption is drawing near."

As in the case of the Second Coming, Josephus did not leave any record or explanation related to salvation of the Christians; for that we depend upon the record of Christian historian Eusebius.

Eusebius: Chapter 5 third paragraph

But the people of the church in Jerusalem had been commanded by a revelation, vouchsafed to approved men there before the war, to leave the city and to dwell in a certain town of Perea called Pella. And when those that believed in Christ had come thither from Jerusalem, then, as if the royal city of the Jews and the whole land of Judea were entirely destitute of holy men, the judgment of God at length overtook those who had committed such outrages against Christ and his apostles, and totally destroyed that generation of impious men.

[We can see the sharp contrast between Christians who left Jerusalem to Pella and a woman Mary who left Pella to Jerusalem.]

Eusebius: Chapter 7 ninth paragraph

But it may be proper to mention also those events which exhibited the graciousness of that all-good Providence which held back their destruction full forty years after their crime against Christ,—during which time many of the apostles and disciples, and James himself the first bishop there, the one who is called the brother of the Lord, were still alive, and dwelling in Jerusalem itself, remained the surest bulwark of the place. Divine Providence thus still proved itself long-suffering toward them in order to see whether by repentance for what they had done they might obtain pardon and salvation; and in addition to such long-suffering, Providence also furnished wonderful signs of the things which were about to happen to them if they did not repent.

If the Jewish nation, which persecuted Jesus and Christians (based upon the New Testament accounts), was destroyed along with their temple, or worship center, according to divine Providence, it certainly can be said that the Christian Church was saved, redeemed, or liberated by God.

Resurrection/taken-up (so-called rapture)
These should be a part of salvation. However, for clarity, I want to deal with each separately.

Matthew 24:31
"And He will send forth His angels with a great trumpet and they will gather together His elect from the four winds, from one end of the sky to the other."

Mark 13:27
"And then He will send forth the angels, and will gather together His elect from the four winds, from the farthest end of the earth to the farthest end of heaven."

John 11:25–26 might be understood in this context.

25. Jesus said to her, "I am the resurrection and the life; he who believes in Me will live even if he dies,
26. and everyone who lives and believes in Me will never die. Do you believe this?"

Just like in the case of the Second Coming and salvation, we should not expect any historical account by a Jewish author to include resurrection and rapture of the Christians. However, if we take what Jesus said and the memory of the authors of the Gospel seriously, we can postulate that resurrection and rapture actually happened in AD 70 in Judea, particularly in Jerusalem. Maybe Josephus did not leave any record about those events because he did not notice or was not interested in them since he was not a Christian. Perhaps they happened to a small group of Christians in the midst of the terrible suffering and turmoil of the Jewish nation. If the whole text that contains the implication of resurrection and rapture is about the AD 70 event, we should not interpret resurrection and rapture as future events separated from the whole text and taken out of context. Even though universal expressions are adopted, it is reasonable to think that some Christians who died due to persecution in Judea were resurrected and that they and some Christians who were in Jerusalem experienced rapture. At least, it is a working hypothesis. If we read the texts with this postulate, the texts make more sense. Also, if we truly believe that resurrection and rapture will happen in the future, does that preclude it from also having happened in AD 70? No, it simply gives more credit to the sayings of Jesus.

It is worth noticing that Eusebius himself interpreted the AD 70 event as the fulfillment of the prophecy of Jesus Christ and the avenging by God for the crimes against Jesus and his disciples. Eusebius devotes the entire chapter 7, The Predictions of Christ, to prove that fact. He quotes from Matthew 24: 19–21, Luke 19: 42–44, Luke 21: 23b–24, Luke 21:20. Chapter 7 paragraph 7 summarizes his confidence: "If any one compares the words of our Saviour with the other accounts of the historian concerning the whole war, how can one fail to wonder, and to admit that the foreknowledge and the prophecy of our Saviour were truly divine and marvelously strange."(Refer to Eusebius: Chapter 5 paragraph 3 and Chapter 7)

Based upon the biblical texts, the comparison of the biblical texts and the accounts of Josephus and Eusebius, and the interpretation of Eusebius, I come to the conclusion that the eschatological statements of the Gospels are all about the AD 70 event, the destruction of the temple, Jerusalem, and Judea and, thus, it is the fulfilled eschatology.

I believe that in the eschatological statements of the Gospels, Jesus was essentially saying to his disciples: You (the disciples or Christians) will be persecuted harshly by the Jews; however, endure that persecution. I will come back and avenge you by destroying the temple, Jerusalem, and the nation of Judea within a generation. I will save you from that destruction and the new Kingdom of God (Christian Church) will be established. It will happen pretty soon but I do not know the exact date, only God knows. Prior to the end of Judea, the gospel will be preached to all nations for the Christian Church to be preserved. Therefore, until I come, be faithful to your duties.

B. The Eschaton in the Epistles

The eschatology of Jesus that predicted the end of Judea was transmitted to the apostles and disciples who then taught and preached it to the non-Jewish world. This generalization of eschaton was effective in universalizing Christianity; however, at the same time, it contributed significantly to the ambiguity of Christian theology. In this section, I will try to convince the reader that the eschaton of the Epistles is, in fact, an allusion to the eschaton in the Gospels, the event that happened in AD 70 — or the fulfilled eschatology. I will present four arguments: the source of knowledge, the imminent coming, the vivid recollection of the sayings of Jesus, and the historical comparison.

Let us read the major relevant texts:

1 Corinthians 15:51–58

51. Behold, I tell you a mystery; we will not all sleep, but we will all be changed,

52. in a moment, in the twinkling of an eye, at the last trumpet; for the trumpet will sound, and the dead will be raised imperishable, and we will be changed.

53. For this perishable must put on the imperishable, and this mortal must put on immortality.

54. But when this perishable will have put on the imperishable, and this mortal will have put on immortality, then will come about the saying that is written, "death is swallowed up in victory.

55. "O death, where is your victory? O death, where is your string?"

56. The sting of death is sin, and the power of sin is the law;

57. but thanks be to God, who gives us the victory through our Lord Jesus Christ.

58. Therefore, my beloved brethren, be steadfast, immovable, always abounding in the work

of the Lord, knowing that your toil is not in vain in the Lord.

1 Thessalonians 1:10

and to wait for His Son from heaven, whom He raised from the dead, that is Jesus, who rescues us from the wrath to come.

1 Thessalonians 2:19

For who is our hope or joy or crown of exultation? Is it not even you, in the presence of our Lord Jesus at His coming?

1 Thessalonians 3:13

so that He may establish your hearts without blame in holiness before our God and Father at the coming of our Lord Jesus with all His saints.

1 Thessalonians 4:13–18

13. But we do not want you to be uninformed, brethren, about those who are asleep, so that you will not grieve as do the rest who have no hope.
14. For if we believe that Jesus died and rose again, even so God will bring with Him those who have fallen asleep in Jesus.
15. For this we say to you by the word of the Lord, that we who are alive and remain until the coming of the Lord, will not precede those who have fallen asleep.
16. For the Lord Himself will descend from heaven with a shout, with the voice of the archangel and with the trumpet of God, and the dead in Christ will rise first.
17. Then we who are alive and remain will be caught up together with them in the clouds to meet the Lord in the air, and so we shall always be with the Lord.
18. Therefore comfort one another with these words.

1 Thessalonians 5:1–7, 23

1. Now as to the times and the epochs, brethren, you have no need of anything to be written to you.
2. For you yourselves know full well that the day of the Lord will come just like a thief in the night.

3.   While they are saying, "Peace and safety!" then destruction will come upon them suddenly like labor pains upon a woman with child, and they will not escape.

4.   But you, brethren, are not in darkness, that the day would overtake you like a thief;

5.   for you are all sons of light and sons of day We are not of night nor of darkness;

6.   so then let us not sleep as others do, but let us be alert and sober.

7.   For those who sleep do their sleeping at night, and those who get drunk get drunk at night.

23. Now may the God of peace Himself sanctify you entirely; and may your spirit and soul and body be preserved complete, without blame at the coming of our Lord Jesus Christ.

2 Thessalonians 1:5–10

5.   This is a plain indication of God's righteous judgment so that you will be considered worthy of the kingdom of God, for which indeed you are suffering.

6.   For after all it is only just for God to repay with affliction those who afflict you,

7.   and to give relief to you who are afflicted and to us as well when the Lord Jesus will be revealed from heaven with His mighty angels in flaming fire,

8.   dealing out retribution to those who do not know God and to those who do not obey the gospel of our Lord Jesus.

9.   These will pay the penalty of eternal destruction, away from the presence of the Lord and from the glory of His power,

10. when He comes to be glorified in His saints on that day, and to be marveled at among all who have believed--for our testimony to you was believed.

2 Thessalonians 2:1–12

1.   Now we request you, brethren, with regard to the coming of our Lord Jesus Christ and our gathering together to Him,

2. that you not be quickly shaken from your composure or be disturbed either by a spirit or a message or a letter as if from us, to the effect that the day of the Lord has come.
3. Let no one in any way deceive you, for it will not come unless the apostasy comes first, and the man of lawlessness is revealed, the son of destruction,
4. who opposes and exalts himself above every so-called god or object of worship, so that he takes his seat in the temple of God, displaying himself as being God.
5. Do you not remember that while I was still with you, I was telling you these things?
6. And you know what restrains him now, so that in his time he will be revealed.
7. For the mystery of lawlessness is already at work; only he who now restrains will do so until he is taken out of the way.
8. Then that lawless one will be revealed whom the Lord will slay with the breath of His mouth and bring to an end by the appearance of His coming;
9. that is, the one whose coming is in accord with the activity of Satan, with all power and signs and false wonders,
10. and with all the deception of wickedness for those who perish, because they did not receive the love of the truth so as to be saved.
11. For this reason God will send upon them a deluding influence so that they will believe what is false,
12. in order that they all may be judged who did not believe the truth, but took pleasure in wickedness

James was written to the Christians who were outside of Judea; the recipients are described in James 1:1:

James, a bond-servant of God and of the Lord Jesus Christ, To the twelve tribes who are dispersed abroad: Greetings.

James 5:1–8
1. Come now, you rich, weep and howl for your miseries which are coming upon you.
2. Your riches have rotted and your garments have become moth-eaten.
3. Your gold and your silver have rusted; and their rust will be a witness against you and will consume your flesh like fire. It is in the last days that you have stored up your treasure!
4. Behold, the pay of the laborers who mowed your fields, and which has been withheld by you, cries out against you; and the outcry of those who did the harvesting has reached the ears of the Lord of Sabaoth.
5. You have lived luxuriously on the earth and led a life of wanton pleasure; you have fattened your hearts in a day of slaughter.
6. You have condemned and put to death the righteous man; he does not resist you.
7. Therefore be patient, brethren, until the coming of the Lord The farmer waits for the precious produce of the soil, being patient about it, until it gets the early and late rains.
8. You too be patient; strengthen your hearts, for the coming of the Lord is near.

The epistle 1 Peter was written to the Christians who were in Asia Minor; the recipients are described in 1 Peter 1:1:

Peter, an apostle of Jesus Christ, To those who reside as aliens, scattered throughout Pontus, Galatia, Cappadocia, Asia, and Bithynia, who are chosen.

1 Peter 1:5–9
5. who are protected by the power of God through faith for a salvation ready to be revealed in the last time.
6. In this you greatly rejoice, even though now for a little while, if necessary, you have been distressed by various trials,
7. so that the proof of your faith, being more precious than gold which is perishable, even though tested by fire, may be found to result in praise and glory and honor at the revelation of Jesus Christ;

8. and though you have not seen Him, you love Him, and though you do not see Him now, but believe in Him, you greatly rejoice with joy inexpressible and full of glory,

9. obtaining as the outcome of your faith the salvation of your souls.

1 Peter 4:7–19

7. The end of all things is near; therefore, be of sound judgment and sober spirit for the purpose of prayer.

8. Above all, keep fervent in your love for one another, because love covers a multitude of sins.

9. Be hospitable to one another without complaint.

10. As each one has received a special gift, employ it in serving one another as good stewards of the manifold grace of God.

11. Whoever speaks, is to do so as one who is speaking the utterances of God; whoever serves is to do so as one who is serving by the strength which God supplies; so that in all things God may be glorified through Jesus Christ, to whom belongs the glory and dominion forever and ever. Amen.

12. Beloved, do not be surprised at the fiery ordeal among you, which comes upon you for your testing, as though some strange thing were happening to you;

13. but to the degree that you share the sufferings of Christ, keep on rejoicing, so that also at the revelation of His glory you may rejoice with exultation.

14. If you are reviled for the name of Christ, you are blessed, because the Spirit of glory and of God rests on you.

15. Make sure that none of you suffers as a murderer, or thief, or evildoer, or a troublesome meddler;

16. but if anyone suffers as a Christian, he is not to be ashamed, but is to glorify God in this name.

17. For it is time for judgment to begin with the household of God; and if it begins with us first, what will be the outcome for those who do not obey the gospel of God?

18. and if it is with difficulty that the righteous is saved, what will become of the godless man and the sinner?

19. Therefore, those also who suffer according to the will of God shall entrust their souls to a faithful Creator in doing what is right.

Many scholars think that 2 Peter was not written by Peter and was written after AD 70. Neither the author nor date is an important issue in this study. What is important is whether or not the eschatological statements of these texts were allusions to the events of AD 70. If these texts were written after AD 70, they would be an example that the end of Judea had become thought of as the end of the world because the fulfilled eschaton was being taught and preached as a coming event to the Gentile Christians even after AD 70.

The recipients of 2 Peter are described in 2 Peter 1:1:

Simon Peter, a bond-servant and apostle of Jesus Christ, To those who have received a faith of the same kind as ours, by the righteousness of our God and Savior, Jesus Christ:

No specific recipient is referenced; however, 2 Peter 3:1 says, "This is now, beloved, the second letter I am writing to you in which I am stirring up your sincere mind by way of reminder." Therefore, regardless of authorship, the recipients should be understood in conjunction with 1 Peter, the Christians who were in Asia Minor.

2 Peter 1:16
For we did not follow cleverly devised tales when we made known to you the power and coming of our Lord Jesus Christ, but we were eyewitnesses of His majesty.

2 Peter 3:1–15
1. This is now, beloved, the second letter I am writing to you in which I am stirring up your sincere mind by way of reminder,
2. that you should remember the words spoken beforehand by the holy prophets and the commandment of the Lord and Savior spoken by your apostles.

3. Know this first of all, that in the last days mockers will come with their mocking, following after their own lusts,

4. and saying, "Where is the promise of His coming? For ever since the fathers fell asleep, all continues just as it was from the beginning of creation."

5. For when they maintain this, it escapes their notice that by the word of God the heavens existed long ago and the earth was formed out of water and by water,

7. But by His word the present heavens and earth are being reserved for fire, kept for the day of judgment and destruction of ungodly men.

8. But do not let this one fact escape your notice, beloved, that with the Lord one day is like a thousand years, and a thousand years like one day.

9. The Lord is not slow about His promise, as some count slowness, but is patient toward you, not wishing for any to perish but for all to come to repentance.

10. But the day of the Lord will come like a thief, in which the heavens will pass away with a roar and the elements will be destroyed with intense heat, and the earth and its works will be burned up.

11. Since all these things are to be destroyed in this way, what sort of people ought you to be in holy conduct and godliness,

12. looking for and hastening the coming of the day of God, because of which the heavens will be destroyed by burning, and the elements will melt with intense heat!

13. But according to His promise we are looking for new heavens and a new earth, in which righteousness dwells.

14. Therefore, beloved, since you look for these things, be diligent to be found by Him in peace, spotless and blameless,

15. and regard the patience of our Lord as salvation; just as also our beloved brother Paul, according to the wisdom given him, wrote to you,

Proof 1: Source of Knowledge

I would argue that if the apostles and the disciples had any knowledge regarding the Second Coming, judgment, the end, and salvation, that knowledge certainly came from Jesus himself. Jesus is believed to have died and resurrected in about AD 30, and immediately the apostles and disciples spread the gospel and teachings of Jesus to the world. They preached, taught, and wrote about the Second coming, judgment, end, and salvation to encourage the Gentile Christians who were under the sort of persecutions the Jewish Christians were experiencing in Judea (1 Thessalonians 2:14: For you, brethren, became imitators of the churches of God in Christ Jesus that are in Judea, for you also endured the same sufferings at the hands of your own countrymen, even as they did from the Jews), to teach them patience and to live holy lives. Also, they used those eschatological teachings to evangelize the Gentiles (Acts 17: 31: because He has fixed a day in which He will judge the world in righteousness through a Man whom He has appointed, having furnished proof to all men by raising Him from the dead). Where did they get this knowledge and these ideas? From whom did they learn? If they learned them from Jesus, their eschatology must be the eschatology of Jesus. If the eschatology of Jesus (Matthew 24:1–51, Mark 13:1–37, Luke 21:5–36) was about AD 70, their eschatology must be about AD 70, too. Is there any possibility that there are two different eschatologies in the Epistles and the Gospels? Is the eschatology in the Epistles one which predicts the end of the world rather than the one in which Jesus predicted the end of the Judea? Arguably the answer seems "No." Where else could they get those eschatological ideas except from Jesus? The apostles, who were absolutely devoted to preserving and teaching what Jesus taught and commanded them, certainly transmitted the eschatology that Jesus taught and preached. This was what Jesus commanded:

Matthew 28:18–20

18. And Jesus came up and spoke to them, saying, "All authority has been given to Me in heaven and on earth.

19. "Go therefore and make disciples of all the nations, baptizing them in the name of the Father and the Son and the Holy Spirit,

20. underline them to observe all that I commanded you; and lo, I am with you always, even to the end of the age."

And the apostles had been faithful to the commandment of their Lord:

1 John 1:1–3
1. What was from the beginning, what we have heard, what we have seen with our eyes, what we have looked at and touched with our hands, concerning the Word of Life—
2. and the life was manifested, and we have seen and testify and proclaim to you the eternal life, which was with the Father and was manifested to us—
3. what we have seen and heard we proclaim to you also, so that you too may have fellowship with us; and indeed our fellowship is with the Father, and with His Son Jesus Christ.

If the passages that contain eschatological statements were written before AD 70, the possibility that the eschatology in the Epistles is the same as the eschatology in the Gospels would be even greater because the writers did not see that the destruction was confined only to Judea and Jerusalem. According to scholars and Church tradition, Peter and Paul are believed to have been martyred in Rome during Nero's persecution.[59] Since Nero died in AD 68, Paul and Peter must have died in or before AD 68. This supports the theory that the letters of Paul and Peter were written before AD 70. Therefore, when they wrote the letters to the Christians and preached to the Gentiles, the destruction of the temple, Jerusalem, and Judea were still future events, but very imminent. James, the brother of Jesus, who wrote the book of James, is believed to have been martyred before AD 70, as well.[60] In the case of Paul, who was neither one of the twelve apostles nor a disciple who knew Jesus in person, certainly, acquired knowledge from the twelve or from some persons who knew firsthand the teachings and predictions of Jesus. Therefore, Paul's knowledge regarding the eschaton must be secondary to that learned from the others, but indirectly from Jesus:

1 Corinthians 15:3
For I delivered to you as of first importance what I also received, that Christ died for our sins according to the Scriptures,

1 Thessalonians 4:15
For this we say to you by the word of the Lord, that we who are alive and remain until the coming of the Lord, will not precede those who have fallen asleep.

These eschatological statements were initially meant as words of encouragement to those Christians facing persecutions in Judea. However, through the use of generalized, universal expressions, they were spread, intentionally or unintentionally, to the non-Jewish Christians who were experiencing similar persecutions like Christians in Judea and, in addition, to the Gentiles in cities like Corinth or Thessalonica or Athens (Acts 17:31) which were not at all affected by the destruction of Judea.
As a result, by their letters, and through their preaching and teaching to both the Gentile Christians and other Gentiles, the message regarding the end of Judea became a message predicting the end of the world.

Proof 2: The Imminent Coming
Jesus's disciples started to preach the Second Coming right after the ascension of Jesus. Because they believed with confidence that the Second Coming was very imminent, the event they spoke of was likely the one referenced at the scene of the ascension:

Acts 1:9–11
9.   And after He had said these things, He was lifted up while they were looking on, and a cloud received Him out of their sight.
10. And as they were gazing intently into the sky while He was going, behold, two men in white clothing stood beside them.
11. They also said, "Men of Galilee, why do you stand looking into the sky? This Jesus, who has been taken up from you into heaven, will come in just the same way as you have watched Him go into heaven."

The Second Coming referenced at the ascension and spoken of by Jesus in the Gospels happened in AD 70. There is little likelihood that the Second Coming in the Epistles is different from the one referenced in the Gospels unless the writers of the Epistles meant a Second Coming that would happen long after Jesus's ascension. However, since both Jesus and his disciples were talking about one event that would happen very soon, and there was no time duration between the ascension of Jesus and the disciples' proclamation of the Second Coming, the Second Coming in the Epistles is almost certainly the same as the one in the Gospels. Therefore, the eschatology in the Epistles should be considered the fulfilled eschatology.

Let us read some relevant texts comparing the Gospel accounts with the Epistles:

In the Gospels

Matthew 24: 34, Mark 13: 30, and Luke 21:32 "Truly I say to you, this generation will not pass away until all these things take place."

Matthew 10:23
"But whenever they persecute you in one city, flee to the next; for truly I say to you, you will not finish going through the cities of Israel until the Son of Man comes."

Matthew 16:28
"Truly I say to you, there are some of those who are standing here who will not taste death until they see the Son of Man coming in His kingdom."

Mark 9:1.
And Jesus was saying to them, "Truly I say to you, there are some of those who are standing here who will not taste death until they see the kingdom of God after it has come with power."

Luke 9:27
"But I say to you truthfully, there are some of those standing here who will not taste death until they see the kingdom of God."

In the Epistles

Romans 13:11
Do this, knowing the time, that it is already the hour for you to awaken from sleep; for now salvation is nearer to us than when we believed.

1 Thessalonians 4:18
Therefore comfort one another with these words.

Paul encouraged Thessalonian Christians to comfort one another with the eschatological hope. This implies that Paul believed that the eschaton was very near.

Philippians 4:5
Let your gentle spirit be known to all men. The Lord is near.

James 5:3, 8
3. Your gold and your silver have rusted; and their rust will be a witness against you and will consume your flesh like fire. It is in the last days that you have stored up your treasure!
8. You too be patient; strengthen your hearts, for the coming of the Lord is near.

1 Peter 1:5
who are protected by the power of God through faith for a salvation ready to be revealed in the last time.
1 Peter 4:7
The end of all things is near; therefore, be of sound judgment and sober spirit for the purpose of prayer.

2 Peter 3:9
The Lord is not slow about His promise, as some count slowness, but is patient toward you, not wishing for any to perish but for all to come to repentance.

The author of 2 Peter defended the delay of the Second Coming. This implies that the Church taught that the Second Coming was very imminent.

1 John 2:18
Children, it is the last hour; and just as you heard that antichrist is coming, even now many antichrists have appeared; from this we know that it is the last hour.

Proof 3: The Vivid Recollection of the Sayings of Jesus
The major relevant texts in the Epistles omit all references regarding the particular locations (Jerusalem, temple, Judea), the people (the Jews and the Jewish Christians), and historical settings (armies, famine, swords, captivity), of the eschatological statements of the Gospels. Instead, they exceedingly focus upon the Signs / the Second Coming, Resurrection / taken-up, and Salvation. However, when we read the eschatological statements of the Epistles, we can still find the references to the sayings of Jesus, as expressed, for instance, in 2 Peter 3:2: "you should remember the words spoken beforehand by the holy prophets and the commandment of the Lord and Savior spoken by your apostles."

Angels

1 Thessalonians 4:16
For the Lord Himself will descend from heaven with a shout, with the voice of the archangel and with the trumpet of God, and the dead in Christ will rise first.

2 Thessalonians 1:7
and to give relief to you who are afflicted and to us as well when the Lord Jesus will be revealed from heaven with His mighty angels in flaming fire,

Matthew 13:39–50

39. and the enemy who sowed them is the devil, and the harvest is the end of the age; and the reapers are angels.

40. "So just as the tares are gathered up and burned with fire, so shall it be at the end of the age.

41. "The Son of Man will send forth His angels, and they will gather out of His kingdom all stumbling blocks, and those who commit lawlessness,

42. and will throw them into the furnace of fire; in that place there will be weeping and gnashing of teeth.

49. "So it will be at the end of the age; the angels will come forth and take out the wicked from among the righteous,

50. and will throw them into the furnace of fire; in that place there will be weeping and gnashing of teeth.

Matthew 16:27

"For the Son of Man is going to come in the glory of His Father with His angels, and will then repay every man (holistic expression) according to his deeds.

Matthew 24:31

"And He will send forth His angels with a great trumpet and they will gather together His elect from the four winds, from one end of the sky to the other.

Matthew 25:31

"But when the Son of Man comes in His glory, and all the angels with Him, then He will sit on His glorious throne.

Mark 13:27

"And then He will send forth the angels, and will gather together His elect from the four winds, from the farthest end of the earth to the farthest end of heaven.

Trumpet

1 Corinthians 15:52
in a moment, in the twinkling of an eye, at the last trumpet; for the trumpet will sound, and the dead will be raised imperishable, and we will be changed.

1 Thessalonians 4:16
For the Lord Himself will descend from heaven with a shout, with the voice of the archangel and with the trumpet of God, and the dead in Christ will rise first.

Matthew 24:31
"And He will send forth His angels with a great trumpet and they will gather together His elect from the four winds, from one end of the sky to the other.

Thief / sudden coming / on the alert

1 Thessalonians 5:1–4
1. Now as to the times and the epochs, brethren, you have no need of anything to be written to you.
2. For you yourselves know full well that the day of the Lord will come just like a thief in the night.
3. While they are saying, "Peace and safety!" then destruction will come upon them suddenly like labor pains upon a woman with child, and they will not escape.
4. But you, brethren, are not in darkness, that the day would overtake you like a thief;

2 Peter 3:10
But the day of the Lord will come like a thief, in which the heavens will pass away with a roar and the elements will be destroyed with intense heat, and the earth and its works will be burned up.

Matthew 24:42–43

42. "Therefore be on the alert, for you do not know which day your Lord is coming.
43. "But be sure of this, that if the head of the house had known at what time of the night the thief was coming, he would have been on the alert and would not have allowed his house to be broken into.

Matthew 25:6

"But at midnight there was a shout, 'Behold, the bridegroom! Come out to meet him.'

Mark 13:32–37

32. "But of that day or hour no one knows, not even the angels in heaven, nor the Son, but the Father alone.
33. "Take heed, keep on the alert; for you do not know when the appointed time will come.
34. "It is like a man away on a journey, who upon leaving his house and putting his slaves in charge, assigning to each one his task, also commanded the doorkeeper to stay on the alert.
35. "Therefore, be on the alert--for you do not know when the master of the house is coming, whether in the evening, at midnight, or when the rooster crows, or in the morning--
36. in case he should come suddenly and find you asleep.
37. "What I say to you I say to all, 'Be on the alert!'"

Luke 12:39–40

39. "But be sure of this, that if the head of the house had known at what hour the thief was coming, he would not have allowed his house to be broken into.
40. "You too, be ready; for the Son of Man is coming at an hour that you do not expect."

Luke 21:34–36

34. "Be on guard, so that your hearts will not be weighted down with dissipation and drunkenness and the worries of life, and that day will not come on you suddenly like a trap;

35. for it will come upon all those who dwell on the face of all the earth.

36. "But keep on the alert at all times, praying that you may have strength to escape all these things that are about to take place, and to stand before the Son of Man."

In the temple of God/the man of lawlessness/Satan

2 Thessalonians 2:3–10

3. Let no one in any way deceive you, for it will not come unless the apostasy comes first, and the man of lawlessness is revealed, the son of destruction,

4. who opposes and exalts himself above every so-called god or object of worship, so that he takes his seat in the temple of God, displaying himself as being God.

5. Do you not remember that while I was still with you, I was telling you these things?

6. And you know what restrains him now, so that in his time he will be revealed.

7. For the mystery of lawlessness is already at work; only he who now restrains will do so until he is taken out of the way.

8. Then that lawless one will be revealed whom the Lord will slay with the breath of His mouth and bring to an end by the appearance of His coming;

9. that is, the one whose coming is in accord with the activity of Satan, with all power and signs and false wonders,

10. and with all the deception of wickedness for those who perish, because they did not receive the love of the truth so as to be saved.

Matthew 13:37–41

37. And He said, "The one who sows the good seed is the Son of Man,

38. and the field is the world (universal expression); and as for the good seed, these are the sons of the kingdom; and the tares are the sons of the evil one;
39. and the enemy who sowed them is the devil, and the harvest is the end of the age; and the reapers are angels.
40. "So just as the tares are gathered up and burned with fire, so shall it be at the end of the age.
41. "The Son of Man will send forth His angels, and they will gather out of His kingdom all stumbling blocks, and those who commit lawlessness,

Matthew 24:15
"Therefore, when you see the abomination of desolation which was spoken of through Daniel the prophet, standing in the holy place (let the reader understand),

Matthew 25:41
"Then He will also say to those on His left, 'Depart from Me, accursed ones, into the eternal fire which has been prepared for the devil and his angels

Mark 13:14
"But when you see the abomination of desolation standing where it should not be (let the reader understand), then those who are in Judea must flee to the mountains.

Fire

1 Corinthians 3:12–15
12. Now if any man builds on the foundation with gold, silver, precious stones, wood, hay, straw,
13. each man's work will become evident; for the day will show it because it is to be revealed with fire, and the fire itself will test the quality of each man's work.

14. If any man's work which he has built on it remains, he will receive a
    reward.
15. If any man's work is burned up, he will suffer loss; but he himself will
    be saved, yet so as through fire.

2 Peter 3:7, 10–12

7. But by His word the present heavens and earth are being reserved for
    fire, kept for the day of judgment and destruction of ungodly men.
10. But the day of the Lord will come like a thief, in which the heavens will
    pass away with a roar and the elements will be destroyed with intense
    heat, and the earth and its works will be burned up.
11. Since all these things are to be destroyed in this way, what sort of
    people ought you to be in holy conduct and godliness,
12. looking for and hastening the coming of the day of God, because of
    which the heavens will be destroyed by burning, and the elements
    will melt with intense heat!

Matthew 3:10–12

10. "The axe is already laid at the root of the trees; therefore, every tree
    that does not bear good fruit is cut down and thrown into the fire.
11. "As for me, I baptize you with water for repentance, but He who is
    coming after me is mightier than I, and I am not fit to remove His
    sandals; He will baptize you with the Holy Spirit and fire.
12. "His winnowing fork is in His hand, and He will thoroughly clear His
    threshing floor; and He will gather His wheat into the barn, but He
    will burn up the chaff with unquenchable fire."

This is a saying of John the Baptist. Since he is describing the act of Jesus
at the end, this might be considered as a saying of Jesus.

Matthew 13:40–50

40. "So just as the tares are gathered up and burned with fire, so shall it
    be at the end of the age.

41. "The Son of Man will send forth His angels, and they will gather out of His kingdom all stumbling blocks, and those who commit lawlessness,

42. and will throw them into the furnace of fire; in that place there will be weeping and gnashing of teeth.

49. "So it will be at the end of the age; the angels will come forth and take out the wicked from among the righteous,

50. and will throw them into the furnace of fire; in that place there will be weeping and gnashing of teeth.

Matthew 22:5–7

5. "But they paid no attention and went their way, one to his own farm, another to his business,

6. and the rest seized his slaves and mistreated them and killed them.

7. "But the king was enraged, and he sent his armies and destroyed those murderers and set their city on fire.

Matthew 25:41

"Then He will also say to those on His left, 'Depart from Me, accursed ones, into the eternal fire which has been prepared for the devil and his angels

Luke 12:49

"I have come to cast fire upon the earth; and how I wish it were already kindled!

Blessed

1 Peter 4:14

If you are reviled for the name of Christ, you are blessed, because the Spirit of glory and of God rests on you.

Matthew 5:11

"Blessed are you when people insult you and persecute you, and falsely say all kinds of evil against you because of Me.

<u>Reward to ministry</u>

1 Corinthians 3:12–15

12. Now if any man builds on the foundation with gold, silver, precious stones, wood, hay, straw,

13. each man's work will become evident; for the day will show it because it is to be revealed with fire, and the fire itself will test the quality of each man's work.

14. If any man's work which he has built on it remains, he will receive a reward.

15. If any man's work is burned up, he will suffer loss; but he himself will be saved, yet so as through fire.

1 Thessalonians 2:19

For who is our hope or joy or crown of exultation? Is it not even you, in the presence of our Lord Jesus at His coming?

Matthew 24:45–47

45. "Who then is the faithful and sensible slave whom his master put in charge of his household to give them their food at the proper time?

46. "Blessed is that slave whom his master finds so doing when he comes.

47. "Truly I say to you that he will put him in charge of all his possessions."

Proof 4: Historical Comparison

Since the historical accounts of the first-century Jewish community mostly depend upon the works of Josephus who was not a Christian, it is not easy to connect the eschatological statements in the Epistles to history. However, some possible implications that might connect them to AD 70 event are detected.

<u>Peace</u>

1 Thessalonians 5:3

While they are saying, "Peace and safety!" then destruction will come upon them suddenly like labor pains upon a woman with child, and they will not escape.

Eusebius: Chapter 8. The Signs which preceded the War

7. But what follows is still more terrible; for a certain Jesus, the son of Ananias, a common countryman, four years before the war, when the city was particularly prosperous and peaceful, came to the feast, at which it was customary for all to make tents at the temple to the honor of God, and suddenly began to cry out: A voice from the east, a voice from the west, a voice from the four winds, a voice against Jerusalem and the temple, a voice against bridegrooms and brides, a voice against all the people.' Day and night he went through all the alleys crying thus

The man of lawlessness

2 Thessalonians 2:3–10

3. Let no one in any way deceive you, for it will not come unless the apostasy comes first, and the man of lawlessness is revealed, the son of destruction,
4. who opposes and exalts himself above every so-called god or object of worship, so that he takes his seat in the temple of God, displaying himself as being God.
5. Do you not remember that while I was still with you, I was telling you these things?
6. And you know what restrains him now, so that in his time he will be revealed.
7. For the mystery of lawlessness is already at work; only he who now restrains will do so until he is taken out of the way.
8. Then that lawless one will be revealed whom the Lord will slay with the breath of His mouth and bring to an end by the appearance of His coming;
9. that is, the one whose coming is in accord with the activity of Satan, with all power and signs and false wonders,
10. and with all the deception of wickedness for those who perish, because they did not receive the love of the truth so as to be saved.

Josephus: Book 5 Chapter 1 fourth paragraph

And now there were three treacherous factions in the city, the one parted from the other. Eleazar and his party, that kept the sacred first-fruits, came against John in their cups. Those that were with John plundered the populace, and went out with zeal against Simon. This Simon had his supply of provisions from the city, in opposition to the seditious.

Josephus: Book 6 Chapter 9 fourth paragraph

Many also of those that had been put in prison by the tyrants were now brought out; for they did not leave off their barbarous cruelty at the very last: yet did God avenge himself upon them both, in a manner agreeable to justice. As for John, he wanted food, together with his brethren, in these caverns, and begged that the Romans would now give him their right hand for his security, which he had often proudly rejected before; but for Simon, he struggled hard with the distress he was in, fill he was forced to surrender himself, as we shall relate hereafter; so he was reserved for the triumph, and to be then slain; as was John condemned to perpetual imprisonment.

Fire

1 Corinthians 3:12–15

12. Now if any man builds on the foundation with gold, silver, precious stones, wood, hay, straw,

13. each man's work will become evident; for the day will show it because it is to be revealed with fire, and the fire itself will test the quality of each man's work.

14. If any man's work which he has built on it remains, he will receive a reward.

15. If any man's work is burned up, he will suffer loss; but he himself will be saved, yet so as through fire.

2 Peter 3:7, 10–12

7. But by His word the present heavens and earth are being reserved for fire, kept for the day of judgment and destruction of ungodly men.

10. But the day of the Lord will come like a thief, in which the heavens will pass away with a roar and the elements will be destroyed with intense heat, and the earth and its works will be burned up.

11. Since all these things are to be destroyed in this way, what sort of people ought you to be in holy conduct and godliness,

12. looking for and hastening the coming of the day of God, because of which the heavens will be destroyed by burning, and the elements will melt with intense heat!

Josephus: Book 5 Chapter 1 fourth paragraph

And if at any time he was freed from those that were above him, which happened frequently, from their being drunk and tired, he sallied out with a great number upon Simon and his party; and this he did always in such parts of the city as he could come at, till he set on fire those houses that were full of corn, and of all other provisions. The same thing was done by Simon, when, upon the other's retreat, he attacked the city also; as if they had, on purpose, done it to serve the Romans, by destroying what the city had laid up against the siege, and by thus cutting off the nerves of their own power. Accordingly, it so came to pass, that all the places that were about the temple were burnt down, and were become an intermediate desert space, ready for fighting on both sides of it; and that almost all that corn was burnt, which would have been sufficient for a siege of many years. So they were taken by the means of the famine, which it was impossible they should have been, unless they had thus prepared the way for it by this procedure.

Josephus: Book 6 Chapter 9 fourth paragraph

And now the Romans set fire to the extreme parts of the city, and burnt them down, and entirely demolished its walls.

Doom of the rich

James 5:1–3
1. Come now, you rich, weep and howl for your miseries which are coming upon you.
2. Your riches have rotted and your garments have become moth-eaten.
3. Your gold and your silver have rusted; and their rust will be a witness against you and will consume your flesh like fire. It is in the last days that you have stored up your treasure!

Eusebius: Chapter 6. The Famine which oppressed them

2. "For the wealthy," he says, "it was equally dangerous to remain. For under pretense that they were going to desert men were put to death for their wealth. The madness of the seditions increased with the famine and both the miseries were inflamed more and more day by day.

Considering four aspects of the eschaton in the Epistles (source of knowledge, the imminent coming, vivid recollection to the sayings of Jesus, and the historical comparison), I argue that the eschaton referenced in the Epistles is, in fact, an allusion to the eschaton in the Gospels: the event that happened in AD 70, and thus a fulfilled eschatology.

What the eschatology meant for the Jewish Christians and the Jews in Judea extended to the Gentile Christians and the Gentiles outside Judea. What Jesus told his apostles about the end of Judea to prepare, encourage, and warn them against laziness and negligence toward the coming persecution from the Jews, was also heard by Gentile Christians who would come under similar persecution in their own countries. These non-Jewish Christians were, in general, under constant persecution because of the differences between their Christian teachings, beliefs, and ethics over against the socio-cultural-political-religious institutions and teachings of their countries of origin; Acts 19 provides a good example (conflict in Ephesus regarding Artemis' business). Therefore, the eschatological statements Jesus delivered to his Jewish apostles and disciples who would soon face horrible persecutions from the Jews were positively and effectively applied to non-Jewish Christians experiencing a similar persecution from their own nations:

1 Thessalonians 2:14

For you, brethren, became imitators of the churches of God in Christ Jesus that are in Judea, for you also endured the same sufferings at the hands of your own countrymen, even as they did from the Jews;

2 Thessalonians 1:5–7

5. This is a plain indication of God's righteous judgment so that you will be considered worthy of the kingdom of God, for which indeed you are suffering.

6. For after all it is only just for God to repay with affliction those who afflict you,

7. and to give relief to you who are afflicted and to us as well when the Lord Jesus will be revealed from heaven with His mighty angels in flaming fire.

1 Peter 1:6

6. In this you greatly rejoice, even though now for a little while, if necessary, you have been distressed by various trials;

1 Peter 4:12–14

12. Beloved, do not be surprised at the fiery ordeal among you, which comes upon you for your testing, as though some strange thing were happening to you;

13. but to the degree that you share the sufferings of Christ, keep on rejoicing, so that also at the revelation of His glory you may rejoice with exultation.

14. If you are reviled for the name of Christ, you are blessed, because the Spirit of glory and of God rests on you.

James 1:2
Consider it all joy, my brethren, when you encounter various trials.

1 John 3:13
Do not be surprised, brethren, if the world hates you.

Ironically, the Gentile Christians' belief that the world would soon come to an end might have encouraged more persecution, thus reinforcing the apostles' warning.

Interestingly we can find that there were some skeptics among the first-century Christians regarding the notion of the imminent Coming and the end of the world:

2 Thessalonians 2:1–3
1. Now we request you, brethren, with regard to the coming of our Lord Jesus Christ and our gathering together to Him,
2. that you not be quickly shaken from your composure or be disturbed either by a spirit or a message or a letter as if from us, to the effect that the day of the Lord has come.
3. Let no one in any way deceive you, for it will not come unless the apostasy comes first, and the man of lawlessness is revealed, the son of destruction,

2 Peter 3:1–9
1. This is now, beloved, the second letter I am writing to you in which I am stirring up your sincere mind by way of reminder,
2. that you should remember the words spoken beforehand by the holy prophets and the commandment of the Lord and Savior spoken by your apostles.
3. Know this first of all, that in the last days mockers will come with their mocking, following after their own lusts,
4. and saying, "Where is the promise of His coming? For ever since the fathers fell asleep, all continues just as it was from the beginning of creation."

5. For when they maintain this, it escapes their notice that by the word of God the heavens existed long ago and the earth was formed out of water and by water,

6. through which the world at that time was destroyed, being flooded with water.

7. But by His word the present heavens and earth are being reserved for fire, kept for the day of judgment and destruction of ungodly men.

8. But do not let this one fact escape your notice, beloved, that with the Lord one day is like a thousand years, and a thousand years like one day.

9. The Lord is not slow about His promise, as some count slowness, but is patient toward you, not wishing for any to perish but for all to come to repentance.

Conservative and liberal scholars differ in their opinions regarding the authorship and date of 2 Thessalonians and 2 Peter,[61] and I will not spend the space to discern one from another. It is, however, worth noticing that though there were skeptics among the first-century Christians regarding the eschaton of the world, their opinions were effectively dismissed by authoritative Christian leaders. Second Thessalonians 2: 2 suggests that there were some Christians who said that "the day of the Lord has come." We are not sure whether those Christians were Jewish or Gentile, and whether the letter was written before AD 70 or after. The phrase "a message or a letter as if from us" implies that they could be the Jewish Christians since 2 Thessalonians was superficially attributed to Paul who was one of the Jewish leaders. Regardless of their race, if they said that "the day of the Lord has come" in conjunction with the end of Judea, AD 70, right before or sometime after AD 70, they were correct. Intentionally or unintentionally—and ironically—their claim was dismissed by Church leaders who quoted the very sayings of Jesus which predicted the end of Judea (verse 3. "Let no one in any way deceive you, for it will not come unless the apostasy comes first, and the man of lawlessness is revealed, the son of destruction").

Also 2 Peter 3: 4 suggests that there were some Gentile Christians who did not believe that the world would come to the end in association with the Second Coming. And since the Coming of Jesus was associated with Judea only, not the whole world, they were right. However, just like in 2 Thessalonians, their doubt was dismissed by Church leaders using a saying of Jesus (verse 3. "Know this first of all, that in the last days mockers will come with their mocking, following after their own lusts"), a logic elicited from Genesis accounts (verses 5–7), and apologetics for delay in terms of loving patience of Jesus (verses 8–9). Now we know that these apologies have been successfully effective for about 2,000 years. Even after AD 70, when Jesus's prediction was fulfilled, Christians have been waiting for the Coming of Jesus and the end of the world.

The irony in the texts is that when Jesus told his disciples about some prior events to the eschaton of Judea, he meant "the persecution from the Jews," "the Jewish Christians' apostasy due to the Jewish persecution," "the Jewish false prophets," and "the lawless Jewish Zealots." However, those contexts were applied to the Gentile Christians who were under the persecution from their own people and who were waiting for the end of the world. Thus, the Jews, who became the enemy of the people of God in the Gospels, turned to non-Jewish Gentiles who would persecute Christians or Gentile Christians who would ironically delude their fellow Christians in the Epistles.

This kind of irony is found in 1 John and 2 John in terms of the anti-Christ. The Jewish antichrists predicted by Jesus in the Gospels turned to the Christian antichrists who denied the Apostolic identity of Jesus.

1 John 2:18–19, 22

18. Children, it is the last hour; and just as you heard that antichrist is coming, even now many antichrists have appeared; from this we know that it is the last hour.
19. They went out from us, but they were not really of us; for if they had been of us, they would have remained with us; but they went out, so that it would be shown that they all are not of us.

22. Who is the liar but the one who denies that Jesus is the Christ? This is the antichrist, the one who denies the Father and the Son.

1 John 4:3
and every spirit that does not confess Jesus is not from God; this is the spirit of the antichrist, of which you have heard that it is coming, and now it is already in the world.

2 John 1:7
For many deceivers have gone out into the world, those who do not acknowledge Jesus Christ as coming in the flesh This is the deceiver and the antichrist.

Even though the Gospel's eschaton of Judea became understood as the eschaton of the world in the Epistles, it is worth noticing that this expanded eschatology has a positive aspect. Gentile Christians received the message of the eschaton of Judea predicted by Jesus, but also his teachings regarding the salvation at his Coming which became the basis of Christian ethics and morality. 2 Peter verses 11 and 14 summarize this aspect found throughout the Epistles:

2 Peter 3:11, 14
11. Since all these things are to be destroyed in this way, what sort of people ought you to be in holy conduct and godliness,
14. Therefore, beloved, since you look for these things, be diligent to be found by Him in peace, spotless and blameless,

By means of these strong ethical assertions, along with apologies, the belief in the imminent end of the world would consolidate the various Christian communities into one ethical body, which, doubtlessly, contributed to the sustainability of the Christian religion.

C. The Eschaton in the Revelation

The Revelation is traditionally believed to have been written in the time of Domitian, AD 90–95, by the Apostle John during the persecution.[62] Eusebius strengthened that view.[63] If so, the book was written after AD 70, the destruction of the temple, Jerusalem, and Judea, and as such after the "end of Judea" had already been transformed into the "end of the world" as expressed in the Epistles. After AD 70, the Christian Church in Judea was saved from the Jewish persecution, but both the Jewish and Gentile Christians faced more powerful and systematic persecutions from the Roman Empire. I think the author, who had experienced the Jewish persecution, witnessed the destruction of the Jewish nation, and was currently experiencing persecution under the Roman Empire, projected the eschaton spoken by Jesus in the Gospels to be first the end of the persecuting Roman Empire and, then, the end of the world. This notion of the end of the world had been proclaimed and was a believed truth for Christians at that time. In other words, the author who was waiting for the end of the world envisioned first the end of the persecuting Roman Empire, followed after a period of the seven seals, by the Second Coming of Jesus (19:11–21), and ultimately the end of the world. The writer seems not to have had any clear notion of whether there would be another coming at the end of the world or not (20:7–10) since Jesus mentioned only one coming as reported in the Gospels.

In the Epistles, the Second Coming of Christ instantly results in the end of the world. However, in the Revelation, it is prolonged by one thousand years after the end of the evil Roman authority. One thousand years should be understood as a reflection of the promised reign of the devoted disciples, as stated in Matthew 19: 27–29 and Luke 22:28–30.[64] After one thousand years, John imagined a day when the whole world would turn against the Christians and the LORD would destroy that world and save the Christians just as the LORD had destroyed the persecuting Jewish nation and saved the Christians. In John's mind, the persecuting entity might be expanded from Judea to the Roman Empire and then to the whole world. In this context, the eschatons in the Revelation are nothing but the projected allusion of the already happened AD 70 event. Since the Revelation is filled with universal expressions, as are the Gospels and the Epistles, the reader should understand their rhetorical aspect with regard to the destruction of the Roman Empire described in chapter 4 through 19: the realm of the "whole world" or on earth is really confined to the Roman-Greek world at the time of the writing.

Therefore, readers of the Revelation should keep in mind that there are two eschatons in the book: The eschaton of the Roman Empire and the eschaton of the world, and these two eschatons are separated by an era of one thousand years.

On the basis of this acknowledgment, the Revelation is divided into five sections:

I.   Synopsis of the Christian Churches
     Chapter 1–3 The Seven Churches in Asia Minor
II. Vision to the Eschaton of the Roman Empire
     Chapter 4–19 The Seven Seals, Trumpets, and Bowls
III. The Intermediate Era
     Chapter 20:1–6 The Thousand Years of Reign
IV. Vision to the Eschaton of the World
     Chapter 20:7–22:6 The New Jerusalem
V.   The final Epilogue
     Chapter 22:7–21 Come Lord Jesus

The purpose of this writing is to prove that the eschatology of the New Testament was fulfilled in the termination of Judea in AD 70: That Jesus's prediction of eschaton became interpreted in the Epistles as the end of the world; and, in the Revelation, as the end of the persecution by the Roman Empire, the medium through which the final end of the world would be realized. First, I will restate the aspiration for the imminent Coming of Jesus Christ expressed in the final epilogue in order to convince readers that this aspiration cannot be different from what Jesus predicted in the

Gospels. This longing for the return of Christ, expressed in the Epistles and the Revelation, is an extended allusion to the AD 70 event. And then I will study section II, the majority of the Revelation, to prove that the vision was for an end of the persecuting Roman Empire, the incumbent political authority to the author and Christians at that time, but not the whole world as it has come to be understood.

Let us read the final epilogue 22: 6–21:

6. And he said to me, "These words are faithful and true"; and the Lord, the God of the spirits of the prophets, sent His angel to show to His bond-servants the things which must soon take place.

7. "And behold, I am coming quickly Blessed is he who heeds the words of the prophecy of this book."

8. I, John, am the one who heard and saw these things And when I heard and saw, I fell down to worship at the feet of the angel who showed me these things.

9. But he said to me, "Do not do that I am a fellow servant of yours and of your brethren the prophets and of those who heed the words of this book. Worship God."

10. And he said to me, "Do not seal up the words of the prophecy of this book, for the time is near.

11. "Let the one who does wrong, still do wrong; and the one who is filthy, still be filthy; and let the one who is righteous, still practice righteousness; and the one who is holy, still keep himself holy."

12. "Behold, I am coming quickly, and My reward is with Me, to render to every man according to what he has done.

13. "I am the Alpha and the Omega, the first and the last, the beginning and the end."

14. Blessed are those who wash their robes, so that they may have the right to the tree of life, and may enter by the gates into the city.

15 Outside are the dogs and the sorcerers and the immoral persons and the murderers and the idolaters, and everyone who loves and practices lying.

16. "I, Jesus, have sent My angel to testify to you these things for the churches I am the root and the descendant of David, the bright morning star."

17. The Spirit and the bride say, "Come " And let the one who hears say, "Come" And let the one who is thirsty come; let the one who wishes take the water of life without cost.

18. I testify to everyone who hears the words of the prophecy of this book: if anyone adds to them, God will add to him the plagues which are written in this book;

19. and if anyone takes away from the words of the book of this prophecy, God will take away his part from the tree of life and from the holy city, which are written in this book.

20. He who testifies to these things says, "Yes, I am coming quickly" Amen Come, Lord Jesus.

21. The grace of the Lord Jesus be with all. Amen.

The epilogue serves as the conclusion to the book which encompasses both eschatons: the end of the persecuting Roman Empire and that of the world. The section is full of aspiration for the imminent Second Coming of Jesus. Is this aspiration different from what Jesus prophesied in the Gospels and what the apostles and disciples desired in the Epistles? It cannot be. Jesus referenced only one Second Coming in the Gospels, and those apostles and disciples who preserved what Jesus said also mentioned only one Second Coming in the Epistles. Therefore, if the author of the Revelation, who lived in 90s in the context of continued persecution, wrote about the imminent Second Coming of Jesus, that Coming should be the same as the one in the Gospels and the Epistles. It was not written long after AD 70 when the disciples continued to believe the Second Coming of Jesus was imminent. If the author were John, one of the apostles, that possibility increases. Verse 6 says that the contents of the book must soon take place. And verse 10 confirms that the time is near. The phase "I am coming quickly" is repeated in verses 7, 12, and 20, with emphasizing words "behold" and "yes." These all resonate with the eschatological expressions found in the Gospels and Epistles. In terms of the mode of Coming, Revelation 1:7 "behold, he is coming with the clouds, and every

eye will see Him, even those who pierced Him; and all the tribes of the
earth will mourn over Him" very much resonates with Matthew 24:30,
Mark 13:26; 14:62, Luke 21:27, and Acts 1: 11. The author of the book
expected the imminent Coming of Jesus, as promised in the Gospels,
which would bring first the end of the persecuting Roman Empire, the
reign of the saints, and then, sometime after, the end of the world. Since
Jerusalem was already destroyed at that time, the author envisioned that
the New Jerusalem was coming down out of heaven from God (21: 2;
10) at the end of the world. Thus, it can be said that the eschatology of
the Revelation is, in fact, an extended allusion to the AD 70 event, the
destruction of the temple, Jerusalem, and Judea.

A second concept, the notion of the reign of the saints, provides another
possible proof that the eschatology of the Revelation was an allusion to
the AD 70 event. In Matthew 19:27–29 and Luke 22:28–30, Jesus uses
imagery of a throne, promising his apostles that they would reign over
the people of God (judging the twelve tribes of Israel) when he came
back. This reign should be understood by the reader as the Apostolic
leadership within the Christian Church after AD 70. Though omitted in
the eschatology of the Epistles, this notion was generalized and repeated
throughout the Revelation, embodied in terms of one thousand years and
the New Jerusalem, repeating the imagery of the thrones.[65] Just like sin
and judgment, the notion of reign should be confined to the realm of Judea
and the Church. However, it came to be expanded to the world with the
saints, not just apostles, ultimately reigning over the world. Is the reign of
the saints depicted in the Revelation different from what Jesus promised
in the Gospels? If it is not, the eschatology of the Revelation would be
considered as an extended allusion to AD 70 event.

Section II (chapter 4 –19), which contains the visions of the seven seals,
trumpets, and bowls, must be about the persecuting Roman Empire.
Revelation 1:1 clearly sets the time frame of the contents of the book:
"The Revelation of Jesus Christ, which God gave Him to show to His
bond-servants, the things which must soon take place; and He sent and
communicated it by His angel to His bond-servant John."

The contents of the Revelation were "things which must soon take place." Since chapter 20 mentions about one thousand years, the imminence expressed in verse 1 should be applied up to chapter 19. If the book was written in the 90s on the island called Patmos,[66] the visions in the book must be about the same time and location, and arguably the time and the realm of the Roman Empire would fit those conditions. Some modern scholars think that the Revelation was written before AD 70 and identifies the number 666 (13:18) with Nero who died in AD 68.[67] Even if this date is adopted, the conclusion would be same. Whatever the arguments about dates, as long as the persecution described in the Revelation is identified with that of the Roman Empire, Domitian or Nero, the contents of section II (chapter 4–19) is inevitably related to the Roman Empire, and the Second Coming and the end described in chapter 19 should be understood as the end of the persecuting Roman Empire.

Imagery of the woman in section II supports this theory. In chapter 16, the judgment of the seven bowls is completed and chapter 17 clearly states that the object of the judgment is the great harlot (the woman in verses 3, 4, 6, 7, 9, 18, and Babylon the Great in verse 5). Verse 5 also says that the name of the woman is mystery and then implies in verse 9 that the wise person might know the identity of the woman who sits on the seven mountains. Ancient Rome was situated on the seven hills (Aventine Hill, Caelian Hill, Capitoline Hill, Esquiline Hill, Palatine Hill, Quirinal Hill, and Viminal Hill)[68] and chapter 17:18 confirms again that the woman is the city: "The woman whom you saw is the great city, which reigns over the kings of the earth." The whole of chapter 18 describes the impact of the destruction of Babylon the Great and makes clear that city is Rome. Therefore section II (chapter 4–19) is not about the end of the world, it is about the end of the persecution by the Roman Empire: the city of Rome (the great harlot, the woman, Babylon the Great), the evil emperor (the beast), the evil royal adviser (the false prophet), and eventually the evil spirit (the devil or Satan) who works behind them.

Conclusion: Chapter 2. The Judgment on Judea Became the Judgment on the World and The End of Judea Became the End of the World

Let me summarize how I view the eschatology of the New Testament. Jesus prophesied the imminent Jewish persecution of his apostles and disciples, which would come right after his death and the initiation of the Jerusalem church. In that prophecy, Jesus seems to say, "Don't worry too much. I will come back and judge the evil doers and nation. I will avenge you and save you. I will come back soon, even though some will think I am late. I don't know the exact date I will be coming, however, there will be certain signs to warn you. So, don't be lazy but be faithful to who I am and what I told you."

This prophecy of Jesus was fulfilled in AD 70. Before AD 70, the apostles and disciples preached the gospel to the Gentiles. The Gentile Christians soon faced the same kind of persecutions as the Jewish Christians had from their own people because of differences in the Christian socio-political-cultural-religious settings. As a result, the apostles and disciples intentionally or unintentionally said to the Gentile Christians: "Be patient! The Lord will come soon and save you and us from judgment and destruction. When the Lord comes back, the present world will end."

Before or after AD 70, some Christians became skeptical about what the apostles and the disciples said. However, their skepticism was effectively dealt with by the persuasive effort of the leaders of the Christian Church. Soon, the Christian Church that was begun by the apostolic tradition faced another challenge, one that came from their own Christian groups. Called heretics, the non-apostolic minority Christian groups were suppressed by and severed from the majority apostolic Christians. As a result, even after AD 70, Christians began to look for the Second Coming of Jesus Christ. This transferred, expanded, and generalized eschatology was used effectively to keep Christians in unity, to educate them ethically, and to evangelize the world. In the midst of this, the Christian Church faced more powerful, institutionalized, and systematic persecution from the Roman Empire, primarily because of Rome's conflicting theology of emperor-worship. Since Christians confessed and believed that Jesus Christ is the Son of God (or God) and the only true king, the persecution from the Roman emperor who claimed to be a god and sole king was harsh.

Against the background of this formidable persecution, the Revelation was written. In it, the Second Coming of Jesus was applied first to the end of the evil Roman Empire and subsequently projected to the end of the world.

This explanation is a hypothesis. However, it is a plausible hypothesis. When we read the New Testament from this viewpoint, we can understand the primary meaning of the texts better.

Based upon this hypothesis, it can be said that the New Testament eschatology is about the end of evil or the evil nation or evil authority, not the end of the world. Now we know, through science, that the earth, even the universe, will not remain forever as it is. As some scientists say, this planet might be destroyed by a comet or natural disaster or by humans, and, as a result, humankind might be annihilated in the near future. However, this scientific eschatology should be distinguished from biblical eschatology. The Christian religion is political in its essence. We talk about king, throne, reign, kingdom, and people. Therefore, Christian eschatology should be discussed within the scope of politics. God destroyed the ancient nations of Israel and Judea and the city of Jerusalem and the temple by the hand of the Assyrian and Babylonian Empires in the Old Testament. Likewise, New Testament eschatology should reflect the context of Judea and the Christian Church, that is, the new Israel or new kingdom of God, in relation to the Roman Empire. And therefore, the judgment on Judea can be compared to the judgment on the Church, not the world.

When we admit that New Testament eschatology is the already-fulfilled eschatology, we can have more confidence in the Christian religion. It presents Jesus as the one who kept his promise of coming back soon. Jesus's promise to come back in the future inevitably elicits a measure of skepticism and uncertainty. When we know that Jesus already came and kept his promise, we can have stronger confidence in what the Gospel says regarding his life, identity, and teaching. We can also have a clearer picture about what the Christian Church is and what it should be like and do. Eventually we will have stronger faith in Jesus. For evangelism, the fulfilled eschatology would eventually bring better benefits because the statement, "Jesus already came back" as a historical fact offers more credibility to the world than "Jesus will come back."

Even though the New Testament eschatology is the fulfilled eschatology, Christians are to apply that to the present and future life of the Church. When this fulfilled eschatology is applied, we need to consider an important condition which can constitute and justify the Second Coming of Jesus. The condition must be that the Second Coming of Jesus should be a genuine wish for all Christians of the world or to all members of a faith community. In other words, I don't think a Christian student who will graduate from high school or college on Saturday will appreciate if Jesus comes back on Friday. I don't think a Christian couple who will marry on Sunday evening will appreciate if Jesus comes back on that Sunday morning. When Jesus comes back, it must be a joyous occasion surpassing all earthly pleasures.

Universal persecution of the Christian community must be the condition which constitutes and justifies the Second Coming of Jesus. Before AD 70 and after the Pentecost, all Christians in Judea were under persecution without exception. They were persecuted regardless of age, sex, or social status by the Jewish authority. They were persecuted based on their religious identity, only because they were Christians. Under that circumstance, the Second Coming of Jesus could be the wish of the whole Judean Christian community and be justified. The same thing happened to the Gentile Christians at that time. They were persecuted based upon their religious choice and identity and thus the persecution on them was unexceptional and collective. The wish for the Second Coming of Jesus was not held merely by some Gentile Christians, but of all at that time. Later under the harsh Roman persecution, both the Jewish and Gentile Christians were persecuted based on their religious preference and thus the wish for the Second Coming of Jesus was intensified and justified.

I think under certain conditions, the fulfilled eschatology of the New Testament can be applied to a community or a nation or even the world. There must be total political persecution on all Christians in a region along with the collective wish for the Coming of Jesus from all Christians in that region. If the whole Christian community of a nation is under the political persecution solely based upon their religious identity, they are purely innocently, and all members of that community—without exception—wish for the Coming of Jesus, one might say, "Jesus might come back soon to save you from the persecution and might carry out justice by punishing the evil nation, because God did that for His people who were in Judea, and therefore he might do that again. Do not lose hope and continue to be faithful to Jesus and his teachings." If it is to be applied to the whole world, the condition must be that the entire Christian community on the earth is under universal political-totalistic persecution and all Christians on the earth wish for the Coming of Jesus. When the gospel left Palestinian soil, the sin of Judea became interpreted as the sin of the world; by the same measure and thereby the end of Judea became the end of the world. Then naturally the only savior of the Judea became the only savior of the world.

CHAPTER 3
The Only Savior of Judea Became
the Only Savior of the World

The only savior of Judea should have transitioned to the only savior of the "Church," not of the "world." Jesus was the only savior of the people of Judea; the one who could save them from the imminent destruction of their nation, and especially the destruction of Jerusalem. And those who were saved by Jesus constituted the primitive Christian Church. From the Christian perspective, therefore, Jesus was the savior who delivered Christians from destruction and persecution, but more than that, Jesus was the founder of the Christian Church, the New Israel, the New Kingdom of God. Moreover, Jesus is the constant redeemer and sustainer of that kingdom, keeping his followers from the judgment of God; he is the eternal Messiah, Christ, or King, of that kingdom. However, when the sin of Judea was expanded to be the sin of the world; and the end of Judea, to the end of the world, explicitly or implicitly, Jesus, the only savior of Judea, was also transformed into the only savior of the world.

A. The Meaning of Salvation

When we talk about savior (σωτήρ), defining salvation (σωτήριος) becomes important. What is the definition of salvation? Saved from what? The New Testament calls Jesus a savior (Matthew 1:21 and Luke 2:11), however, it does not provide a clear definition. We may know the meaning from what Jesus said in the Gospels and its context that was proclaimed by his apostles and disciples.

Let us read Matthew 3:2 and 10:

2. "Repent, for the kingdom of heaven is at hand"
10. "The axe is already laid at the root of the trees; therefore, every tree that does not bear good fruit is cut down and thrown into the fire."

These are sayings of John the Baptist in preparation for the arrival of Jesus and are instructive regarding the meaning of salvation. In these verses, salvation means salvation from the final judgment on the evil Jews. Repentance is the starting point. It is implied that those who repent would welcome Jesus and thus would be saved from the imminent final judgment on the Jews.

Let us read Matthew 24:22 and Luke 21:28:

Matthew 24:22
"Unless those days had been cut short, no life would have been saved; but for the sake of the elect those days will be cut short."

Luke 21:28
"But when these things begin to take place, straighten up and lift up your heads, because your redemption is drawing near."

In these sayings from Jesus, salvation clearly means saved from the final judgment, destruction, and persecution. The elect and the disciples will be saved at the end. In the Gospels, we can find numerous examples that relate the notion of salvation to the end. Therefore, the meaning of "savior" or "salvation" cannot be separated from the eschatological setting and context of the Gospels, that is, the AD 70 event. The same terms used by the apostles and disciples in the New Testament should be interpreted in this setting and context because they preached, taught, and proclaimed what Jesus said.

Therefore, to the Jewish Christians, as expressed in the Gospels, the meaning of salvation was "being saved from the judgment and destruction on Judea and subsequently from the Jewish persecution." This fundamental meaning of salvation changed when the gospel left Palestine and Christianity became universalized. To the Gentiles Christians, salvation, as expressed in the Epistles, came to mean being saved from the persecution of their own people and ultimately from the judgment and destruction of the world. To Jewish and Gentile Christians, salvation, as understood in Revelation, meant being saved from the Roman persecution, the judgment and destruction on the Roman Empire, and subsequently judgment and destruction of the world."

From the viewpoint of contemporary Christians, salvation should be understood as expressed in the Gospels: collectively and in the context of the fulfilled eschaton. Today, when someone says, "You are saved by Jesus," it is ambiguous. "Saved from what?" you might ask. It becomes simply personal, employing the present tense, therefore losing a sense of collectiveness, historicity, and the reality of persecution which comes from the eschatological setting and context of the Gospels. If it is "saved from sin," and we separate sin from the sin of Judea and the related eschatological explanation, it becomes personal and promotes an uneasy theology that justifies Christian immorality, because a Christian continues to sin.

The only reasonable answer is "Saved from sin of the Church, collectively," even though without the eschatological context this answer delivers only half of the story. In the North American context, "You are saved by Jesus," absent a persecuting entity, limits salvation to "the Church." You are saved by Jesus because you have become a part of the Church for which Jesus died. His death means that the Church, in a collective sense, is free from the wrath of God. You are saved because you have become a part of the already-saved Church.

Some Christians still believe that the world will come to an end soon, and Christians will be saved from that destruction by Jesus. To them "You are saved by Jesus" means "You will escape the judgment and destruction of the world." However, this approach is unpersuasive because, as noted in the previous chapter, this claim requires the condition for the Second Coming: an international entity as the agent of persecution of all Christians on the earth. Without this condition, the claim becomes void. Some Christians are concerned about what will happen to them after death. To them, "You are saved by Jesus" means "when you die, you will go to heaven, not hell." This idea is based upon a dualistic worldview which has no biblical basis and lacks the notion of justice. Also, with this claim, salvation loses a sense of collectiveness, historicity, and a notion of persecution, which are the important subjects of salvation in the Gospels. Therefore, the primary meaning of salvation found in the Gospels, "being saved from the judgment and destruction on Judea and subsequently from the Jewish persecution," should be kept in this discussion. The subject of salvation will be explored in more detail in Section III.

In this context and understanding, I will study some exclusive passages in the New Testament and demonstrate how the only savior of Judea became the only savior of the world.

B. Studying the Relevant Exclusive Passages

In the Gospels, Jesus was born as the savior of Judea[69] and later was revealed to be the only savior of Judea. The most well-known exclusive passage of the Gospels is John 14:6 when Jesus answered, "I am the way and the truth and the life. No one comes to the Father except through me." This verse is, in fact, the only verse that can be called exclusive in the Gospels. Also, this verse certainly has significance as an explicit saying of Jesus himself. Let us consider the context. The verse belongs within Chapter 14–16, known as the Last Sermon of Jesus. According to the Gospel of John, this sermon was delivered during and right after the Last Supper. After this sermon, Jesus prayed to God (chapter 17) and then was arrested (chapter 18). Let us read the text that contains the verse:

John 14:1–11

1. "Do not let your hearts be troubled. Trust in God; trust also in me.
2. In my Father's house are many rooms; if it were not so, I would have told you. I am going there to prepare a place for you.
3. And if I go and prepare a place for you, I will come back and take you to be with me that you also may be where I am.
4. You know the way to the place where I am going."
5. Thomas said to him, "Lord, we don't know where you are going, so how can we know the way?"
6. Jesus answered, "I am the way and the truth and the life. No one comes to the Father except through me.
7. If you really knew me, you would know my Father as well. From now on, you do know him and have seen him."
8. Philip said, "Lord, show us the Father and that will be enough for us."
9. Jesus answered: "Don't you know me, Philip, even after I have been among you such a long time? Anyone who has seen me has seen the Father. How can you say, 'Show us the Father'?
10. Don't you believe that I am in the Father, and that the Father is in me? The words I say to you are not just my own. Rather, it is the Father, living in me, who is doing his work.
11. Believe me when I say that I am in the Father and the Father is in me; or at least believe on the evidence of the miracles themselves.

I will present two reasons why verse 6 presents Jesus as the only savior of Judea, not of the world. First, Jesus's main audience was the eleven apostles (since Judas was taken out of the twelve). In verses 2 and 3, Jesus tells them that he would go to the Father and would be back to take them to the Father. When Jesus said to the apostles in verse 4, "You know the way to the place where I am going," Thomas asked Jesus (v. 5), "Lord, we don't know where you are going, so how can we know the way?" In answer to that particular question, Jesus said to Thomas and the apostles, "I am the way and the truth and the life. No one comes to the Father except through me (v.6)." Therefore, by the context of conversation, "no one" should mean none of the eleven apostles, not none of the human beings.

Verse 6, when applied to the eleven apostles in the context of eschatology, could be paraphrased thus: "I am the way and the truth and the life to the Father. Therefore, none of you comes to the Father except through me, when I come back." This verse may be extended to the broader circle of the followers of Jesus at that time: "No one" equals "none of the disciples." Since the Jewish disciples already had the new identity as the followers of Jesus or the people of the new Kingdom of God, "no one" might be interpreted as "none of the Christians."

And even more so, this verse may be extended to the Jews at that time: "No one" as "none of the Jews." Even though the negative universal expression "no one" was adopted, verse 6 should be applied, at best, to the Jews who would live in the time of the end in Judea. In this context, the statement in verse 6 was true to the apostles or the Jewish disciples or the Jews at that time, because only Christians were intentionally saved from the destruction of Judea by Jesus. Indeed, the statement might be always true for Christians, because we all are saved from the wrath of God through Jesus exclusively.

However, "no one" is hardly understood as "none of the human beings." Also, the term "God the Father" was a way Jesus described his relationship with God. Jesus was speaking unconventionally by referring to God as the Father. The dialogue becomes dominantly about the relationship between God and Jesus, with his claim of God as "father." In the text, we can see even the disciples who had lived in the Jewish tradition having difficulty understanding what they could not see (v. 8). Harder still for Gentiles, with no concept of the Father or any knowledge or experience about Jesus, to understand the statement, "No one comes to the Father except through me." If so, how can this statement be applied to all the people who don't understand the meaning at all besides Jesus's historically and culturally bounded audiences.

Therefore, verse 6 must be applied to those who had a concept of God and knowledge or experience of Jesus as the Son of God, or, at least, to those who had lived in the line of that tradition.[70] If verse 6 was proclaimed and applied to non-Jewish people, it would be totally out of the context. While verse 6 was true to the Jews at that time it was written, it could not be true to those non-Jewish people who lived outside the Judean territory and tradition.

In this sense and context, Jesus was seen as the only savior of Judea. When a Jew became a Christian in Judea before AD 70, it was very clear that he or she or his family or her family would be saved from the imminent judgment, destruction,[71] and persecution by becoming a member of the holy Church.[72] In other words, Jesus saved the Jewish Christians from the sin of Judea, the wrath of God toward Judea, the destruction of Judea, and Jewish persecution, by bestowing on them the new identity: the people of the New Israel.

This limited notion of Jesus as the only savior of Judea appears elsewhere in the New Testament, more broadly describing him (explicitly or implicitly) as the only savior of the world. This follows the expanded and generalized concept of sin and judgment (or end). Let me present some examples:

Roman 3:23–24 implicitly presents Jesus as the only savior of the world, apparently based upon the universalization of sin.

23. for all have sinned and fall short of the glory of God,
24. being justified as a gift by His grace through the redemption which is in Christ Jesus;

Romans 13:11 (implicitly) and Philippians 3:20–21 (explicitly) present Jesus as the only savior of the world based upon the universalized eschaton.

Romans 13:11
Do this, knowing the time, that it is already the hour for you to awaken from sleep; for now salvation is nearer to us than when we believed.

Philippians 3:20–21
20. For our citizenship is in heaven, from which also we eagerly wait for a Savior, the Lord Jesus Christ;

21. who will transform the body of our humble state into conformity with the body of His glory, by the exertion of the power that He has even to subject all things to Himself.

Titus 2 implies that Jesus is the only savior of the world based upon universalized sin:

11. For the grace of God has appeared, bringing salvation to all men

1 Timothy 2:5 and 1 John 4:14 explicitly present Jesus as the only savior of the world based upon the implied universalized sin and judgment.

1 Timothy 2:5
For there is one God, and one mediator also between God and men, the man Christ Jesus,

1 John 4:14
We have seen and testify that the Father has sent the Son to be the Savior of the world.

Another example is Acts 16:31. In the second missionary journey (Acts 16), Paul and Silas were imprisoned in Philippi. At midnight, miraculously, all the doors of the prison were opened and every prisoner's chains were unfastened. The jailer thought that the prisoners had escaped and therefore tried to kill himself. At that moment, Paul said to him, "Do not harm yourself, for we are all here." The surprised and moved jailer fell down before Paul and Silas and said, "Sirs, what must I do to be saved?" Paul and Silas replied (v 31), "Believe in the Lord Jesus, and you will be saved, you and your household." This statement should be understood in the eschatological context. In this case, however, this jailer and his family were not affected by the destruction of temple, Jerusalem, and Judea in AD 70. Philippi was located on the east cost of Macedonia, not even close to Palestine. Paul and Silas's proclamation was based upon the supposition that the world was under sin and, as a result, would end soon. In this context, the only savior of Judea became the only savior of the world. If

Acts 16:31 is not understood in the eschatological context, the meaning of salvation must be limited to the Church: "You and your household will be the people of God, the people of the New Israel, the Christian Church, and, as a result, you and your household will be saved from the sin of the Church and therefore the wrath of God toward the Church for which Christ died." In this case, the meaning of salvation will differ from the meaning found in the Gospels. It will also contradict a saying of Paul himself in Romans 13:11b that describes salvation as a chronological event: "for now salvation is nearer to us than when we believed."

We might take a glance at that moment when the only savior of Judea became the only savior of the world. Acts 13 contains the record of the first missionary journey of Paul and Barnabas and Paul's sermon to the Jews at the synagogue in Pisidian Antioch. Acts 13:46 provides the pivotal moment that turned the mission from the Jews to the Gentiles: "Paul and Barnabas spoke out boldly and said, 'It was necessary that the word of God be spoken to you first; since you repudiate it and judge yourselves unworthy of eternal life, behold, we are turning to the Gentiles.'" The salvation offered to—and refused by—the Jews was therefore made to the Gentiles. In Paul's sermon to the Jews on the Sabbath, verse 23 clearly presents Jesus as the only savior of Israel (Judea): "From the descendants of this man, according to promise, God has brought to Israel a Savior, Jesus." However, on the next Sabbath when nearly the whole city assembled to hear the word of the Lord (v 44), this only savior of Israel turned into the only savior of the world: "For so the Lord has commanded us, 'I have placed you as a light for the Gentiles, that you may bring salvation to the end of the earth" (verse 47, quoted from Isaiah 49:6b). How did the savior of Israel become the savior of the world in a week? In his sermon to the Jews, Paul identified Jesus within the history of Israel as the promised Messiah. After a week, Jesus was presented to the Gentiles who had no messianic expectation, as the savior of the world. This text can only be understood in the context of universalized eschatology.

Acts 16:31, therefore, is understood in this context. When the gospel was preached to the Jews who were outside of Judea, Jesus's prophesy about the end of Judea could be meaningful to them because many Jews went back to Jerusalem to observe the Passover, and the destruction of Jerusalem happened during that holy season.[73] But what did the Gentiles hear and understand? Paul and Barnabas must have decided that for Jesus's words to make sense to the Gentiles, they should preach salvation to the end of the world. Therefore, the message of the eschaton of Judea became a message about the eschaton of the world, and therefore Jesus, the only savior of Judea, became the only savior of the world.

Acts 4:12 is another exclusive verse which is often quoted to identify Jesus as the only savior of the world. Let us look at the text:

Acts 4:1–12

1. As they were speaking to the people, the priests and the captain of the temple guard and the Sadducees came up to them,

2. being greatly disturbed because they were teaching the people and proclaiming in Jesus the resurrection from the dead.

3. And they laid hands on them and put them in jail until the next day, for it was already evening.

4. But many of those who had heard the message believed; and the number of the men came to be about five thousand.

5. On the next day, their rulers and elders and scribes were gathered together in Jerusalem;

6. and Annas the high priest was there, and Caiaphas and John and Alexander, and all who were of high-priestly descent.

7. When they had placed them in the center, they began to inquire, "By what power, or in what name, have you done this?"

8. Then Peter, filled with the Holy Spirit, said to them, "Rulers and elders of the people,

9. if we are on trial today for a benefit done to a sick man, as to how this man has been made well (σέσωσται),

10. let it be known to all of you and to all the people of Israel, that by the name of Jesus Christ the Nazarene, whom you crucified, whom God raised from the dead--by this name this man stands here before you in good health.

11. "He is the stone which was rejected by you, the builders, but which became the chief cornerstone.
12. "And there is salvation (σωτηρία) in no one else; for there is no other name under heaven that has been given among men by which we must be saved (σωθῆναι)."

I will present two reasons why, in spite of the universal expressions, verse 12 does not identify Jesus as the only savior of the world: the scope of the conversation and the contextual meaning of salvation in the text.

First, just like John 14:1–11, the conversation in the text is strictly confined to the Jews, and verse 12 was particularly proclaimed to the Jewish leaders. In chapter 3, Peter and John raised a man up who had been lame from his mother's womb. Due to this incident, they were imprisoned. The next day they stood before the Jewish authority for the trial. Verses 5 and 6 detail who was present at the trial; verses 7 to 11 are only understood in the Jewish context. Therefore "men" and "we" in verse 12 should be understood as "the Jews" and the verse can be paraphrased as "and there is salvation in no one else; for there is no other name under heaven that has been given among the Jews by which the Jews must be saved." In this sense, at best, verse 12 presents Jesus as the only savior of the Jews or Judea.

Second, the meaning of "salvation" and "be saved" in verse 12 does not necessarily mean the spiritual or religious meaning of salvation. The words "σωτηρία" for "salvation" and "σωθῆναι" for "be saved" were used in verse 12. "σωθῆναι" is aorist, passive, infinitive of "σῴζω" which means "I save, heal, preserve, or rescue." "σωτηρία" is the noun form of "σῴζω" and therefore means "healing, prosperity, deliverance, preservation, salvation, or safety." Even in verse 9 of the text, σέσωσται (perfect, passive, indicative, third person, singular of σῴζω) is used as "has been made well." Therefore, the meaning of "salvation" or "to save" in Greek should be determined by the context.

An excellent example is found in Acts chapter 27 and 28. The narrative is about Paul's attempted voyage from Caesarea to Rome through the Mediterranean Sea. On their way to Rome, the ship faced a storm and the crew and the prisoners including Paul risked their lives. However, all of them were saved through a divine intervention. Let us read the verses which contain the words σωτηρία and σῴζω:

Acts 27:20, 31, 34

20. Since neither sun nor stars appeared for many days, and no small storm was assailing us, from then on all hope of our being saved (σῴζεσθαι) was gradually abandoned.
31. Paul said to the centurion and to the soldiers, "Unless these men remain in the ship, you yourselves cannot be saved (σωθῆναι)."
34. "Therefore I encourage you to take some food, for this is for your preservation (σωτηρίας), for not a hair from the head of any of you will perish."

Acts 28:4

4. When the natives saw the creature hanging from his hand, they began saying to one another, "Undoubtedly this man is a murderer, and though he has been saved (διασωθέντα) from the sea, justice has not allowed him to live."

The words in the verses mean simply physical deliverance or preservation: salvation from a physical illness or destruction or death. The words have nothing to do with the spiritual or religious meaning of "salvation" or "to save." These words do not mean "salvation by Jesus" or "saved by Jesus" or "being a member of the Christian Church." Therefore, when the contextual meaning of the words are considered, at least Acts 4:12 is talking about the physical recovery from the illness or weakness and can be paraphrased as "and there is healing in no one else; for there is no other name under heaven that has been given among men by which we must be made well."

If we combine both the scope of the conversation and the contextual meaning of salvation in the text, verse 12 can be paraphrased as "and there is healing in no one else; for there is no other name under heaven that has been given among the Jews by which the Jews must be made well." When we consider the healing ministry of Jesus, and the Jews on whom he performed the most miracles, this interpretation seems to fit better to the theme of the Gospels.

Also, this word study, in terms of the physical meaning of salvation, reaffirms the primary meaning of salvation found in the Gospels: "being saved from the judgment and destruction on Judea and subsequently from the Jewish persecution."

Conclusion: Chapter 3. The Only Savior of Judea Became the Only Savior of the World

To the Jews, who could save them from the imminent destruction of Judea in AD 70? Of course, not all Jews were killed in AD 70. Jesus implied that there would be some survivors by virtue of the elect: Matthew 24:22: "Unless those days had been cut short, no life would have been saved; but for the sake of the elect those days will be cut short." As we already read, according to Josephus, three million Jews from all over Judea were shut up in Jerusalem and suffered unspeakable afflictions. The historian says that 1,100,000 Jews perished by famine and sword, and that the rest of the rioters and robbers, being betrayed by each other after the taking of the city, were slain. And the tallest of the youths and those who were distinguished for beauty were preserved for the triumph. Of the rest of the multitude, those who were over seventeen years of age were sent as prisoners to labor in the works of Egypt, while still more were scattered through the provinces to meet their death in the theaters by the sword and by beasts. Those under seventeen years of age were carried away to be sold as slaves, and of these alone the number reached 90,000. Even from today's viewpoint, the casualty is beyond imagination. And numerous Jews were killed in the various cities of Judea during the war. If some Jews were saved from that destruction of Jerusalem and saved from the war because they believed in Jesus and became Christians, who would argue against the idea that Jesus was the only savior of Judea? However, when the gospel was preached out of Judea and changed to appeal to an audience of Gentiles, the sin of Judea became the sin of the world and the judgment on Judea became the judgment on the world. And therefore, the only savior of Judea became the only savior of the world.

Conclusion of Section I. Universalizing of Christianity: Judea Became the World

In the first century, Christianity was rapidly universalized. Jesus, as the promised Messiah, was concerned about the sin of his people, the Jews in Judea. He repudiated the legalistic and hypocritical lifestyle of the Jews and tried to restore the true nature of the law. And he prophesied the coming divine judgment on the unrepentant Judea—the Jews in a collective sense. At the same time, as the savior of his people, he provided himself as the way to be saved from the coming doomsday for Judea. Also, he comforted the afflicted and alienated Jews by giving hope for a new nation—the Kingdom of God—which was, in fact, the burgeoning Christian Church. However, all of these ideas were rapidly generalized and universalized when the gospel left the Palestinian soil and was preached to Gentiles outside the tradition of Judaism. It was at this point that the context that had been Judea became the world. The sin of Judea became the sin of the world; the judgment on Judea became the judgment on the world. And, naturally, the Messiah sent to save the Jews became the only savior of the world.

Since this universalization happened before AD 70, the destruction of the temple, Jerusalem, and Judea itself was viewed by Christians as a local incident—not recognized for its true meaning—and the universalized Christian faith kept growing. A question arises: Who was responsible for this distortion? The first disciples? Or Paul? Further study will need to be done to offer a plausible answer. At least in this study I am confident that if we read the New Testament without recognizing this universalization, we will not understand the primary meaning of the text itself. In other words, when we read the New Testament from the perspective of this universalization, we can interpret the text better.

The effects on evangelism of the universalization of sin and a theology of eschaton are easy to see. Presenting Jesus as the only savior to a world where all human beings are under sin and awaiting final destruction was enormously attractive. Certainly, the growth or success of Christianity in human history owes a great debt to this distortion. However, as always, something that is not true has a price to pay. Due to this universalization, Christian theology became ambiguous. Even today, this distorted eschatology causes some troubles in society.

Being honest may not be so effective for evangelism. However, for the long term, honesty will accomplish the true intention of God toward the human race. When Christianity is presented without original sin or total depravity and with the fulfilled eschatology, the future of our religion will belong to the future of the human race.

In the next section, I will examine some distortions caused by this universalization of the Christian religion.

SECTION II
Thoughts on Distortions

The Christian religion was universalized when it left Palestine in the first century. When the world was "Judaized" by the disciples, the Church in Judea became situated in the Judaized world and non-Jewish Gentiles were treated as Jews. That universalization inevitably resulted in a certain distortion because the world had never had a covenant with God and was fundamentally different from Judea, the covenantal nation. In that sense, a non-Jewish Gentile could not be the same as a Jew. The gospel (εὐαγγέλιον, good news), proclaimed to the Jews by Jesus and his apostles, was then proclaimed to the non-Jewish Gentiles with some distortions and without a clear explanation of why or how these two groups could be the same. In the early stage of the Church there were efforts on the part of some Jewish Christians to make Gentile Christians into Jews by circumcision (a covenantal requirement). However, their efforts were quashed by the Council of Jerusalem in about AD 50.[74] In fact, the Council of Jerusalem did not address the actual problem correctly. Let us read a relevant text in Acts 15:1–31:

Acts 15:1–31

1. Some men came down from Judea and began teaching the brethren, "Unless you are circumcised according to the custom of Moses, you cannot be saved."

2. And when Paul and Barnabas had great dissension and debate with them, the brethren determined that Paul and Barnabas and some

others of them should go up to Jerusalem to the apostles and elders concerning this issue.

3. Therefore, being sent on their way by the church, they were passing through both Phoenicia and Samaria, describing in detail the conversion of the Gentiles, and were bringing great joy to all the brethren.

4. When they arrived at Jerusalem, they were received by the church and the apostles and the elders, and they reported all that God had done with them.

5. But some of the sect of the Pharisees who had believed stood up, saying, "It is necessary to circumcise them and to direct them to observe the Law of Moses."

6. The apostles and the elders came together to look into this matter.

7. After there had been much debate, Peter stood up and said to them, "Brethren, you know that in the early days God made a choice among you, that by my mouth the Gentiles would hear the word of the gospel and believe.

8. "And God, who knows the heart, testified to them giving them the Holy Spirit, just as He also did to us;

9. and He made no distinction between us and them, cleansing their hearts by faith.

10. "Now therefore why do you put God to the test by placing upon the neck of the disciples a yoke which neither our fathers nor we have been able to bear?

11. "But we believe that we are saved through the grace of the Lord Jesus, in the same way as they also are."

12. All the people kept silent, and they were listening to Barnabas and Paul as they were relating what signs and wonders God had done through them among the Gentiles.

13. After they had stopped speaking, James answered, saying, "Brethren, listen to me.

14. "Simeon has related how God first concerned Himself about taking from among the Gentiles a people for His name.

15. "With this the words of the Prophets agree, just as it is written,

16. 'After these things I will return, and I will rebuild the Tabernacle of David which has fallen, and I will rebuild its ruins, and I will restore it,

17. So that the rest of mankind may seek the Lord, and all the Gentiles who are called by my name,'

18. says the Lord, who makes these things known from long ago.

19. "Therefore it is my judgment that we do not trouble those who are turning to God from among the Gentiles,

20. but that we write to them that they abstain from things contaminated by idols and from fornication and from what is strangled and from blood.

21. "For Moses from ancient generations has in every city those who preach him, since he is read in the synagogues every Sabbath."

22. Then it seemed good to the apostles and the elders, with the whole church, to choose men from among them to send to Antioch with Paul and Barnabas--Judas called Barsabbas, and Silas, leading men among the brethren,

23. and they sent this letter by them, "The apostles and the brethren who are elders, to the brethren in Antioch and Syria and Cilicia who are from the Gentiles, greetings.

24. "Since we have heard that some of our number to whom we gave no instruction have disturbed you with their words, unsettling your souls,

25. it seemed good to us, having become of one mind, to select men to send to you with our beloved Barnabas and Paul,

26. men who have risked their lives for the name of our Lord Jesus Christ.

27. "Therefore we have sent Judas and Silas, who themselves will also report the same things by word of mouth.

28. "For it seemed good to the Holy Spirit and to us to lay upon you no greater burden than these essentials:

29. that you abstain from things sacrificed to idols and from blood and from things strangled and from fornication; if you keep yourselves free from such things, you will do well. Farewell."

30. So when they were sent away, they went down to Antioch; and having gathered the congregation together, they delivered the letter.

31. When they had read it, they rejoiced because of its encouragement.

According to verse 1, some Jewish Christians came down to Antioch and informed the Gentile Christians that their salvation depended upon their participation in Jewish customs, especially circumcision. Since Jesus was the savior of the Jews, they believed it was necessary to be a Jew to be saved; by participating in their customs, a Gentile Christian could share the same religious tradition as other Jewish Christians. According to verse 5, that position was reaffirmed by some Jewish Christians at the Council of Jerusalem. After much debate however (v 7), they concluded that it was not even necessary for a Gentile Christian to be a Jew (v 19).

In fact, that conclusion did not resolve the problem. The real problem was not whether a Gentile should be circumcised and observe the Law of Moses, but their absence in the whole covenantal history of the Jews. How could a Gentile relate to Jesus, who embodied the culmination of the long history of the people of God? Once a person believed in Jesus, whether Jew or Gentile, he or she became a Christian. Once a Gentile became a Christian, it was not easy to go back and make him or her a Jew; he or she already shared the Christian identity with other Jewish Christians. The conclusion at the Council might elicit the unity of Christians but did not address the actual problem. Logically speaking, Jesus was the only savior of the Jews. So for a Gentile to be saved, he or she first must be a Jew, in order to inherit the salvation promised by the Messiah. Making a Gentile Christian into a Jew was an effort on the part of some Jewish Christians to endow them with a retroactive salvation—the salvation Jesus offered the Jews.

When the Church of Antioch sent missionaries to the Gentiles (Acts 13), it should have modified the content of the gospel for its non-Jewish audience. These missionaries needed to find a way to communicate to the Gentiles—who were not the people of God and did not share their history or their expectation of Messiah—what Jesus offered them. These guidelines for the missionaries should have been provided before the Gentile mission started, not after. At least, they should have explained that because of its sin against God, Judea would come to an end. Instead the message became universalized and the Gentile Christians came to believe that the whole world was under sin and would therefore be destroyed. This is precisely how the distortion of the gospel happened. When the missionaries were successful in appealing to their fears and offering the attraction of salvation, that success was on the basis of the universalization: the world became Judaized and Gentiles were treated like Jews.

Somehow Jewish Christians in Jerusalem did not get a chance to participate in the process of the evangelism carried out by the church of Antioch. When they recognized a problem, it was already late: A gentile became a Christian because he or she was treated like a Jew even before he or she became a Jew according to their law. Therefore, in Acts 15, they tried to fix the problem that had already happened. They tried to make a gentile Christian who was treated like a Jew implicitly (through the Judaized world) a Jew again explicitly (through circumcision). However, it was too late. Their argument could not have much persuasion because a gentile already became a Christian and was in their faith community already. Before the gospel was preached to the Gentiles, the Apostles should have to clarify the content of the gospel: How Jesus the savior and Messiah of the Jews should be introduced to the Gentile who knew nothing about their tradition, the tradition of the people of God, and who did not wait the promised Messiah. The guidelines should be provided before the Gentile mission started, not after. At least, they had to be clear about that Judea would come to an end, not the world, due to the sin of Judea. However, apparently, they did not and the distortion happened.

It seems to me that the universalization happened unintentionally by the missionaries when they adopted the universal expressions which the Apostles and leaders of Jerusalem church transmitted carelessly. Later the Apostles and leaders accepted the result along with the distortions. Maybe that's why even the Gospels that were written after universalization contain some universal expressions in describing sin and the end. I can think of two possible ways the gospel should have been introduced to the Gentiles to avoid these distortions. First, adopting the perspective of the conservative Jewish Christians, a gentile could become a Jew prior to accepting Jesus as the Son of God and Christ (Messiah). In this case, circumcision might be employed before baptism, not after, and then a converted Gentile-Jewish Christian would share the messianic tradition with their fellow Jewish Christians and then share salvation in the new kingdom of God, Christian Church, because Jesus came as the savior of the Jews. The second relies on education. If circumcision was not favored, prior to baptism, a gentile should understand the identity of the Christian Church as the new kingdom of God which replaces Judea or Israel, the identity of Jesus as the Lord of that Kingdom, and believing Jesus demonstrated by baptism as entering the gate of that kingdom; since the only requirement to enter that kingdom is to believe and accept the identity of Jesus, it is called grace; Jesus atoned Christian Church once and for all and thereby Christian Church is preserved by God as the holy Kingdom of God on earth; and then salvation means to be a part of the Christian Church because the Christian Church is to be saved from the destruction of Judea In these ways, I think, Judaization of the world could be prevented and the gospel preached by Jesus could be preserved intact.

For centuries Jews had lived in the tension between keeping the Law and repenting of sin when they inevitably failed. Because of this history, when a Jew became a Christian, repentance of sin had a clear message. Repentance was necessary to be reborn as a citizen of the new kingdom of God which Jesus, as the Messiah, would save soon from destruction. In this case, a citizen of the old kingdom of God (Judea), which was waiting for the Messiah (Christ), became a citizen of the new kingdom of God that confesses Jesus as the promised Messiah (Christ). Such was not the case for Gentiles who became Christians. Instead, because Gentiles' prior culture and religion was not tied to systems of law and repentance,[75] the identity of the Christian Church as the new kingdom of God with Jesus as Christ (one who reigns) of that kingdom should have trumped the ideas of sin and repentance. How to be a part of the new kingdom of God was the primary matter to a gentile, and the answer was faith, to believe and accept the identity of Jesus as the Son of God and Christ. In Christianity a gentile, a citizen of a secular kingdom, was invited to be a citizen of the new kingdom of God through faith, not according to flesh. Instead the message they received—repentance and forgiveness of sin, based upon Judaized world and universalized sin—was proclaimed prior to faith associated with the identity of Jesus and confession: The cross of Jesus preceded the reign of Christ.

Imagine a Möbius strip and you will understand how the distortion happened: the same material had been twisted and the inside became the outside; the same terms applied to the Jews by Jesus and his apostles were applied to the Gentiles without distinguishing the difference between the two groups.

In this sense, apostolic leadership failed but Paul might be saved. It was not the responsibility of Paul, but the disciples who saw, heard, and touched Jesus and knew what the gospel was. Since Paul wrote most of the New Testament books besides the Gospels, the distortions are found mostly in his writings, particularly his longest letter to the Romans. Paul may be excused from responsibility of these distortions if he was faithful to what the disciples transmitted to him. After all he did not receive the exact instruction how to preach to the Gentiles from them, and he never encountered Jesus physically, but knew facts such as his death and resurrection, the Second Coming and the end, along with the already universalized concepts.

The purpose of this section is not to call out who was responsible for the distortions or when the distortions exactly happened, but to understand that they happened. Knowing that will help us interpret the biblical accounts of the New Testament more accurately and restore the Christian faith as it was originally intended by Jesus.

CHAPTER 1
The Distorted Gospel: From Reign To Cross

The gospel, presented in both the Old and New Testaments, meant "the reign of God" in contrast to "the reign of man." Let us read some Isaiah passages:

בָּשַׂר: To bear good news

Isaiah 40:9
Get yourself up on a high mountain, O Zion, bearer of good news (תְמַבַשֶׂרֶת),
Lift up your voice mightily, O Jerusalem, bearer of good news (תְמַבַשֶׂרֶת);
Lift it up, do not fear Say to the cities of Judah, "Here is your God!"

Isaiah 41:27
"Formerly I said to Zion, 'Behold, here they are ' And to Jerusalem, 'I will give a messenger of good news (מְבַשֵׂר).'

Isaiah 52:
7. How lovely on the mountains are the feet of him who brings good news (מְבַשֵׂר), who announces peace and brings good news of happiness, who announces salvation, And says to Zion, "Your God reigns!"
8. Listen! Your watchmen lift up their voices, they shout joyfully together; for they will see with their own eyes when the LORD restores Zion.
9. Break forth, shout joyfully together, you waste places of Jerusalem; For the LORD has comforted His people, He has redeemed Jerusalem.

10. The LORD has bared His holy arm In the sight of all the nations, That all the ends of the earth may see The salvation of our God.

Isaiah 60:6

"A multitude of camels will cover you, The young camels of Midian and Ephah; All those from Sheba will come; They will bring gold and frankincense, And will bear good news (יְבַשֵּׂרוּ) of the praises of the LORD.

Isaiah 61:

1. The Spirit of the Lord GOD is upon me, Because the LORD has anointed me To bring good news (רְשֵׂבַּל) to the afflicted; He has sent me to bind up the brokenhearted, To proclaim liberty to captives And freedom to prisoners;

2. To proclaim the favorable year of the LORD And the day of vengeance of our God; To comfort all who mourn,

3. To grant those who mourn in Zion, Giving them a garland instead of ashes, The oil of gladness instead of mourning, The mantle of praise instead of a spirit of fainting So they will be called oaks of righteousness, The planting of the LORD, that He may be glorified.

In the texts, the title of "good news" meant the restoration or the salvation of Jerusalem, or Zion, and the content of "good news" was "the reign of God" and its benefits to the people of God. It implies that Jerusalem, or "the people of God," was destroyed due to "the reign of man," however, it would be restored by "the reign of God."[76]

Let us look at the relevant passages in the New Testament:

εὐαγγέλιον: good news or gospel

Mark 1:1, 14, 15

1. The beginning of the gospel (εὐαγγελίου) of Jesus Christ, the Son of God

14. Now after John had been taken into custody, Jesus came into Galilee, preaching the gospel (εὐαγγέλιον) of God,

15. and saying, "The time is fulfilled, and the kingdom of God is at hand; repent and believe in the gospel (εὐαγγελίῳ)."

Matthew 4:23
Jesus was going throughout all Galilee, teaching in their synagogues and proclaiming the gospel (εὐαγγέλιον) of the kingdom, and healing every kind of disease and every kind of sickness among the people.

Matthew 9:35
Jesus was going through all the cities and villages, teaching in their synagogues and proclaiming the gospel (εὐαγγέλιον) of the kingdom, and healing every kind of disease and every kind of sickness.

Matthew 11:5
the blind receive sight the lame walk, the lepers are cleansed and the deaf hear, the dead are raised up, and the poor have the gospel (εὐαγγελίζονται) preached to them.

Luke 4:18–19 (Quoted from Isaiah 61:1–2)
18. "The spirit of the LORD is upon me, because he anointed me to preach the gospel (εὐαγγελίσασθαι) to the poor. He has sent me to proclaim release to the captives, and recovery of sight to the blind, to set free those who are oppressed
19. To proclaim the favorable year of the LORD."

Luke 4:43
But He said to them, "I must preach (the gospel) (εὐαγγελίσασθαί) the kingdom of God to the other cities also, for I was sent for this purpose."

Luke 8:1
Soon afterwards, He began going around from one city and village to another, proclaiming and preaching (the gospel) (εὐαγγελιζόμενος) the kingdom of God. The twelve were with Him,

Luke 16:16
"The Law and the Prophets were proclaimed until John; since that time the gospel (εὐαγγελίζεται) of the kingdom of God has been preached, and everyone is forcing his way into it.

In the New Testament, the gospel or "the good news" Jesus brought to the Jews was "the good news of God" and "the good news of the kingdom of God." Therefore, the gospel meant "the good news" God, himself, proclaimed to the Jews and was about the kingdom over which God, himself, reigns. Particularly, at the beginning of his ministry, Jesus quoted Isaiah 61:1–2 at the synagogue of Nazareth (Luke 4:18–19). That clearly implies that the gospel Jesus proclaimed was the gospel mentioned in Isaiah. Therefore, the gospel of the New Testament was directly related to the gospel of the Old Testament, which was, the kingdom of God, or the reign of God, which was coming close to the Jews. In fact, "the good news" meant the imminent birth of the Christian Church in which God reigns. This subject will be discussed further in the next section. Jesus encouraged the Jews to be a part of the new kingdom. And the way to get into that kingdom was to believe and accept the identity of Jesus as the Son of God and the Messiah or Christ of the kingdom of God. With that acceptance came an invitation to become the people of Jesus:

Matthew 16:15–17
15. He said to them, "But who do you say that I am?"
16. Simon Peter answered, "You are the Christ, the Son of the living God."
17. And Jesus said to him, "Blessed are you, Simon Barjona, because flesh and blood did not reveal this to you, but my Father who is in heaven."

John 20:31
but these have been written so that you may believe that Jesus is the Christ, the Son of God; and that believing you may have life in His name.

Jesus called the people of God to be the new people of God. Salvation in Christ required Jews to repent of their legalistic lifestyles, to turn away from the old kingdom toward the new kingdom. In this sense, the mission of Jesus and John the Baptist were closely related. In addition to being circumcised, Gentiles were baptized when they converted to Judaism. Only Jews who acknowledged that they did not live as the people of God but rather lived like the Gentiles (who did not have the Law) could respond to John the Baptist's message of repentance and be baptized. That's why the baptism of John was called the baptism of repentance which meant regeneration:

Mark 1:4
John the Baptist appeared in the wilderness preaching a baptism of repentance for the forgiveness of sins.

Luke 3:3
And he came into all the district around the Jordan, preaching a baptism of repentance for the forgiveness of sins;

Acts 13:24
after John had proclaimed before His coming a baptism of repentance to all the people of Israel.

Acts 19:4
Paul said, "John baptized with the baptism of repentance, telling the people to believe in Him who was coming after him, that is, in Jesus."

Those Jews who believed and accepted Jesus as the Son of God and Christ formed the new faith community, the first Christian Church in Jerusalem (Acts 1). The proclamation of that Church to the Jews was "Repent of your old way of life and what you did to Jesus, and believe and accept that Jesus, whom you killed, was the Son of God and the Messiah (Christ) you were waiting for. Do this and you will be a part of the new kingdom of God over which Jesus reigns and therefore be saved from the imminent destruction of the old kingdom." Peter and the newly converted Paul preached the same message to the Jews.

Peter in Jerusalem

Acts 2:36–40

36. "Therefore let all the house of Israel know for certain that God has made Him both Lord and Christ--this Jesus whom you crucified."
37. Now when they heard this, they were pierced to the heart, and said to Peter and the rest of the apostles, "Brethren, what shall we do?"
38. Peter said to them, "Repent, and each of you be baptized in the name of Jesus Christ for the forgiveness of your sins; and you will receive the gift of the Holy Spirit.
39. "For the promise is for you and your children and for all who are far off, as many as the Lord our God will call to Himself."
40. And with many other words he solemnly testified and kept on exhorting them, saying, "Be saved from this perverse generation!"

Paul in Damascus right after conversion

Acts 9:18–22

18. And immediately there fell from his eyes something like scales, and he regained his sight, and he got up and was baptized;
19. and he took food and was strengthened. Now for several days he was with the disciples who were at Damascus,
20. and immediately he began to proclaim Jesus in the synagogues, saying, "He is the Son of God."
21. All those hearing him continued to be amazed, and were saying, "Is this not he who in Jerusalem destroyed those who called on this name, and who had come here for the purpose of bringing them bound before the chief priests?"
22. But Saul kept increasing in strength and confounding the Jews who lived at Damascus by proving that this Jesus is the Christ.

The Jews had the history and the capacity to understand their culpability, their error in not recognizing Jesus as the long-awaited Messiah. However, the Gentiles did not have the context to understand who Jesus was. They had not lived in that Jewish tradition of Messianic expectation. It certainly did not make sense preaching Jesus as Messiah to those who did not wait for him; therefore, instead of explaining the identity of Jesus, they preached: "You all are sinners. The world will soon come to an end. If you don't repent and accept Jesus as the savior, you will perish."

Paul's preaching to the Greeks in Athens illustrates this aspect well:

Acts 17:30–31
30. "Therefore having overlooked the times of ignorance, God is now declaring to men that all people everywhere should repent,
31. because He has fixed a day in which He will judge the world in righteousness through a Man whom He has appointed, having furnished proof to all men by raising Him from the dead."

Here, we notice some distortions and universal expressions. Paul says that all people, not just Jews, should repent. However, this "repent" cannot be the same "repent" Jesus used in Mark 1:15 and Peter used in Acts 2:38, because "sin" means something different to each group, the Jews and the Gentiles. Also, he says that God fixed a day to judge the world. However, God fixed a day to judge Judea. The Gentiles were treated as the Jews in terms of sin and judgment. Interestingly Paul does not mention the name Jesus. Instead he uses the general term "a Man" because the Gentiles did not know who Jesus was and did not wait for the promised Messiah.

In conclusion, the gospel became for the Gentiles this news: "Here is the way to resolve your previous sin and therefore to be saved from the imminent destruction of the world: to believe in the atoning power of Jesus" rather than: "Here is the new kingdom of God, reigned over by Jesus, who is the Son of God and the promised Christ (Messiah) of the kingdom. Believe that Jesus is of God and become a member of that Kingdom." Since Romans is the longest of Paul's letters in the New Testament and presents this distorted gospel in detail, I will analyze Romans chapter 1 to 8 to give a better understanding of these misleading concepts.

CHAPTER 2
The Distorted Gospel in the Romans

Prior individual sin, rather than the collective sin of the people of God, became the main concern of Paul in Romans 3:

Romans 3:25
whom God displayed publicly as a propitiation in His blood through faith. This was to demonstrate His righteousness, because in the forbearance of God He passed over the sins previously committed [τῶν προγεγονότων ἁμαρτημάτων]

This idea is repeated in Romans 5 and 6:

Romans 5:6–10
6. For while we were still helpless, at the right time Christ died for the ungodly.
7. For one will hardly die for a righteous man; though perhaps for the good man someone would dare even to die.
8. But God demonstrates His own love toward us, in that while we were yet sinners, Christ died for us.
9. Much more then, having now been justified by His blood, we shall be saved from the wrath of God through Him.
10. For if while we were enemies we were reconciled to God through the death of His Son, much more, having been reconciled, we shall be saved by His life.

Romans 6:6, 17–18

6. knowing this, that our old self was crucified with Him, in order that our body of sin might be done away with, so that we would no longer be slaves to sin.

17. But thanks be to God that though you were slaves of sin, you became obedient from the heart to that form of teaching to which you were committed,

18. and having been freed from sin, you became slaves of righteousness.

How to resolve the problem of the previous sin? The suggested way by Paul was faith, not just believing the identity of Jesus, but believing in the atoning power of Jesus to remove prior sin. The cross came out to the gate to be applied to the world. Gentiles, even though they had no covenant bounded sin because they had not been "responsible" to uphold the Law, were given the gift of atonement at the moment they converted to the Christian faith. The sin of Judea, the collective sin of the people of God, got set aside; instead, individual prior sin became a concern for the Gentile Christians. The cross of Christ, alleged universal atonement for universal sin, resolved the problem for the Gentiles, therefore, repentance and forgiveness became the entry point to the kingdom.

The message that requires faith became "Jesus Christ died for you. Just believe this and be saved. Jesus is the savior. It is the grace of God," instead of "Jesus the Son of God is the Christ of the Kingdom of God, the Christian Church." The Law comprises works, and failing them allegedly results in sin. Therefore, faith, believing in atonement through Jesus, became more prominent than the commandment and teachings of Jesus.[77] In other words, the atonement of Jesus, a benefit of the reign of Christ for His people, became the gospel itself for the world: For the Gentiles, forgiveness of previous sin through the atoning sacrifice of Jesus Christ became the good news. Entering the gate to the kingdom, therefore, became believing in the atonement alone in the name of grace instead of believing in the identity of Jesus. The Church as the new Kingdom and the reign of Jesus Christ over the Church was the actual good news. However, the actual gospel (kingdom and reign) became something futuristic.[78] The forgiven individuals formed a church that waits for completion instead of being added to the new kingdom of God, established on Pentecost and redeemed by Jesus.

The basis of Christian ethics became ambiguous because the problem was resolved at the gate and the forgiven individuals formed the Church. Here's where the shift happens. The original idea was to "save the people of God from their continual covenantal sin," which, under the Law, required a redemptive sacrifice. Through this redemption they were "saved from the destruction of Judea." With the evangelism of Gentiles, salvation meant "saved from some, or all, previous sin": individual sin, based upon conscience, and this newly universalized "original sin." Salvation also now meant "saved from the imminent end of the world," instead of, "saved from the destruction of Judea." When evangelism for Jesus leapt to the Gentiles, terms and ideas that had meant something particular to Jews became generalized. The scope of sin moved from Judea or the Christian church to the world, and the doctrines of "original" sin and "total depravity" of all human beings became the foundation for the gospel.

The world was treated as if it were Judea; the Gentiles, as Jews. Because the Gentile followers of Jesus were identified with the Jews, they were treated as sinners and asked to repent. Instead of inviting Gentiles into the newly established kingdom of God, which was spiritual in its nature, the missionaries—unintentionally—threatened the world by creating the fear that the end was near. Instead of proclaiming the identity of Jesus to the world, opening the door to the gospel, which was the Christian kingdom reigned by the triune God, they emphasized sin to create the absolute need for Jesus. Even though Jesus never spoke of it, the world began to wait for doomsday, the end of the world.

In Romans, we can see how sin became generalized, to be used as the foundation for the absolute claim for Jesus. Writing moves quickly to the intended conclusion: all human beings of the world are sinners, in other words, all humans are totally depraved.

Generalization in Romans[79]

A group of the people (1:18, 2:17)
  ⇨   All human beings (3:19b, 23)

The Jews or Judea (2:17)
  ⇨   The world (3:19b)

Under the judgment (2:2)
  ⇨   Under sin (3:9b, 23)
  ⇨   Under sin and death (5:12)

Conclusion
All human beings of the world are sinners.

I have stated in Section I that the universal expressions in Romans need to be reinterpreted. Romans 3:9b lacks logic and proof and therefore "all" cannot be interpreted literally. It was Paul's own generalized proclamation. Because he was addressing Jews, when he says "every mouth" and "all the world" (verse 3:19b), what he really meant was "every mouth under the Law" and "all the world under the Law." Likewise, "all" in 3:23 should be understood as "all under the Law." Also, it should be noticed that "all" in 5:12 changes to "many" in the following verses. Which does Paul mean? The following analysis is based upon the supposition that 5:12 was Paul's true intention since he lays out the case for total depravity of human beings in connection with natural death. This will provide the foundation for his absolute claim for Jesus. Even though some universal expressions cannot be interpreted literally because to do so would be illogical, it is clear that this was Paul's intention in writing Romans. "Death" in 5:12 is defined as the physical death; this sentiment is echoed in Paul's writing in I Corinthians 15: 21–22.

In Romans chapters 1 and 2, Paul is, in fact, talking about a particular group of people, not the human race. However, this group becomes generalized and turns into all human beings by 3:19b and 23. In addition, the scope of the nation becomes generalized. In chapter 2, Paul is talking about the Jews, the people of Judea, thus, the nation of Judea. But Judea turns into the world in 3:19b. In chapter 2, Paul says that a group of people, including the Jews, is under the judgment of God. However, "under the judgment of God" turns to "under sin" in 3:9b and 23 and then to "under sin and death" in 5:12. In 5:12 natural death is utilized to set the absolute claim for the total depravity of human beings: No one can deny that all humans will die. He concludes then that all human beings are sinners. As examined in Section I, the intended conclusion is based upon Paul's faulty logic and methodology, not upon objective truth and principles. If one reads Romans uncritically, with a conviction that the writing is correct because it is the word of God, he or she will come to the conclusion intended by Paul, but there will linger a certain degree of ambiguity because it lacks logic and objectivity.

Pointing out their sin to the Gentiles and asking them to repent might be justified. Like everyone else, they are not perfect. Those who live unethical lives always need to repent to come closer to perfection. However, from the viewpoint of ethics, the problem might be universalization. The statement "all human beings are sinners" contradicts the notion of God's justice. From a theological viewpoint, the problem is that the atonement of Jesus, intended for the people of God, was applied to all human beings of the world even though most (Gentiles) had never had a covenant with God. When the gospel spread to non-Jews, the gate was widely opened and whoever entered became a beneficiary of the atonement of Jesus. It is critical here to understand the nature of distortion. Just like a Möbius strip, the same materials exist, but in a twisted order. Pointing out sin and demanding repentance to live as people of God were not wrong at all. However, the message was not "Repent of your previous sin and believe and accept that Jesus is the Son of God and Christ of the kingdom of God. In doing so you will receive the benefit of atonement," but rather "Repent of your previous sin. Believe that Jesus Christ, the Son of God, died for those sins and be saved." The weight of sin moved from Judea and the Church to the world and all human beings. The redemptive atonement of Jesus moved from the Church and Christians to the world and all human beings. The atonement, which should be applied to the Church and Christians who confessed Jesus as the Son of God and Christ of the kingdom of God, was applied to Gentiles who did not understand who Jesus is and were not awaiting the promised Messiah.

Once all human beings became sinners, the notion of faith became ambiguous and distorted. In the Gospels, faith, as the right to be the people of God, meant believing the identity of Jesus. This was contrasted with the human bloodline. Let us read John 1:11–13.

11. He came to His own, and those who were His own did not receive Him.
12. But as many as received Him, to them He gave the right to become children of God, even to those who believe in His name,
13. who were born, not of blood [αἱμάτων] nor of the will of the flesh [σαρκὸς] nor of the will of man [ἀνδρὸς], but of God.

Who were the people of God before Jesus? The answer in general might be the descendants of Abraham, Isaac, and Jacob. In the strictest sense, those who were born as the descendants of the twelve sons of Jacob (Israel) were the people of God. Also, in terms of a physical sign, those who were circumcised were considered to be the people of God, including the circumcised Gentiles.[80] When a Jew, as a descendant of Jacob, believed and received Jesus, descendent of David,[81] as the son of God and the promised Messiah,[82] he or she could be a member of the new kingdom of God through that faith. The same principle was later applied to the Gentiles but without requiring circumcision. This new era was opened by Jesus, the era in which anyone could be a member of the kingdom of God, become children of God, not by blood nor the will of the flesh nor the will of man, but by faith alone. The gate to the good news and its abundant blessings was widely open. It was truly by virtue of the grace of God. However, particularly in Romans and Galatians, faith, along with atonement and grace, is strongly contrasted with works of the Law. If work meant only circumcision (in contrast to faith), there would be no problem because circumcision was closely related to blood and flesh. However, the problem was that, according to Paul, even though the commandment of circumcision was given to Abraham before Moses,[83] circumcision represented works of the Law, and all Jewish Law, including circumcision, was contrasted with faith. Paul does not define with any consistency what is meant by faith. Sometimes in Paul's writings faith is identified with believing the identity of Jesus or believing the promise of God, including all benefits of the gospel. One thing is clear in Paul's writings: he strongly contrasts faith with works of the Law in conjunction with atonement of Jesus. Therefore, faith is identified with believing in the atonement of Jesus. Let us read some relevant texts:

Romans 3:21–31

21. But now apart from the Law the righteousness of God has been manifested, being witnessed by the Law and the Prophets,
22. even the righteousness of God through faith in Jesus Christ for all those who believe; for there is no distinction;
23. for all have sinned and fall short of the glory of God,
24. being justified as a gift by His grace through the redemption which is in Christ Jesus;
25. whom God displayed publicly as a propitiation in His blood through faith. This was to demonstrate His righteousness, because in the forbearance of God He passed over the sins previously committed;
26. for the demonstration, I say, of His righteousness at the present time, so that He would be just and the justifier of the one who has faith in Jesus.
27. Where then is boasting? It is excluded. By what kind of law? Of works? No, but by a law of faith.
28. For we maintain that a man is justified by faith apart from works of the Law.
29. Or is God the God of Jews only? Is He not the God of Gentiles also? Yes, of Gentiles also,
30. since indeed God who will justify the circumcised by faith and the uncircumcised through faith is one.
31. Do we then nullify the Law through faith? May it never be! On the contrary, we establish the Law.

Romans 4:4–5, 13–14

4. Now to the one who works, his wage is not credited as a favor, but as what is due.
5. But to the one who does not work, but believes in Him who justifies the ungodly, his faith is credited as righteousness,
13. For the promise to Abraham or to his descendants that he would be heir of the world was not through the Law, but through the righteousness of faith.
14. For if those who are of the Law are heirs, faith is made void and the promise is nullified;

Romans 5:1, 9, 20–21

1. Therefore, having been justified by faith, we have peace with God through our Lord Jesus Christ
9. Much more then, having now been justified by His blood, we shall be saved from the wrath of God through Him.
20. The Law came in so that the transgression would increase; but where sin increased, grace abounded all the more,
21. so that, as sin reigned in death, even so grace would reign through righteousness to eternal life through Jesus Christ our Lord.

Romans 9:30–32

30. What shall we say then? That Gentiles, who did not pursue righteousness, attained righteousness, even the righteousness which is by faith;
31. but Israel, pursuing a law of righteousness, did not arrive at that law.
32. Why? Because they did not pursue it by faith, but as though it were by works. They stumbled over the stumbling stone

Galatians 2:16

Nevertheless knowing that a man is not justified by the works of the Law but through faith in Christ Jesus, even we have believed in Christ Jesus, so that we may be justified by faith in Christ and not by the works of the Law; since by the works of the Law no flesh will be justified.

Galatians 3:2, 5, 11–13, 23–25

2. This is the only thing I want to find out from you: did you receive the Spirit by the works of the Law, or by hearing with faith?

5. So then, does He who provides you with the Spirit and works miracles among you, do it by the works of the Law, or by hearing with faith?

11. Now that no one is justified by the Law before God is evident; for, "The righteous man shall live by faith."

12. However, the Law is not of faith; on the contrary, "He who practices them shall live by them."

13. Christ redeemed us from the curse of the Law, having become a curse for us—for it is written, "Cursed is everyone who hangs on a tree."

23. But before faith came, we were kept in custody under the law, being shut up to the faith which was later to be revealed.

24. Therefore the Law has become our tutor to lead us to Christ, so that we may be justified by faith.

25. But now that faith has come, we are no longer under a tutor.

In these texts, first, faith is identified with atonement (Romans 3:25a; 5:1, 9). The writer aims to resolve an individual's prior sin (Romans 3:25b), not the sin of the people of God. Therefore, atonement, a benefit for the people of God, is applied to the allegedly sinful Gentiles in advance. Therefore, faith means believing in the atonement of Jesus. Here, we should distinguish the statement "If you believe Jesus is the son of God and Christ, then you will be the people of God and your sin will be forgiven through the atonement of Jesus" from the statement "Jesus, the son of God and Christ, died for the sins you have committed. If you believe this, you will be a people of God."

Second, faith and atonement are contrasted with "works of the Law" or "the Law" or "works" (Romans 3:27, 28; 4:4, 5, 13, 14; 9:32; Galatians 2:16; 3:2, 5, 11, 12). There is no reason for faith or atonement to be contrasted with works of the Law. In the Old Testament, faith, the Law, and atonement stand independently but complementarily. Faith belonged to the people of Israel. Faith meant believing that Yahweh (יְהֹוָה) is God (אֱלֹהִים) and one.[84] That particular God gave the Law to the people of

God. Moreover, God did not even expect that the people of God would observe the Law perfectly. That is precisely why God set up the system of atonement through blood sacrifice; in fact, the sacrificial system was a part of the Law. If Paul denounces the Law totally, that includes atonement and, as a result, the atonement of Jesus loses its connection to the biblical story. Atonement was set up to compensate for the works of the Law (or the Law or the works).[85] In the Gospels, faith meant to believe Jesus as the son of God and the promised Messiah (Christ). To those who had faith and became the new people of God, Jesus gave teachings and even the New Commandment, the Law. When His people violate His Law and teachings, the atonement set up by His own sacrifice compensates for the sin of His people. Therefore, it was not necessary for faith to be contrasted with the Law. And that's why Paul had to defend the Law while denouncing it without a clear and logical explanation for this contradiction: "Do we then nullify the Law through faith? May it never be! On the contrary, we establish the Law" (Romans 3:31); "What shall we say then? Is the Law sin? May it never be! On the contrary, I would not have come to know sin except through the Law" (Romans 7:7); "So then, the Law is holy, and the commandment is holy and righteous and good" (Romans 7:12).

Let me explain these through the patterns:

Comparison of the Old Testament and the Gospels (diagram A)

O.T.		Gospels of N.T.
The people of God (by Blood or circumcision)	≈	The new people of God by Faith
Law as commandments	≈	The New Commandment and teachings of Jesus
Atonement through Animal Sacrifice	≈	Atonement through Sacrifice of Jesus

In the Old Testament, there were the people of God, the Law, and atonement. The people of God were identified by blood (or circumcision) and were supposed to observe the commandments of the Law given by

God. Atonement through animal sacrifice kept the relationship between God and the people. In the Gospels, there were the new people of God, the New Commandment and teachings[86], and atonement. The new people of God were identified with those who believed and received Jesus and were supposed to observe the New Commandment and teachings given by Jesus. And atonement, through the sacrifice of Jesus, kept the relationship between God and the new people. Therefore, faith in the Gospels should correspond to blood (or circumcision) in the Old Testament. Here, faith should mean believing the identity of Jesus. The New Commandment and teachings of Jesus in the Gospels should correspond to the commandments of the Law in the Old Testament. Atonement through the Sacrifice of Jesus in the Gospels should correspond to atonement through animal sacrifice in the Old Testament. This aspect is well paraphrased in Hebrews chapter 9 and 10, comparing the death of Jesus with the sin offering and the Day of Atonement of the Old Testament.

However, in Paul's writings, we can find subtly distorted patterns:

Comparison of the Old Testament and Paul's writings (diagram B)

O.T.   Paul'swritings of N.T.

                                        Faith to be the new people of God
        _____
Works of the Law (or circumcision)   _____
        _____

                                        Atonement through the Sacrifice of Jesus

Works of the Law (or the Law or the works) of the Old Testament should be compared or contrasted with the New Commandment or teachings of Jesus. Instead, those are contrasted with faith and atonement of the New Testament. Therefore, faith is identified with atonement in Paul's writings. Even though circumcision was instituted before the Mosaic Law, circumcision represents the Law in Paul's writings. Since circumcision is, in fact, a part of the Law, and faith corresponds to circumcision in terms of identifying the people of God, faith and circumcision could be contrasted to each other. However, again, the problem is that Paul contrasts not just circumcision but the Law as a whole, including circumcision, with faith.

When we compare diagram A and B, the missing parts are revealed: In the Old Testament, "the people of God by bloodline" and "atonement through animal sacrifice"; in the New Testament, "the New Commandment and teachings of Jesus." In order to better understand the distortions, it is helpful to understand how Paul approaches the two missing parts of the Old Testament and one in the New Testament.

First, for "the people of God by blood" of the Old Testament, Paul adopted an ahistorical approach. Paul skips over the long history of the descendants of the twelve tribes and connects the Christians directly to Abraham and Isaac by utilizing the term "faith and promise." As a result, he ignores the biblical significance of the number twelve and the continuity of the people of God through the tradition of the twelve disciples and 120 saints at Pentecost.[87] Let us read the relevant texts:

Romans 4:1–25
1. What then shall we say that Abraham, our forefather according to the flesh, has found?
2. For if Abraham was justified by works, he has something to boast about, but not before God.
3. For what does the Scripture say? "Abraham believed God, and it was credited to him as righteousness."
4. Now to the one who works, his wage is not credited as a favor, but as what is due.
5. But to the one who does not work, but believes in Him who justifies the ungodly, his faith is credited as righteousness,
6. just as David also speaks of the blessing on the man to whom God credits righteousness apart from works:
7. "Blessed are those whose lawless deeds have been forgiven, and whose sins have been covered.
8. "Blessed is the man whose sin the Lord will not take into account."

9. Is this blessing then on the circumcised, or on the uncircumcised also? For we say, "Faith was credited to Abraham as righteousness."

10. How then was it credited? While he was circumcised, or uncircumcised? Not while circumcised, but while uncircumcised;

11. and he received the sign of circumcision, a seal of the righteousness of the faith which he had while uncircumcised, so that he might be the father of all who believe without being circumcised, that righteousness might be credited to them,

12. and the father of circumcision to those who not only are of the circumcision, but who also follow in the steps of the faith of our father Abraham which he had while uncircumcised.

13. For the promise to Abraham or to his descendants that he would be heir of the world was not through the Law, but through the righteousness of faith.

14. For if those who are of the Law are heirs, faith is made void and the promise is nullified;

15. for the Law brings about wrath, but where there is no law, there also is no violation.

16. For this reason it is by faith, in order that it may be in accordance with grace, so that the promise will be guaranteed to all the descendants, not only to those who are of the Law, but also to those who are of the faith of Abraham, who is the father of us all,

17. (as it is written, "A father of many nations have I made you ") in the presence of Him whom he believed, even God, who gives life to the dead and calls into being that which does not exist.

18. In hope against hope he believed, so that he might become a father of many nations according to that which had been spoken, "So shall your descendants be."

19. Without becoming weak in faith he contemplated his own body, now as good as dead since he was about a hundred years old, and the deadness of Sarah's womb;

20. yet, with respect to the promise of God, he did not waver in unbelief but grew strong in faith, giving glory to God,

21. and being fully assured that what God had promised, He was able also to perform.

22. Therefore it was also credited to him as righteousness

23. Now not for his sake only was it written that it was credited to him,

24. but for our sake also, to whom it will be credited, as those who believe in Him who raised Jesus our Lord from the dead,

25. He who was delivered over because of our transgressions, and was raised because of our justification.

Galatians 3:6–9, 16–29

6. Even so Abraham believed God, and it was reckoned to him as righteousness.

7. Therefore, be sure that it is those who are of faith who are sons of Abraham.

8. The Scripture, foreseeing that God would justify the Gentiles by faith, preached the gospel beforehand to Abraham, saying, "All the nations will be blessed in you

9. So then those who are of faith are blessed with Abraham, the believer.

16. Now the promises were spoken to Abraham and to his seed. He does not say, "And to seeds," as referring to many, but rather to one, "And to your seed," that is, Christ.

17. What I am saying is this: the Law, which came four hundred and thirty years later, does not invalidate a covenant previously ratified by God, so as to nullify the promise.

18. For if the inheritance is based on law, it is no longer based on a promise; but God has granted it to Abraham by means of a promise.

19. Why the Law then? It was added because of transgressions, having been ordained through angels by the agency of a mediator, until the seed would come to whom the promise had been made.

20. Now a mediator is not for one party only; whereas God is only one.

21. Is the Law then contrary to the promises of God? May it never be! For if a law had been given which was able to impart life, then righteousness would indeed have been based on law.

22. But the Scripture has shut up everyone under sin, so that the promise by faith in Jesus Christ might be given to those who believe.

23. But before faith came, we were kept in custody under the law, being shut up to the faith which was later to be revealed.
24. Therefore the Law has become our tutor to lead us to Christ, so that we may be justified by faith.
25. But now that faith has come, we are no longer under a tutor.
26. For you are all sons of God through faith in Christ Jesus.
27. For all of you who were baptized into Christ have clothed yourselves with Christ.
28. There is neither Jew nor Greek, there is neither slave nor free man, there is neither male nor female; for you are all one in Christ Jesus.
29. And if you belong to Christ, then you are Abraham's descendants, heirs according to promise.

Galatians 4:22–31

22. For it is written that Abraham had two sons, one by the bondwoman and one by the free woman.
23. But the son by the bondwoman was born according to the flesh, and the son by the free woman through the promise.
24. This is allegorically speaking, for these women are two covenants: one proceeding from Mount Sinai bearing children who are to be slaves; she is Hagar.
25. Now this Hagar is Mount Sinai in Arabia and corresponds to the present Jerusalem, for she is in slavery with her children.
26. But the Jerusalem above is free; she is our mother.
27. For it is written, "Rejoice, barren women who does not bear; break forth and shout, you who are not in labor; for more numerous are the children of the desolate than of the one who has a husband."
28. And you brethren, like Isaac, are children of promise.
29. But as at that time he who was born according to the flesh persecuted him who was born according to the Spirit, so it is now also.
30. But what does the Scripture say? "Cast out the bondwoman and her son, for the son of the bondwoman shall not be an heir with the son of the free woman."
31. So then, brethren, we are not children of a bondwoman, but of the free woman.

How do the Christians become the people of God, in relation to the people of God in the Old Testament? First, in the Gospels, Jesus is identified with Jacob, or Israel, when he calls the twelve disciples or apostles. Jesus is the new Jacob, starting the new people of God, a direct parallel to the twelve tribes of Jacob in the Old Testament. Since the twelve had such a symbolic and theological meaning, the eleven disciples quickly elected Matthias to complete the number right after the ascension of Jesus.[88] Also, Acts 1:15 states that the first Christian church in Jerusalem, by the time of the Pentecost, was comprised of about 120 members. The twelve as the number of the people of God is well illustrated in Revelation in terms of 24 (12+12) elders, 144,000 (12X12,000) saints, and the description of the new Jerusalem (12 gates, 12 angels, 12 names of the 12 tribes, 12 foundation stones, 12 names of 12 apostles, 12,000 furlongs, 144 [12X12] cubits).[89] In Revelation, the twelve apostles are identified with the twelve tribes, and therefore, the people of God in both Testaments are naturally related or combined through the number 12. Also, James 1:1 calls the Christians in such a manner: "James, a bond-servant of God and of the Lord Jesus Christ, To the twelve tribes who are dispersed abroad: Greetings." Therefore, by the tradition of the Old Testament and the Gospels, when a Gentile was converted as a Christian, he or she was meant to be added to the twelve apostles as a descendant in order to be identified as a member of the people of God. Second, in the Gospels, Jesus as the descendant of David is identified with the promised Messiah or Christ. Therefore, those who believed in and received Jesus become the people under the reign of Messiah or Christ. They are identified as the people of God just as those who were reigned over by kings (messiahs) in the Old Testament were the people of God.

Unlike the Gospels, Paul connected the Christians directly to Abraham and Isaac without identifying Jesus as Jacob (Israel) or the son of David to make them the people of God. How? Three methods are noticed. First, Christians become the descendants of Abraham in terms of a common denominator, faith: Abraham was justified by faith and Christians are justified by faith; therefore, the Christians are the descendants of Abraham (Romans 4, Galatians 3). Second, Christians become the descendants of Abraham by identifying Jesus with Isaac, in terms of a common denominator, promise: Jesus is declared as the promised seed of Abraham because Jesus was promised by God just like Isaac (Galatians 3). Therefore Christians, who belong to Jesus, belong to Abraham. Third, Christians become the descendants of Abraham through being directly identified with Isaac, in terms of promise: Isaac was born by promise and Christians are seen as the fulfillment of the promise (Galatians 4). By this allegorical and ahistorical approach, Paul successfully identified Christians as the people of God not by comparing or contrasting faith with bloodline, but instead by utilizing faith and promise as the common denominator connecting to Abraham. This serves to reinforce the significance of faith that Paul argued for. However, by adopting this approach, the significance of the twelve tribes and disciples, the foundation of the people of God in both Testaments, got overlooked.

Second, as for "the atonement through animal sacrifice" of the Old Testament, Paul basically keeps silent. The death of Jesus can have a theological meaning only when the animal sacrifice of the Old Testament is properly understood and applied. However, Paul speaks of the Law but not the animal sacrifice. Why does Paul keep silent on the animal sacrifice of the Old Testament when he puts a great emphasis on the death of Jesus in conjunction with faith? Three possible reasons might be pondered. First, though "the atonement through sacrifice of Jesus" should be compared or contrasted with "the atonement through animal sacrifice" of the Old Testament, Paul utilized the former to contrast with the Law in conjunction with faith: Faith equals believing the atonement of Jesus. Therefore, he was silent because he already used this New Testament resource to compare or contrast with the Old. Second, "the atonement through the sacrifice of Jesus" was applied to the Gentiles outwardly for their prior sin whereas "the atonement through animal sacrifice" of the Old Testament was exclusively applied to the people of the covenant inwardly. Since the direction of applying the atonement was opposite, Paul was silent; he could not make any logical connection between the two sacrifices. Third, since he had already denounced the Law as a whole, he had to keep silent about animal sacrifice of the Old Testament because "the atonement through animal sacrifice of the Old Testament" was, in fact, a part of the Law and, in nature, that was, grace of God.

Paul's concern regarding the Old Testament is heavily concentrated on the Law constituting works against grace.[90] However, we should remember that the covenant relationship between God and God's people was set on the foundation of grace, not on the people's perfect observance of the Law or perfect works. Leviticus 16:30 solemnly proclaims the grace of God as the foundation of holiness of the people of God: "for it is on this day that atonement shall be made for you to cleanse you; you will be clean from all your sins before the LORD." Works were not the medium through which the relationship between God and Israel was maintained. It was the atonement by animal sacrifice: The Day of Atonement (מֵהַכִּפֻּרִי סוֹיְ), which was the ultimate expression of God's lovingkindness (דְסָׁה).

Third, Paul replaces the New Testament's "New Commandment and teachings of Jesus" with his own ethical approach. Since faith was identified with those Gentiles belief in the atonement of Jesus for previous sin, the problem of sin was resolved "at the gate." Therefore, the converted Christians became sinless and were left without the need for atonement after baptism because "atonement through Jesus" had been applied outwardly to them already. The sinless, converted Christians were not expected to sin after baptism. Rather they were supposed to live holy and godly lives as the people of God. That's why, after stating that previous sin is cleansed, not by works, but by believing in the atonement of Jesus, Paul declares, "May it never be! How shall we who died to sin still live in it?" (Romans 6:2). "What then? Shall we sin because we are not under law but under grace? May it never be!" (Romans 6:15).

However, Paul had to address two problems caused by his universalizing of the gospel. First, what would be the ethical basis for the converted Christians to live holy and godly lives? Second, how to resolve post-baptismal sin, because Christians, in reality, continue to sin after baptism? From the viewpoint of the Old Testament and the Gospels, the answers would be rather simple. Those converted Christians should live up to the New Commandment and teachings of Jesus Christ: The Law of Jesus. When they sin after baptism, the atonement of Jesus would cover their sins collectively; therefore, the Christian Church would continue to maintain the special relationship with God as God's holy kingdom. For an individual, he or she is asked to repent to be sanctified. When an individual acknowledges his or her sin and repents, the atonement and mercy of Jesus Christ continues to redeem him or her from that sin so that he or she may continue to be a member of the holy kingdom of God.[91] To Paul, however, atonement was for the sins committed prior to conversion; and the death and resurrection of Jesus were his main concern, not the New Commandment and teachings of Jesus. Therefore, he employed his own ways to respond to these two problems.

For the first problem: what would be the ethical basis for the converted Christians to live holy and godly lives? Even though Paul mentions "the law of Christ" in 1 Corinthians 9:21 and Galatians 6:2,[92] he does not paraphrase the New Commandment or remind his readers of the teachings of Jesus explicitly. There are, perhaps, two reasons that Paul did not give weight to the New Commandment and teachings of Jesus (the new Law of Jesus). First, because he had not known Jesus in the flesh (John 13:34; 14:15; 15:10), and the teachings were directed to his disciples, not to him. The Jesus he knew was the resurrected Jesus (Acts 9:1–20). Second, since he denounced the Law collectively, he could not emphasize the New Commandment or the reinterpreted Law of Jesus (Matthew 5:17–48) that was, in its nature, the Law. Therefore, he needed to employ his own way to imagine the holy and godly lives of the converted Christians rather than quoting what Jesus said and did directly. His ethical foundation depends upon logical necessity rather than the Law of Jesus: Since you became freed from sin and are under grace, you should be now holy. If not, you must die (Romans 6:7, 14, 18; 8:13).

Paul employs two premises in Romans to support the necessity for converted Christians to live holy and godly lives: "the resurrected ones" and "being in the spirit."

Let us read Romans 6:3–13:

3. Or do you not know that all of us who have been baptized into Christ Jesus have been baptized into His death?
4. Therefore we have been buried with Him through baptism into death, so that as Christ was raised from the dead through the glory of the Father, so we too might walk in newness of life.
5. For if we have become united with Him in the likeness of His death, certainly we shall also be in the likeness of His resurrection,
6. knowing this, that our old self was crucified with Him, in order that our body of sin might be done away with, so that we would no longer be slaves to sin;
7. for he who has died is freed from sin.
8. Now if we have died with Christ, we believe that we shall also live with Him,
9. knowing that Christ, having been raised from the dead, is never to die again; death no longer is master over Him.
10. For the death that He died, He died to sin once for all; but the life that He lives, He lives to God.
11. Even so consider yourselves to be dead to sin, but alive to God in Christ Jesus.
12. Therefore do not let sin reign in your mortal body so that you obey its lusts,
13. and do not go on presenting the members of your body to sin as instruments of unrighteousness; but present yourselves to God as those alive from the dead, and your members as instruments of righteousness to God.

In the text, Paul identifies the Christians with the resurrected Jesus and demands from them holy and godly lives. By utilizing the analogy of immersion at baptism, he encourages Christians to consider themselves as crucified with Jesus when they were baptized. Therefore, after baptism, he argues, they should live like the resurrected ones, just as Jesus was resurrected. This approach, in fact, contradicts what the Gospels present as Christian ethics. In the Gospels, Jesus, in his physical body, taught and set an example for how the people of God, who were also in physical bodies, should live. The followers of Jesus were supposed to imitate the life of Jesus who was in this world, not the resurrected Jesus. "I say" in the New Commandment "you love one another, even as I have loved you" (John 13:34) certainly means Jesus of the physical body, not the resurrected Jesus. Since Jesus as a human being lived a holy and godly life, his life can be an example and his teaching can have meaning to Christians. To help his followers live holy and godly lives, Jesus promised them the Holy Spirit. It should be noted that this promise was made in-between emphasizing his commandments.[93] Therefore the most important role of the Holy Spirit should be helping the disciples to keep the commandments of Jesus. I think that's why the Holy Spirit is called the Helper. Paul's approach, however, is different even though both approaches aim toward the same result. The different approaches do not necessarily mean one is bad or wrong; Paul's teachings, in fact, positively complement the teachings of Jesus. It should be noted that the task of this writing is to understand the distortions that happened by universalized Christianity, not to denounce the ethics presented by Paul.

Paul asks the converted Christians to consider themselves as the resurrected ones. Is this approach applicable? There must be a fundamental difference: the body of Jesus was actually transformed to a spiritual one while the bodies of the converted Christians remain the same. They are not resurrected but have been transformed from the non-people of God to the people of God. The Christian Church, in comparison with Judea or Israel, might be said to be resurrected because it was conceived upon the death of Judea and replaced Judea as a people of God of the world. One could argue that the Christian Church has a transformed and spiritual body not limited to physical land or territory—it is the resurrected kingdom of God. In this sense, the Christian Church as a nation should be distinguished from Judea or Israel or all other secular nations. However, this concept of resurrection cannot be applied to individual converted Christians. Living with the help and guidance of the Holy Spirit should be distinguished from living as the resurrected ones. The former does not deny the body; the latter does.

The second premise is closely related to the first one in terms of denying the body.

Let us read Romans 8:1–15:

1. Therefore there is now no condemnation for those who are in Christ Jesus.
2. For the law of the Spirit of life in Christ Jesus has set you free from the law of sin and of death.
3. For what the Law could not do, weak as it was through the flesh, God did: sending His own Son in the likeness of sinful flesh and as an offering for sin, He condemned sin in the flesh,
4. so that the requirement of the Law might be fulfilled in us, who do not walk according to the flesh but according to the Spirit.
5. For those who are according to the flesh set their minds on the things of the flesh, but those who are according to the Spirit, the things of the Spirit.
6. For the mind set on the flesh is death, but the mind set on the Spirit is life and peace,
7. because the mind set on the flesh is hostile toward God; for it does not subject itself to the law of God, for it is not even able to do so,
8. and those who are in the flesh cannot please God.
9. However, you are not in the flesh but in the Spirit, if indeed the Spirit of God dwells in you But if anyone does not have the Spirit of Christ, he does not belong to Him.
10. If Christ is in you, though the body is dead because of sin, yet the spirit is alive because of righteousness.
11. But if the Spirit of Him who raised Jesus from the dead dwells in you, He who raised Christ Jesus from the dead will also give life to your mortal bodies through His Spirit who dwells in you.

12. So then, brethren, we are under obligation, not to the flesh, to live according to the flesh—

13. for if you are living according to the flesh, you must die; but if by the Spirit you are putting to death the deeds of the body, you will live.

14. For all who are being led by the Spirit of God, these are sons of God.

15. For you have not received a spirit of slavery leading to fear again, but you have received a spirit of adoption as sons by which we cry out, "Abba! Father!"

In the text, Paul assures the reader that the Holy Spirit dwells in the converted Christians. And he asks them to set their mind on the Spirit, not on the flesh, for their holy and godly lives. Further, he declares that the Christians are in the Spirit, not in the flesh (verse 9). He goes on to assert that if they are living according to the flesh, they must die; but if, by the Spirit, they are putting to death the deeds of the body, they will live (verse 13). For the first premise, Paul basically says that the Christians are the resurrected ones, not in the body (σῶμα). Now he says that the Christians are in the Spirit, not in the flesh (σάρξ). In both instances, Paul's approach denies reality. The Christians are, in fact, in the flesh. To Paul, the body and the flesh are used synonymously, in contrast to the resurrected body and the Spirit (verses 10, 11, 13). As stated above, the Christians cannot deny their flesh, their bodies. The role of the indwelling Spirit is to help them live as Jesus did, not to replace their flesh.[94] Living with help and guidance of the indwelling Holy Spirit should be distinguished from living as "ones in the Spirit." The former does not deny the flesh; the latter does. Also, whereas the New Commandment of Jesus is univocal and clearly identifiable, the Law of the Spirit (verse 2) or "according to the Spirit" (verse 5) without the commandments, is ambiguous and indecipherable. It cannot be defined objectively and, therefore, is applied with difficulty to a group of people, the Christians.

Another aspect we should question is, "Is the flesh necessarily evil?" The cause of some sins is certainly related to the flesh, such as sexual immorality or gluttony. However, it is not rational to say that the flesh is the cause of all sins. For example, wrath, pride, and envy are not necessarily related to the flesh; and, on the contrary, marriage certainly requires the flesh.

Paul tries to give an answer to the first problem: What would be the ethical basis for the converted Christians to live holy and godly lives? His answer is that the Christians are the resurrected ones and in the Spirit and, therefore, must live holy and godly lives. Paul's approach to Christian ethics is different from that in the Gospels, which reinterpret the Law and do not necessarily deny the body. Why did Paul neglect the New Commandment and teachings of Jesus and instead adopt his own approaches as we see here? As previously stated, first, because he did not know Jesus who lived as a human and the New Commandment and teachings to his disciples, and second, because he denounced the Law collectively, he could not emphasize the New Commandment. When we consider the second reason, we can see this ethical approach of Paul is a result of a distortion: because Paul contrasted faith with the Law, rather than with the bloodline or circumcision alone, he condemned the Law as a whole. The employed premises reveal anther distortion: that Christians are the resurrected ones and in the Spirit, and therefore granted perfect holy and godly lives, denying the body or the flesh. These premises do not portray the Christians on earth who are struggling to keep the commandments and imitate the life of Jesus with the help and guidance of the Holy Spirit. Why did Paul employ these unrealistic premises? I think it resulted from Paul applying Jesus's atonement outwardly for the prior sins. To Paul, since the previous sins were resolved through faith—believing in the atonement of Jesus—the converted Christians became sinless and should continue to remain sinless. However, the sinless, holy, and godly lives of the Christians do not depend upon simple proclamations like "You are the resurrected ones," "You are in the Holy Spirit," or "Therefore if anyone is in Christ, he is a new creature; the old things passed away; behold, new things have come" (2 Corinthians 5:17). The reality is that converted Christians have physical bodies, and, in a sense, continue to sin because of body or mind.

I believe that Paul himself, even though he employed unrealistic premises, understood that reality. And that reality brings into discussion the second problem caused by Paul's universalizing the gospel: how to resolve post-baptismal sin?

After Paul concluded that all human beings of the world are sinners and that faith, believing in the atonement of Jesus, is the only way to be saved (3:9b, 21–31; 5:12–21), he writes that the saved Christians now can and must live holy and godly lives (6:1–2) because they are the resurrected ones (6:3–13) and in the Spirit (8:1–15). We should interpret Romans 7:15–25 in this context.

Romans 7:15–25

15. For what I am doing, I do not understand; for I am not practicing what I would like to do, but I am doing the very thing I hate.
16. But if I do the very thing I do not want to do, I agree with the Law, confessing that the Law is good.
17. So now, no longer am I the one doing it, but sin which dwells in me.
18. For I know that nothing good dwells in me, that is, in my flesh; for the willing is present in me, but the doing of the good is not.
19. For the good that I want, I do not do, but I practice the very evil that I do not want.
20. But if I am doing the very thing I do not want, I am no longer the one doing it, but sin which dwells in me.
21. I find then the principle that evil is present in me, the one who wants to do good.
22. For I joyfully concur with the law of God in the inner man,
23. but I see a different law in the members of my body, waging war against the law of my mind and making me a prisoner of the law of sin which is in my members.
24. Wretched man that I am! Who will set me free from the body of this death?
25. Thanks be to God through Jesus Christ our Lord! So then, on the one hand I myself with my mind am serving the law of God, but on the other, with my flesh the law of sin.

Since the tense of the text is the present and Christians continue to experience a sort of conflict between the desire of the mind and the desire of the flesh, the text might be thought to express the conflicting desires of the converted Christians seen through Paul's own experience. However, the text should be understood as the past experience of Paul when he was a Jew, not a Christian. The Law, the flesh, is the dominant word in the text and Paul identifies himself with the flesh in verse 18. The text is the description of a frustrating condition Paul experienced as a Jew, bound to the Jewish Law, not in the Spirit, not freed by faith or grace. If the text is the description of the condition of post-baptismal Christians, it will logically contradict what Paul said in chapter 6 (verses 11, 12) and 8 (verse 9, 13), which deny the body of the Christians and demand holy and godly lives. The text is neither describing the condition of the post-baptismal sin nor presenting the solution to that. After his conclusion that all human beings of the world are the sinners, and because he believes the atonement of Jesus is the only way to be saved from prior sin (covered in chapter 1–5), Paul states that the converted Christians should live holy and godly lives (covered in 6:1–8:15). In this context, Romans 7:15–25 should be interpreted as Paul's flashback to the frustrating condition when he was under the Law and in the body.

Following 8:15, Paul must address the problem of post-baptismal sin because he knew that, in spite of his assertion for holy and godly living of the converted Christians, it was inevitable for them to continue to sin in some degree. Paul's way to answer the problem of post-baptismal sin is found in 8:29–39.

Romans 8:29–39

29. For those whom He foreknew (προέγνω), He also predestined (προώρισεν) to become conformed to the image of His Son, so that He would be the firstborn among many brethren;
30. and these whom He predestined (προώρισεν), He also called; and these whom He called, He also justified; and these whom He justified, He also glorified.

31. What then shall we say to these things? If God is for us, who is against us?

32. He who did not spare His own Son, but delivered Him over for us all, how will He not also with Him freely give us all things?

33. Who will bring a charge against God's elect (ἐκλεκτῶν)? God is the one who justifies;

34. who is the one who condemns? Christ Jesus is He who died, yes, rather who was raised, who is at the right hand of God, who also intercedes for us.

35. Who will separate us from the love (ἀγάπης) of Christ? Will tribulation, or distress, or persecution, or famine, or nakedness, or peril, or sword?

36. Just as it is written, "For your sake we are being put to death all day long; we were considered as sheep to be slaughtered."

37. nor height, nor depth, nor any other created thing, will be able to separate us from the love (ἀγάπης) of God, which is in Christ Jesus our Lord.

From the viewpoint of both the Old Testament and the Gospels, post-baptismal sin of the people of God should be covered by the atonement of Jesus. However, since Paul applied atonement outwardly to the previous sins (the pre-baptismal sin), he first had to employ the unrealistic premise of converted Christians becoming sinless. He then moved to foreknowledge (verse 29), predestination (verses 29 and 30), election (verse 33), and the love of Christ or God (verses 35 and 39) to replace the role of Jesus's atonement. How was the proper relationship between God and the people of God maintained in the Old Testament? Atonement. In the New Testament, it should be atonement, too: Matthew 1:21 says, "She will bear a Son; and you shall call His name Jesus, for He will save His people from their sins." The proper relationship between God and the Church should be maintained through the atonement of Jesus. Since Paul applied atonement of Jesus to the world outwardly, he had to adopt something else that could maintain the proper relationship between God and the converted Christians. That something was foreknowledge, predestination, election, and the love of Christ. The first three point to the unilateral action of God. They convey a certain sense of fatalism and provide a sense of security for the converted Christians. The love of God or Christ is a general term; however, in the text, it is utilized to replace the atonement of Jesus. The statement is true:

35. Who will separate us from the love (ἀγάπης) of Christ? Will tribulation, or distress, or persecution, or famine, or nakedness, or peril, or sword?
38. For I am convinced that neither death, nor life, nor angels, nor principalities, nor things present, nor things to come, nor powers,
39. nor height, nor depth, nor any other created thing, will be able to separate us from the love (ἀγάπης) of God, which is in Christ Jesus our Lord.

Any danger, threat, or created thing will be unable to separate Christians from the love of God or Christ. However, the question still remains: What happens when a Christian sins after baptism?

Paul impressively resolved the contradiction about how Christians could live holy and godly lives after baptism by employing the unilateral action and love of God: Christians can and must live holy and godly lives and will not be separated from God, even when they sin after baptism. This logical contradiction of being both holy and forgiven is nothing but a result of Paul's distorting Jesus's atonement for prior sin. This contradiction raises another confusing question: What is the role of repentance for the Christians?

Let us go back to Diagram A and B. Paul replaces the missing third part, "the New Commandment and teachings of Jesus" of the New Testament with his own ethical approaches, which, I believe to be the result of the distortion. Distortion happened when Paul unnecessarily contrasted the Law with faith—applying the atonement of Jesus to the world outwardly for previous sin—and when he denounced the Law. He had to adopt his own ethic without the Law, based upon the unrealistic premise for the logically necessary holy and godly lives of the converted Christians. He further had to employ the unilateral action and love of God to replace the atonement of Jesus.

Summary on Distortion

Distortion happened on the distorted foundation due to the Judaized world: All human beings are sinners and thus the end of the world is imminent. To resolve this problem, the distorted gospel was offered to the Gentiles. The gospel meant "the reign of God," thus "the reign of Christ," however; a major benefit of that reign (forgiving sin) became the good news: From reign to the cross. The atonement of Jesus—which should be applied to the Christians for sins violating the new commandment and teachings of Jesus—was applied outwardly to the world (Gentiles) for their previous sins, based upon the original sin and conscience. In this process, the theological concept of atonement, initially pertinent primarily to the nation of Judea and then the Christian Church, became solely individualized. Faith came to mean believing in the atoning power of Jesus, instead of believing in the identity of Jesus. The theological concept of salvation, primarily pertinent to the nation, also became solely individualized. Salvation came to mean "saved from individual previous sin" not "saved from the sin of the people of God." The imminent end of Judea became the imminent end of the world; therefore, the end of the world came to be always futuristic. At this point Christian ethics becomes ambiguous, because the Law and works were denounced in the process of enhancing faith by believing in the atonement. The role of Jesus became primarily as savior of the world rather than the King (Messiah or Christ) of the Christian Church.

In the New Testament, both the normative paradigm of Christianity and the distorted paradigm of Christianity are found. In general, it can be said that the normative paradigm is found in the Gospels and the distorted paradigm, in Romans. I shall compare both paradigms by diagrams.

CHAPTER 3
Two Paradigms in the New Testament

Life Span of a Christian

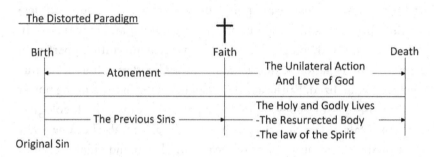

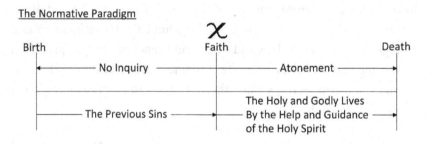

In the distorted paradigm, faith means believing in the atoning power of Jesus (✝). In the normative paradigm, faith means believing and receiving the identity of Jesus (Son of God and Messiah or Christ [Χριστός], therefore, marked as chi (𝒳). When we consider the previous sins in the normative case, we must think about both kinds of Christians, Jewish and Gentile. For the Jewish Christians, previous sins mean the biblical sins that violated Jewish Law. When Jews became Christians, their post-baptismal sins also mean biblical sins, but this time it means the sins that violate the new commandment and teachings of Jesus. Therefore, it can be said that, for the Jewish Christians, both sins are covered by the atonement of Jesus.

However, for the Gentile Christians, previous sins mean the non-biblical sins that violated the natural law or conscience and positive law. These sins are not covered by the blood of Jesus which was shed for His people. Therefore, from the biblical point of view, these sins bear no connection to Jewish Law and therefore are unrelated to the atonement of Jesus. Instead each individual is responsible for his or her own previous sin. When a Gentile believes and receives Jesus as the Son of God and Christ, he or she becomes a new citizen of the kingdom of God. At that moment, a new life starts, akin to the life of Israel, begun with God's covenant with Moses at Mount Sinai. God did not inquire about Israel's past when he gave the Ten Commandments; likewise, with these new Gentile followers of Christ: Their previous sin is neither punished by God nor covered by the atonement of Jesus.

In the distorted paradigm, since previous sin is covered by the atonement of Jesus, the post-baptismal sin is covered by the unilateral action of God (election and predestination) and the inseparable love of God or Jesus. In comparison with the normative paradigm, the unilateral action of God and inseparable love of God or Jesus, in fact, replaces the atonement of Jesus. Since both paradigms are found in the New Testament, the Christians may become confused hearing both—a sort of the mixed paradigm at church.

Christian Church or the Kingdom of God

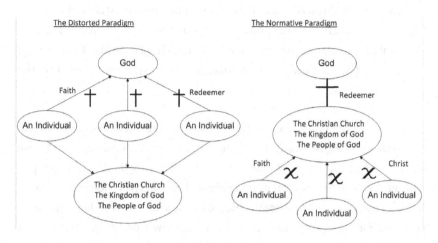

In both paradigms, the Christian Church means the one universal, invisible, ecumenical Church, not a denomination or a local church. In the distorted paradigm, an individual is united with God first through faith— believing the atonement of Jesus through the cross; Jesus is primarily and initially identified as the redeemer—then voluntarily joins into the church. Whereas, in the normative paradigm, an individual joins into the already redeemed, established Christian Church through faith, that is, believing and receiving the identity of Jesus who is primarily and initially identified as the one who reigns, the Christ or Messiah and the Son of God.

Since both paradigms are found in the New Testament, a denomination or a church somehow projects both aspects and elements. There are pros and cons in both paradigms.

The distorted paradigm might be effective in evangelism because it presupposes that all human beings are sinners and the end of the world is imminent. Since this paradigm points out sin of an individual and presents the solution to that problem, it carries power and emotion at conversion. However, since a resolved individual constitutes the Christian Church in a voluntary manner, unity and ethics of the Christian Church can be weak. Jesus as the mediator becomes prominent but Jesus as the sovereign and educator becomes ambiguous. Also, in comparison to other religions, the presupposition of this paradigm puts the Christian Church in an exclusive position.

On the other hand, the normative paradigm might not be effective in evangelism because it does not presuppose that all human beings are sinners and the end of the world is imminent. To be effective or successful in evangelism, the Christian Church must demonstrate the superiority of the reign of Christ in comparison with other kinds of reigns. However, since an individual must be a member of the one universal, invisible, ecumenical Christian Church and be bound to the new commandment and teachings of Christ in order to be a beneficiary of the reign of Christ, unity and ethics of the Christian Church can be strong. Jesus can be clearly seen as the sovereign, the educator, and the mediator. Those who believe in the identity of Jesus become the people of God and then live up to the new commandment and teachings of Jesus, and the Christian Church is redeemed by the atonement of Jesus. Also, in relation to other religions, the presupposition of this paradigm puts the Christian Church in an inclusive position.

In the next section, I will revisit the Christian religion based upon the normative paradigm in an effort to restore the true nature of Christianity.

SECTION III
The Restored Christianity: Christianity without Total Depravity and with the Fulfilled Eschatology

Context of Messianic Expectation

What is the Christian religion? This question asks a more fundamental question: Who was Jesus? According to the New Testament, the most credible answer to the question is that Jesus was the promised Messiah, or Christ, to the people of Israel/Judea. Let us read the Old Testament passages that sets the foundation for the Messianic expectation.

2 Samuel 7:4–16

4. But in the same night the word of the LORD came to Nathan, saying,

5. "Go and say to My servant David, 'Thus says the LORD, "Are you the one who should build Me a house to dwell in?

6. "For I have not dwelt in a house since the day I brought up the sons of Israel from Egypt, even to this day; but I have been moving about in a tent, even in a tabernacle.

7. "Wherever I have gone with all the sons of Israel, did I speak a word with one of the tribes of Israel, which I commanded to shepherd My people Israel, saying, 'Why have you not built Me a house of cedar?'"'

8. "Now therefore, thus you shall say to My servant David, 'Thus says the LORD of hosts, "I took you from the pasture, from following the sheep, to be ruler over My people Israel.

9. "I have been with you wherever you have gone and have cut off all your enemies from before you; and I will make you a great name, like the names of the great men who are on the earth.

10. "I will also appoint a place for My people Israel and will plant them, that they may live in their own place and not be disturbed again, nor will the wicked afflict them any more as formerly,

11. even from the day that I commanded judges to be over My people Israel; and I will give you rest from all your enemies The LORD also declares to you that the LORD will make a house for you.

12. "When your days are complete and you lie down with your fathers, I will raise up your descendant after you, who will come forth from you, and I will establish his kingdom.

13. "He shall build a house for My name, and I will establish the throne of his kingdom forever.

14. "I will be a father to him and he will be a son to Me; when he commits iniquity, I will correct him with the rod of men and the strokes of the sons of men,

15. but My lovingkindness shall not depart from him, as I took it away from Saul, whom I removed from before you.

16. "Your house and your kingdom shall endure before Me forever; your throne shall be established forever."'"

The concept of Messiah מָשִׁיחַ (the anointed one) was not a part of the original plan when God called the Israelites out of Egypt. God was the King and there were only the priests between God and the people of Israel. According to 1 Samuel chapter 8, the people of Israel asked Samuel to give them a king like all other nations. That request was granted, reluctantly, by God. The king of Israel was distinguished from the kings of all other nations because only the one who was anointed by God could be the king of Israel. This meant that the king of Israel was God's commissioned ruler: In fact, it was God who was in charge; the king ruled over the people of God with the approval of God. First Samuel 15:1 illustrates this aspect

well: Then Samuel said to Saul, "The LORD sent me to anoint you as
king over His people, over Israel; now therefore, listen to the words of
the LORD." The first messiah was Saul (1 Samuel 10:1). However, he
failed in the messianic role as a commissioned ruler because he acted
like a king who had nobody over him. Therefore, God anointed another
person and set him as the messiah of Israel. The second messiah was
David. David was anointed by Samuel according to the order of God (1
Samuel 16:12–13; later he was anointed twice more as the king of Judea
and Israel). After David conquered all their enemies and restored the
land which was promised to Abraham by God, he intended to build the
temple for God. God was so impressed by his intention that God made
the unconditional promise to David: the sons of David would continue
to be the king of Israel (2 Samuel 7:16). We know that Solomon, the son
of David, was anointed by Zadok, the priest, and Nathan, the prophet (1
Kings 1:34, 39, 45), but we don't know whether other descendants of David
were anointed or not. However, it was clear that only descendants of David
could be the messiahs of Judea, from the time the nation was divided into
the northern kingdom of Israel and the southern kingdom of Judea after
Solomon. Israel, the northern kingdom, was destroyed by the Assyrians in
721 (or 722) BC; Judea, the southern kingdom, in 586 (or 587) BC. The
last messiah, the son of David, was Zedekiah. His tragic end is described
in 2 Kings 25:1–7. The death of his sons was the last scene Zedekiah saw
before he was blinded. During the Hasmonean dynasty (142 BC–63 BC,
the Jewish dynasty during inter-testament period), there were Jewish
kings. However, they were not the descendants of David, but Levites.
The Jewish kingdom fell under Roman control in 63 BC. Soon, the Jews
faced a worse political situation. The Herodian dynasty was set up in
37 BC: a non-Jewish Idumaean (Idumaea was biblical Edom), Herod,
became the king of Judea by the power of Roman authority. He was the
first non-Jewish king in Jewish history. The Jews naturally eagerly waited
for the messiah, the Jewish king, a descendant of David, during the reign
of Herod. Jesus was born in the last years of the reign of Herod. According
to the Gospels, the first Christian group was a group of Jews who believed
and received Jesus as the messiah of the Jews. Therefore, Christianity

must be defined by the relationship between the life of Jesus—as the messiah of the Jews—and the Jewish nation or people.

Jesus was, however, the unique messiah. He brought a surprise to his fellow Jews who were waiting for their messiah to liberate them from foreign oppression and Roman rule. Understanding this uniqueness of Jesus as Messiah is critical in understanding the true nature of the Christian religion, following, as it does, Old Testament tradition.

First, Jesus was a descendant of David, but the Son of God.[95] According to Matthew's genealogy (Matthew 1:1–16) and Luke's genealogy (Luke 3:23–38), Jesus was legally a descendent of David by Joseph's lineage; however, his origin was claimed to be directly from God by means of the virgin birth. Sometimes a king was called or considered as a god or the son of God in the ancient world. For example, the ancient Egyptian pharaohs were often deputized for Horus, the sun god, to rule over the people with authority. Likewise, Psalm 2 describes the messiah of Israel as the son of God (verse 7 and 12). However, unlike all other "anointed ones" of Israel who had a human origin, Jesus was claimed intrinsically as the God, or the actual only son of God, in the New Testament. Even though this divinity of Jesus was prophesied in the Old Testament (Isaiah 9:6 and Ezekiel 34), it was a surprise to the Jews who knew only the human messiahs. Let us read the relevant Old Testament accounts:

Isaiah 9:1–7

1. But there will be no more gloom for her who was in anguish; in earlier times He treated the land of Zebulun and the land of Naphtali with contempt, but later on He shall make it glorious, by the way of the sea, on the other side of Jordan, Galilee of the Gentiles.
2. The people who walk in darkness Will see a great light; Those who live in a dark land, The light will shine on them.
3. You shall multiply the nation, You shall increase their gladness; They will be glad in Your presence As with the gladness of harvest, As men rejoice when they divide the spoil.

4. For You shall break the yoke of their burden and the staff on their shoulders, The rod of their oppressor, as at the battle of Midian.

5. For every boot of the booted warrior in the battle tumult, And cloak rolled in blood, will be for burning, fuel for the fire.

6. For a child will be born to us, a son will be given to us; And the government will rest on His shoulders; And His name will be called Wonderful Counselor, Mighty God (גִּבּוֹר אֵל), Eternal Father (אֲבִיעַד), Prince of Peace.

7. There will be no end to the increase of His government or of peace, On the throne of David and over his kingdom, To establish it and to uphold it with justice and righteousness From then on and forevermore The zeal of the LORD of hosts will accomplish this.

Ezekiel 34:1–31

1. Then the word of the LORD came to me saying,

2. "Son of man, prophesy against the shepherds of Israel Prophesy and say to those shepherds, 'Thus says the Lord GOD, "Woe, shepherds of Israel who have been feeding themselves! Should not the shepherds feed the flock?

3. "You eat the fat and clothe yourselves with the wool, you slaughter the fat sheep without feeding the flock.

4. "Those who are sickly you have not strengthened, the diseased you have not healed, the broken you have not bound up, the scattered you have not brought back, nor have you sought for the lost; but with force and with severity you have dominated them.

5. "They were scattered for lack of a shepherd, and they became food for every beast of the field and were scattered.

6. "My flock wandered through all the mountains and on every high hill; My flock was scattered over all the surface of the earth, and there was no one to search or seek for them."'"

7. Therefore, you shepherds, hear the word of the LORD:

8. "As I live," declares the Lord GOD, "surely because My flock has become a prey, My flock has even become food for all the beasts of the field for lack of a shepherd, and My shepherds did not search for

My flock, but rather the shepherds fed themselves and did not feed My flock;

9. therefore, you shepherds, hear the word of the LORD:

10. 'Thus says the Lord GOD, "Behold, I am against the shepherds, and I will demand My sheep from them and make them cease from feeding sheep So the shepherds will not feed themselves anymore, but I will deliver My flock from their mouth, so that they will not be food for them."'"

11. For thus says the Lord GOD, "Behold, I Myself will search for My sheep and seek them out.

12. "As a shepherd cares for his herd in the day when he is among his scattered sheep, so I will care for My sheep and will deliver them from all the places to which they were scattered on a cloudy and gloomy day.

13. "I will bring them out from the peoples and gather them from the countries and bring them to their own land; and I will feed them on the mountains of Israel, by the streams, and in all the inhabited places of the land.

14. "I will feed them in a good pasture, and their grazing ground will be on the mountain heights of Israel There they will lie down on good grazing ground and feed in rich pasture on the mountains of Israel.

15. "I will feed My flock and I will lead them to rest," declares the Lord GOD.

16. "I will seek the lost, bring back the scattered, bind up the broken and strengthen the sick; but the fat and the strong I will destroy I will feed them with judgment.

17. "As for you, My flock, thus says the Lord GOD, 'Behold, I will judge between one sheep and another, between the rams and the male goats.

18. 'Is it too slight a thing for you that you should feed in the good pasture, that you must tread down with your feet the rest of your pastures? Or that you should drink of the clear waters, that you must foul the rest with your feet?

19. 'As for My flock, they must eat what you tread down with your feet and drink what you foul with your feet!'"

20. Therefore, thus says the Lord GOD to them, "Behold, I, even I, will judge between the fat sheep and the lean sheep.
21. "Because you push with side and with shoulder, and thrust at all the weak with your horns until you have scattered them abroad,
22. therefore, I will deliver My flock, and they will no longer be a prey; and I will judge between one sheep and another.
23. "Then I will set over them one shepherd, My servant David, and he will feed them; he will feed them himself and be their shepherd.
24. "And I, the LORD, will be their God, and My servant David will be prince among them; I the LORD have spoken.
25. "I will make a covenant of peace with them and eliminate harmful beasts from the land so that they may live securely in the wilderness and sleep in the woods.
26. "I will make them and the places around My hill a blessing And I will cause showers to come down in their season; they will be showers of blessing.
27. "Also the tree of the field will yield its fruit and the earth will yield its increase, and they will be secure on their land Then they will know that I am the LORD, when I have broken the bars of their yoke and have delivered them from the hand of those who enslaved them.
28. "They will no longer be a prey to the nations, and the beasts of the earth will not devour them; but they will live securely, and no one will make them afraid.
29. "I will establish for them a renowned planting place, and they will not again be victims of famine in the land, and they will not endure the insults of the nations anymore.
30. "Then they will know that I, the LORD their God, am with them, and that they, the house of Israel, are My people," declares the Lord GOD.
31. "As for you, My sheep, the sheep of My pasture, you are men, and I am your God," declares the Lord GOD.

Both texts describe the future messiah for the people of Israel: On the throne of David and over his kingdom (Isaiah 9:7) and my servant David (Ezekiel 34:23–24). The described future messiah was unique in that he would not be a simple human being, but divine. Isaiah 9:6b says, "And His name will be called Wonderful Counselor, Mighty God (גִּבּוֹר אֵל), Eternal Father (אֲבִיעַד), Prince of Peace." If the future messiah were a human being like all other messiahs of Israel or Judah, the expressions like Mighty God (גִּבּוֹר אֵל) and Eternal Father (אֲבִיעַד) would not be used. Also, in Ezekiel 34:1–31, the will of God to participate directly in the reign of the future messiah is strongly emphasized by the repeated use of "I":

Verse 10: I will demand, I will deliver
Verse 11: I Myself will search
Verse 12: I will care for
Verse 13: I will bring, I will feed
Verse 14: I will feed
Verse 15: I will feed, I will lead
Verse 16: I will seek, I will destroy, I will feed
Verse 17: I will judge
Verse 20: I, even I, will judge
Verse 22: I will deliver, I will judge
Verse 25: I will make
Verse 26: I will make, I will cause
Verse 27: I have broken
Verse 29: I will establish

In the midst of "I"s, however, in verses 23 and 24, "I" is replaced by "one shepherd," "My servant David," and "he." Therefore, the divinity of Jesus, who was a descendant of David, was prophesied in the Old Testament and, accordingly, was fully manifested in the Gospels.

Second, Jesus did not come to liberate or save Judea from the Roman rule as the Jews expected, but rather to start the new Israel and to save his followers from the coming destruction of the Jewish nation (AD 70). At the beginning of his ministry, he called the twelve disciples in correspondence to the twelve tribes of the Israel. Creating a new kind of Israel was in his mind from the beginning of his ministry, as was preparing them for the imminent destruction of the Jewish nation. There are no directly relevant Old Testament passages that can be applied to this new

Israel. However, the rhetorical hope and vision aspired to in Deutero-Isaiah (Isaiah 40–55) and Trito-Isaiah (Isaiah 56–66), for Israel to be restored from the Babylonian captivity, can be interpreted as a hope and vision for the New Israel, especially when the life of Jesus is understood as a nation, not just an individual. This aspect will be discussed in detail under the section, "The Life of Jesus as a Nation." Meanwhile, in the midst of rhetorical hope and vision, expressed in Trito-Isaiah (Isaiah 56–66), for the restored Israel from the Babylonian captivity, we can find an implication for the New Nation in terms of a new name:

Isaiah 62:1–2
1. For Zion's sake I will not keep silent, And for Jerusalem's sake I will not keep quiet, Until her righteousness goes forth like brightness, And her like a torch that is burning.
2. The nations will see your righteousness, And all kings your glory; And you will be called by a new name Which the mouth of the LORD will designate.

Isaiah 65:13–15
13. Therefore, thus says the Lord GOD, "Behold, My servants will eat, but you will be hungry Behold, My servants will drink, but you will be thirsty Behold, My servants will rejoice, but you will be put to shame.
14. "Behold, My servants will shout joyfully with a glad heart, But you will cry out with a heavy heart, And you will wail with a broken spirit.
15. "You will leave your name for a curse to My chosen ones, And the Lord GOD will slay you But My servants will be called by another name.

It was envisioned that the restored Jerusalem would be called by a new name (62:2) and the servants of God by another name (65:15). Since name means identity, a new name or another name means a new identity. Since the Christian Church (ἐκκλησία) was the only name which succeeded the Israelite or Judean tradition in actual history, those texts might be considered as the prophetic expressions for the New Israel started by Jesus Christ. However, it would be wiser to find the basis of the New

Israel directly from the accounts of the Gospels such as calling the twelve disciples or the parable of new wine, because there are various and controversial interpretations regarding the Isaiah passages.

Malachi chapter 4 should be considered as a prophecy of the destruction of Jerusalem in AD 70:

Malachi 4:1–6
1. "For behold, the day is coming, burning like a furnace; and all the arrogant and every evildoer will be chaff; and the day that is coming will set them ablaze," says the LORD of hosts, "so that it will leave them neither root nor branch."
2. "But for you who fear My name, the sun of righteousness will rise with healing in its wings; and you will go forth and skip about like calves from the stall.
3. "You will tread down the wicked, for they will be ashes under the soles of your feet on the day which I am preparing," says the LORD of hosts.
4. "Remember the law of Moses My servant, even the statutes and ordinances which I commanded him in Horeb for all Israel.
5. "Behold, I am going to send you Elijah the prophet before the coming of the great and terrible day of the LORD.
6. "He will restore the hearts of the fathers to their children and the hearts of the children to their fathers, so that I will not come and smite the land with a curse."

The main theme of the Hebrew prophecy before the Babylonian exile was to warn of the destruction of Jerusalem, an event that happened in 587 BC. However, since Malachi was written after the return from exile, "the coming of the great and terrible day of the LORD" in verse 5 should be understood as another terrible destruction of Jerusalem, one that would happen in the future. That event would happen in AD 70 at the hand of the Romans. In addition, Jesus himself identified John the Baptist, who warned the imminent divine judgment, with Elijah, mentioned in verse 5:

Matthew 3:7–10

7.   But when he (John the Baptist) saw many of the Pharisees and
     Sadducees coming for baptism, he said to them, "You brood of vipers,
     who warned you to flee from the wrath to come?

8.   "Therefore bear fruit in keeping with repentance;

9.   and do not suppose that you can say to yourselves, 'We have Abraham
     for our father'; for I say to you that from these stones God is able to
     raise up children to Abraham.

10. "The axe is already laid at the root of the trees; therefore, every tree
     that does not bear good fruit is cut down and thrown into the fire

Matthew 11:13–14

13. "For all the prophets and the Law prophesied until John.

14. "And if you are willing to accept it, John himself is Elijah who was to
     come.

Third, unlike all previous messiahs, Jesus provided himself as the sacrifice
for the New Israel, and this sacrifice was once for all. Just like the New
Israel, there are no directly relevant Old Testament passages we can apply
to the atonement of the messiah. Many Christians relate Isaiah 53 to
the sufferings and death of Jesus and as a messianic prophecy. I think,
however, "he" or "the servant" of Isaiah 53 meant the nation, Judah. As in
the case of the New Israel, when the life of Jesus is understood as a nation,
Isaiah 53 or the servant songs of Isaiah, will be related to the sufferings
and death of Jesus, because the life of Jesus as a nation recapitulated the
history of Israel or Judah. This aspect will also be discussed in detail under
the section, "The Life of Jesus as a Nation." Besides an analogy between
the life of Jesus and the history of Israel or Judah in terms of suffering and
death, we can find clear indications for the meaning of the suffering and
death of Jesus in the Gospels. Jesus presented himself as the sacrificial
lamb of the Passover. He himself spoke of the meaning of his death to the
twelve disciples on the Passover meal:

Matthew 26:26–28

26. While they were eating, Jesus took some bread, and after a blessing, He broke it and gave it to the disciples, and said, "Take, eat; this is My body."
27. And when He had taken a cup and given thanks, He gave it to them, saying, "Drink from it, all of you;
28. for this is My blood of the covenant, which is poured out for many for forgiveness of sins.

Mark 14:22–24

22. While they were eating, He took some bread, and after a blessing He broke it, and gave it to them, and said, "Take it; this is My body."
23. And when He had taken a cup and given thanks, He gave it to them, and they all drank from it.
24. And He said to them, "This is My blood of the covenant, which is poured out for many.

Luke 22:17–20

17. And when He had taken a cup and given thanks, He said, "Take this and share it among yourselves;
18. for I say to you, I will not drink of the fruit of the vine from now on until the kingdom of God comes."
19. And when He had taken some bread and given thanks, He broke it and gave it to them, saying, "This is My body which is given for you; do this in remembrance of Me."
20. And in the same way He took the cup after they had eaten, saying, "This cup which is poured out for you is the new covenant in My blood.

Just as the Passover lamb was sacrificed to save the people of God from the divine wrath in the Old Testament, Jesus presented himself as the sacrificial Passover lamb to save His people from the imminent wrath of God that fell on Judea in AD 70. However, this sacrificial aspect of the promised messiah was certainly hidden to the Jews at that time.

Fourth, through his resurrection, Jesus became the eternal, everlasting messiah, the Messiah of the New Israel. Therefore, the Christian Church as the New Israel has only one Messiah forever, no successors to Jesus Christ. Let us read Isaiah 9: 6–7 again:

Isaiah 9:6–7

6. For a child will be born to us, a son will be given to us; And the government will rest on His shoulders; And His name will be called Wonderful Counselor, Mighty God (גִּבּוֹר אֵל), Eternal Father (אֲבִיעַד), Prince of Peace.

7. There will be no end to the increase of His government or of peace, On the throne of David and over his kingdom, To establish it and to uphold it with justice and righteousness From then on and forevermore The zeal of the LORD of hosts will accomplish this.

Verse 6 says that the child's name will be "Eternal Father" (אֲבִיעַד). If the born-child were called "Eternal Father," there could not be any successor of that child. The child was expected to rule eternally. However, to the Jews at the time of Jesus who were accustomed to the succession of the messiah, this eternal reign of the promised messiah was apparently hidden from their perception.

Just like the promised messiah, the kingdom reigned by that messiah, the Christian Church, was unique in comparison with the old kingdom of Israel or Judea. Not just new chronologically, but also the nature of the nation was new. Unlike the old kingdom which was homogeneous and determined by bloodline, anyone could be a member of the new kingdom by believing and receiving Jesus as the Son of God and Christ. Therefore the new kingdom was inclusive and multi-racial in nature. In addition, the new kingdom was not bound to a geographical terrain and limit; unlike the old kingdom, which was absolutely bound to the Promised Land and later Judean province under the Roman rule. Therefore, the new kingdom was a nation, but unique: without land but multi-racial. In this respect, the Christian Church, the new kingdom, was and is spiritual, without a body (land) but with the people and the ruler. A couple of Isaiah passages imply that the restored Israel would be a multi-racial nation, and this implication might be understood as a vision toward the new kingdom, the Christian Church:

Isaiah 49:6

He says, "It is too small a thing that You should be My Servant To raise up the tribes of Jacob and to restore the preserved ones of Israel; I will also make You a light of the nations So that My salvation may reach to the end of the earth."

Isaiah 56:6–7

6. "Also the foreigners who join themselves to the LORD, To minister to Him, and to love the name of the LORD, To be His servants, everyone who keeps from profaning the Sabbath And holds fast My covenant;

7. Even those I will bring to My holy mountain And make them joyful in My house of prayer Their burnt offerings and their sacrifices will be acceptable on My altar; For My house will be called a house of prayer for all the peoples."

While considering the above aspects related to Jesus the Messiah, I continue with "The Life of Jesus and The Church as the Fulfilled Kingdom of God," in order to define the true nature of the Christian religion.

CHAPTER 1
The Life of Jesus

A. Life as a Person, the Promised Messiah

To define the Christian religion correctly, it is most important to understand the life of Jesus who founded it. The life of Jesus as a person can be diagramed as follows based upon the accounts of the Gospels:

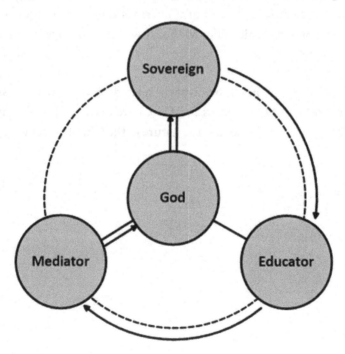

Jesus was the Son of God (or God) and came down to his people as the promised messiah (Sovereign). He educated the people who believed and received his sovereign identity (Educator), died for them (Mediator), and rose and ascended to his Father. His appearance was so meaningful and powerful to the Jews because it happened during a time of foreign rule and oppression (Herod and the Roman Empire). Moreover, it was prophetic because it happened not long before the destruction of Jerusalem and the Jewish nation (AD 70). Let us take a close look at the life of Jesus, based upon the accounts in the Gospels.

a. Jesus as the Sovereign: The Son of God and the Messiah (Christ)

First, Jesus presented himself publicly as the sovereign to the Jews. Jesus as the sovereign means Jesus as the Son of God and the promised Messiah (Christ). The Son of God clarifies his divine origin and claims for sovereignty in heaven. Messiah (Christ) is his formal title over the earthly Kingdom, establishing his claims for sovereignty on earth: Both entitle him to sovereignty. The images used to denote the sovereign are king, lord, shepherd, groom, and friend. King and lord are the most important and the major images. Jesus was the King and the Lord, but not in a dictatorial way, more like shepherd, groom, and friend. Corresponding to these images, the images for the Christians are the people, children, sheep, bride, and friend. The term friend defies any hierarchical order and, therefore, is used mutually.

Jesus is the Son of God. In John 5:36–39, Jesus presented three arguments for himself being the Son of God in addition to the testimony of John the Baptist: his works, the confidence of the Father, and prophecies of Scripture.

John 5:36–39

36. "But the testimony which I have is greater than the testimony of John; for the works which the Father has given Me to accomplish--the very works that I do--testify about Me, that the Father has sent Me.

37. "And the Father who sent Me, He has testified of Me. You have neither heard his voice at any time nor seen his form.
38. "You do not have His word abiding in you, for you do not believe Him whom He sent.
39. "You search the Scriptures because you think that in them you have eternal life; it is these that testify about Me."

Even before Jesus appeared in public, John the Baptist testified about Jesus as the Son of God in terms of his preexistence, the one who bestows the Holy Spirit, and the one who has the right and authority to judge (Matthew 3:11–12, Mark 1:7–8, Luke 3:16–17, John 1:15, 26–34). Since John's testimony of the coming Messiah was made before the public appearance of Jesus, and John did not recognize Jesus until he baptized him, John's testimony was divine, true, and credible. Besides John's testimony, Jesus's very works prove his divine origin. The miracles and signs Jesus performed were the things that only the Son of God could do, and his works were good deeds, manifesting the love of God toward his people. Above all the miracles and signs, the resurrection definitively proved Jesus was the Son of God (Romans 1:4). God, the Father himself, testified about Jesus as his Son at Jesus's baptism and at the transfiguration on a high mountain (Matthew 3:16–17, 17:5, Mark 1:10–11, 9:7, Luke 3:21–22, 9:35). Finally, the Scripture (the Old Testament) testifies that the coming Messiah would be of divine origin (Isaiah 9:6 and Ezekiel 34).

The Son of God means that Jesus is the legal heir of God (Matthew 21:38). Moreover, Jesus is the only begotten Son of God (John 1:14; 3:16, 18; 1 John 4:9). If there are two sons, the right to inherit could be disputed. However, since there is only one son, no dispute is found. This fact means that Jesus is the sovereign who inherits the title of God, the power and authority of God, and the possessions of God; his claims are primarily for sovereignty over the kingdom of God in heaven. When Jesus came to the people of God on earth, all inheritance was bestowed to him by God, his Father. Jesus himself claimed this completed inheritance:

Matthew 9:6, 8

6.   "But so that you may know that the Son of Man has on to forgive sins"--then He said to the paralytic, "Get up, pick up your bed and go home."

8.   But when the crowds saw this, they were awestruck, and glorified God, who had given such authority to men.

Matthew 11:27

"All things have been handed over to Me by My Father; and no one knows the Son except the Father; nor does anyone know the Father except the Son, and anyone to whom the Son wills to reveal Him.

Matthew 28:18

And Jesus came up and spoke to them, saying, "All has been given to Me in and on earth.

Mark 2:10

"But so that you may know that the Son of Man has authority on earth to forgive sins"--He said to the paralytic

Luke 10:22

"All things have been handed over to Me by My Father, and no one knows who the Son is except the Father, and who the Father is except the Son, and anyone to whom the Son wills to reveal Him."

John 5:22, 26–27

22.   "For not even the Father judges anyone, but He has given all judgment to the Son,

26.   "For just as the Father has life in Himself, even so He gave to the Son also to have life in Himself;

27.   and He gave Him authority to execute judgment, because He is the Son of Man.

John 10:18
"No one has taken it away from Me, but I lay it down on My own initiative I have to lay it down, and I have to take it up again This commandment I received from My Father."

John 16:15
"All things that the Father has are Mine; therefore, I said that He takes of Mine and will disclose it to you.

John 17:2
even as You gave Him authority over all flesh, that to all whom You have given Him, He may give eternal life.

John 17:10
and all things that are Mine are Yours, and Yours are Mine; and I have been glorified in them

Therefore, Jesus as the Son of God means that Jesus is the mightiest sovereign of all because he has all power of God (omnipotent) and inherits all the possessions of God. Since God is the creator of the universe, Jesus has all rights and authority over the universe. However, Jesus has a particular and special right and authority over the kingdom of God on earth. He is directly involved in its politics as the Son of God, because God created the earthly kingdom with a special interest and purpose for it (Leviticus 20:26, Palm 135:4, Malachi 3:17).

Jesus is the Christ (Messiah). Jesus as the Christ (Messiah) means that Jesus is the legal and ideal king of the kingdom of God on earth. The messiah of Israel, unlike the kings of other nations, was appointed and commissioned by God to rule over God's kingdom on earth and had to be a descendant of David. A messiah, like David, was supposed to be humble before God and obey the commandments of God and take care of the people of God with the heart of God, like a good shepherd. Jesus manifested true messiah-ship during his ministry. He always obeyed God, his Father, and carried out his will, not his own (Matthew 12:50, 18:14,

26:39, 42; Mark 14:36; Luke 22:42; John 5:30, 6:38–40, 8:38, 10:37, 14:10, 31, 17:7–8). He identified himself as the good shepherd (Matthew 9:36, Mark 6:34, John 10:11–15). Not just identifying, he demonstrated his loving-kindness to the people of God (Matthew 4:23–24, 8:16, 9:12, 35, 10:1, 8, 12:15, 14:35–36, 19:2, Mark 1:34, 2:17, Luke 4:16–21, 5:31, 7:21, 9:6). He truly loved, embraced, and healed those who suffered, the weak, and the alienated people of God. Jesus was indeed the promised Christ (Messiah) of the kingdom of God and for God's people on earth.

Therefore, Jesus was (is and will be) the Son of God and the Christ (Messiah). This means that Jesus is the sovereign of the kingdom of God in heaven and on earth, possesses that kingdom, and is the legal, ideal, and omnipotent king of that kingdom.

Jesus presented himself as the sovereign to the Jews. However, only some Jews believed and received his identity and became followers and disciples. Eventually Jesus was rejected by the Jewish authority and crucified by the law of the Romans. The following parable told by Jesus about three days before his crucifixion illustrates well this aspect of the slain sovereign:

Matthew 21:33–39 (Mark 12:1–8, Luke 20:9–15)
33. "Listen to another parable. There was a landowner who planted a vineyard and put a wall around it and dug a wine press in it, and built a tower, and rented it out to vine- growers and went on a journey.
34. "When the harvest time approached, he sent his slaves to the vine-growers to receive his produce.
35. "The vine-growers took his slaves and beat one, and killed another, and stoned a third.
36. "Again he sent another group of slaves larger than the first; and they did the same thing to them.
37. "But afterward he sent his son to them, saying, 'They will respect my son.'
38. "But when the vine-growers saw the son, they said among themselves, 'This is the heir; come, let us kill him and seize his inheritance.'
39. "They took him, and threw him out of the vineyard and killed him.

In this parable, Jesus identifies himself with the sovereign (the Son of God). Jesus never said directly that he was the promised Messiah (Christ) or the Son of God; rather he called himself the son of man. However, from his birth to death, the most significant and primary identity of Jesus was the sovereign. When Jesus was born, the magi from the east identified him as the king of the Jews: Matthew 2:2 "Where is He who has been born King of the Jews? For we saw his star in the east and have come to worship Him." During the public ministry, the disciples worshipped Jesus and confessed that Jesus was the Son of God (Matthew 13:34). Moreover, when Peter identified him as the sovereign, he willingly accepted that identity:

Matthew 16:16–20 (Mark 8:29)
16. Simon Peter answered, "You are the Christ, the Son of the living God."
17. And Jesus said to him, "Blessed are you, Simon Barjona, because flesh and blood did not reveal this to you, but My Father who is in heaven.
18. "I also say to you that you are Peter, and upon this rock I will build My church; and the gates of Hades will not overpower it.
19. "I will give you the keys of the kingdom of heaven; and whatever you bind on earth shall have been bound in heaven, and whatever you loose on earth shall have been loosed in heaven."
20. Then He warned the disciples that they should tell no one that He was the Christ.

Finally, when he was crucified, the plaque indicating his crime, the reason of the crucifixion, was put up above his head. The plaque read, "This is Jesus the king of the Jews," written in three languages: Hebrew, Latin, and Greek (Matthew 27:37, Luke 23:38, John 19:19–20). Right after his death, the Roman centurion witnessed that Jesus was the Son of God (Matthew 27:54, Mark 15:39). Above all, John 20:31 confirms that the purpose of writing the Gospels was to make the readers believe that Jesus is the Christ and the Son of God: "but these have been written so that you may believe that Jesus is the Christ, the Son of God; and that believing you may have life in his name."

Jesus was born, lived, and died as the sovereign. He came to the Jews as their sovereign, however, becoming the sovereign only to those who believed his identity and received his sovereignty (Luke 12:32). Throughout his life, the sovereign was the most significant, primary identity of Jesus and, therefore, it should precede all other identities. The meaning of the gospel, faith, and salvation, which are related to this identity, should be defined under this section.

Defining the Gospel

The term "gospel" (from the Old English gōd-spell, good news, εὐαγγέλιον in Greek) was not a New Testament creation. When Jesus and his disciples said "gospel," they certainly borrowed the term from the Hebrew Scriptures. John the Baptist, who opens the gospel (Mark 1:1) is the same as "the voice of the wilderness," an echo of Isaiah 40:1–4. Elsewhere (Matthew 3:1–6, Mark 1:1–5, Luke 3:1–6, John 1:19–23), he is identified with "the bearer of good news" in Isaiah 40:9 and Isaiah 52:7. Moreover, Jesus himself quoted Isaiah 61:1–2 proclaiming that the gospel had been fulfilled (Luke 4:16–21). Therefore, we need to know what gospel meant in the Old Testament to understand its meaning in the New.

In the Old Testament, the gospel means "the direct reign of God" in association with the restoration of Jerusalem:

Isaiah 40:9–11
9. Get yourself up on a high mountain, O Zion, bearer of good news (מְבַשֶּׂרֶת), Lift up your voice mightily, O Jerusalem, bearer of good news (מְבַשֶּׂרֶת); Lift it up, do not fear Say to the cities of Judah, "Here is your God!"
10. Behold, the Lord GOD will come with might, With his arm ruling for Him Behold, his reward is with Him And his recompense before Him.
11. Like a shepherd He will tend his flock, In his arm He will gather the lambs And carry them in his bosom; He will gently lead the nursing ewes.

Isaiah 52:6–10

6. "Therefore My people shall know My name; therefore, in that day I
   am the one who is speaking, 'Here I am.'"
7. How lovely on the mountains Are the feet of him who brings good
   news (מְבַשֵּׂר), Who announces peace And brings good news of
   happiness, Who announces salvation, And says to Zion, "Your God
   reigns!"
8. Listen! Your watchmen lift up their voices, They shout joyfully
   together; For they will see with their own eyes When the LORD
   restores Zion.
9. Break forth, shout joyfully together, You waste places of Jerusalem;
   For the LORD has comforted his people, He has redeemed Jerusalem.
10. The LORD has bared his holy arm In the sight of all the nations, That
    all the ends of the earth may see The salvation of our God.

Isaiah 61:14

1. The Spirit of the Lord GOD is upon me, Because the LORD has
   anointed me To bring good news (לְבַשֵּׂר) to the afflicted; He has sent
   me to bind up the brokenhearted, To proclaim liberty to captives And
   freedom to prisoners;
2. To proclaim the favorable year of the LORD And the day of vengeance
   of our God; To comfort all who mourn,
3. To grant those who mourn in Zion, Giving them a garland instead
   of ashes, The oil of gladness instead of mourning, The mantle of
   praise instead of a spirit of fainting So they will be called oaks of
   righteousness, The planting of the LORD, that He may be glorified.
4. Then they will rebuild the ancient ruins, They will raise up the former
   devastations; And they will repair the ruined cities, The desolations
   of many generations.

בָּשַׂר (basar) in Hebrew means the news. It meant the news of "the direct
reign of God" that would bring the restoration of Jerusalem. It was
associated with liberation from captivity, salvation from oppression, and
tending to the people of God. Certainly, that news was good news to the
people of God.

In the New Testament, the gospel, or the good news, means "the imminent coming of the Kingdom of God":

Mark 1:1, 14–15
1.   The beginning of the gospel of Jesus Christ, the Son of God.
14. Now after John had been taken into custody, Jesus came into Galilee, preaching the gospel of God,
15. and saying, "The time is fulfilled, and the kingdom of God is at hand; repent and believe in the gospel."

Matthew 3:1–2
1.   Now in those days John the Baptist came, preaching in the wilderness of Judea, saying,
2.   "Repent, for the kingdom of heaven is at hand."

Matthew 4:17, 23
17. From that time Jesus began to preach and say, "Repent, for the kingdom of heaven is at hand."
23. Jesus was going throughout all Galilee, teaching in their synagogues and proclaiming the gospel of the kingdom, and healing every kind of disease and every kind of sickness among the people.

Matthew 10:7
"And as you go, preach, saying, 'The kingdom of heaven is at hand.'

Matthew 24: 14
"This gospel of the kingdom shall be preached in the whole world as a testimony to all the nations, and then the end will come.

Luke 4:43
But He said to them, "I must preach the kingdom of God to the other cities also, for I was sent for this purpose."

Luke 10:9
and heal those in it who are sick, and say to them, 'The kingdom of God
has come near to you.'

Luke 16:16
"The Law and the Prophets were proclaimed until John; since that time
the gospel of the kingdom of God has been preached, and everyone is
forcing his way into it.

In these texts, the gospel of Jesus means "the kingdom of God is near"
(Mark 1:15). In addition, it is revealed that the kingdom of God is
equivalent to the kingdom of heaven. To the Jews of Jesus's time who
suffered under the Roman occupation and the corrupt Jewish authority,
that news was certainly the good because it meant the restoration of Israel
and salvation from oppressions. Those who believed that news became
a part of the coming kingdom of God and thus benefited from all the
blessings of the messianic reign. They were saved from the destruction of
Jerusalem and Judea and became the eternal citizens of the kingdom of
God on earth and in heaven.

How is "the coming of the kingdom of God" (gospel of the New Testament)
related to "the direct reign of God" (gospel of the Old Testament)? Since
the kingdom of God meant the kingdom reigned over by God, the coming
of the kingdom of God certainly implied the direct reign of God. Since
Jesus, as the Son of God, reigned over the coming kingdom of God, the
gospels of the both Testaments meant intrinsically the same.

Since the gospel "the kingdom of God is near" contains an element of
time, we need to define the term according to the historical timeline. If
the news was "the kingdom of God is far way," it certainly could not be
the good news to the Jews of Jesus's time. Therefore, for the gospel to
have a meaning for first-century Jews, and to be the good news, the term
should be defined in the first-century historical context. The definition
of the gospel is absolutely related to the existence of the Christian church.

Therefore, more details will be discussed in chapter 2, "Christian Church as the Fulfilled Kingdom of God."

Definitions of the Gospel

Timeline	Definition
From John the Baptist and Jesus to the Pentecost	The kingdom of God is near
From the Pentecost to AD 70	The kingdom of God is already here, but not yet consummated
After AD 70	The kingdom of God is here

The Christian Church is the kingdom of God or the kingdom of heaven. Her appearance and completion were foretold by John the Baptist and Jesus during their ministries. The first Christian church was born in Jerusalem on the day of the Pentecost when the Holy Spirit came upon about 120 disciples; it was consummated in AD 70 when the temple, Jerusalem, and Judea were destroyed, and the Christian church was saved from that destruction and, as a result, became liberated from the Jewish persecution. Pentecost was very near in time to the ministries of John the Baptist and Jesus. We do not know how many years John the Baptist ministered. However, if we consider the end of his ministry and the start of Jesus's ministry, Pentecost would be within four years (based upon three and a half years of ministry, as quantified in the Gospel of John). Therefore, from the viewpoint of John the Baptist and Jesus, the coming of the kingdom of God was very imminent. It was so close that, to Jesus, the kingdom was already present in terms of the spirit of God being on earth (Matthew 12:28). Therefore, the gospel proclaimed to the Jews by John the Baptist and Jesus was "The kingdom of God is near," and we can reasonably assume that Pentecost was around AD 30.

At Pentecost, the kingdom of God was born in Jerusalem as the Christian church and the mustard seed of Christendom (Matthew 13:31). All benefits and blessings by virtue of the messianic reign were manifested in that church. The Jerusalem church as the kingdom of God was rapidly expanding by the guidance of the Holy Spirit, however, it was companioned by persecution. The gospel was preached to the regions beyond Judea and the Jews and, at the same time, the kingdom of God was moving rapidly toward her consummation in AD 70. During that period, the gospel should be defined as "The kingdom of God is already here, but not yet consummated." Even from the viewpoint of John the Baptist and Jesus, AD 70 was not far away. It was just one generation (forty years) away from their contemporaries. Therefore, to them, not only the inauguration of the kingdom of God, but also the consummation of that kingdom was imminent. That was why both Jesus and John the Baptist foretold the beginning and completion, and urging repentance was an important part of their proclamation of the gospel (Matthew 3:1–10, 4:17). In this sense, Pentecost meant the end: from the viewpoint of the New Kingdom, the Christian church, and the end of Judea, it started at Pentecost in AD 30 and was completed in AD 70. After AD 70 when the Old Kingdom of God was completely destroyed, the New Kingdom of God, the Christian church, was already present around the world through the urged evangelism. Therefore, the gospel after AD 70 should be defined as "The kingdom of God is here." As I presented in the previous sections, the consummation of the kingdom of God became futuristic in the process of evangelization (the end of Judea became the end of the world) even after AD 70. This futuristic view should be corrected today. Christendom as the new kingdom of God is very present on earth, and the Lord Jesus Christ reigns over that kingdom. Therefore, the definition of the gospel today should be "The kingdom of God is here" and should be the same in the future.

If the initial gospel was "the kingdom of God is near," it led naturally to the next question: How to enter that kingdom? Where the gospel had to do with introducing the kingdom of God, faith was concerned with how to enter that kingdom. They entered that kingdom who believed the identity of Jesus as the sovereign of that kingdom and received his sovereignty. Therefore, faith, believing Jesus as the Son of God and the Christ (Messiah) was (is) the primary faith of Christianity. However, the word "faith" is used in more than one way in Christian life. Those who became a part of the kingdom of God through primary faith still needed another kind of faith to live a Christian life; that was (is), secondary faith. Christians, holding to primary faith, needed to rely constantly upon the mercy and power of the Son of God (Christ) to live as the people of God in this life, to be freed from sin, sickness, and all kinds of physical, social, and spiritual difficulties, pains, and sufferings, and to keep the commandments of the Lord in good conscience.

How can the people access these two kinds of faith? For the people during the ministry of Jesus, it was to believe what Jesus proclaimed. After the ascension of Jesus, it was to believe what the Apostles, disciples, or witnesses preached. After the death of the first eyewitnesses, it was to believe what was written by them, particularly, the accounts in the Gospels. I will call this faith "faith for faith." Let us have a close look at these three faiths.

Defining Faith: Three Kinds of Faith

Primary Faith: Believing Jesus as the Son of God and the Christ (Messiah)

This faith is concerned with the sovereign identity and is the most important and fundamental faith of Christianity. By this faith, anyone could (can) enter the kingdom of God and be a citizen of that kingdom. In the Old Testament, those who were the descendants of Israel (Jacob) became the people of God, and primary faith for them was to believe that the Yahweh who was revealed to the patriarchs is the Elohim (God) who created the universe and their only sovereign. In the New Testament, primary faith of the people of God was (is) to believe that the historical Jesus is the Christ (the good sovereign) and the Son of God (the omnipotent sovereign). Whoever had (has) that faith could (can) enter the kingdom of God. In the Gospels, this primary faith was immanent among the people who followed and came up to Jesus. After Pentecost, this primary faith was explicitly asked of the Jews and Gentiles. Since both the title (the Christ) and the origin (the Son of God) point to sovereignty, the word "believe" has a dual meaning: acknowledge and receive. To believe in Jesus actually means to both acknowledge the sovereign identity of Jesus and to receive his sovereignty. If someone acknowledges Jesus as the Christ and the Son of God but does not receive his sovereignty, he or she cannot be said to "believe" and be a part of the kingdom of God. Also, someone cannot receive Jesus's sovereignty without acknowledging him as the Christ and the Son of God. Therefore, primary faith is paraphrased in this way: It is to acknowledge the fact that the historical Jesus—the Son of God and only heir of God—came down on earth with all inherited authority and became the legal and ideal Christ (Messiah) of the people of God; it is also to receive and obey the sovereignty of Jesus Christ, the Son of God.

The main texts for primary faith:

Matthew 14:33
And those who were in the boat worshiped Him, saying, "You are certainly God's Son!"

Matthew 16:15–17
15. He said to them, "But who do you say that I am?"
16. Simon Peter answered, "You are the Christ, the Son of the living God."
17. And Jesus said to him, "Blessed are you, Simon Barjona, because flesh and blood did not reveal this to you, but My Father who is in heaven.

Matthew 26:63–64a
63. But Jesus kept silent And the high priest said to Him, "I adjure You by the living God, that You tell us whether You are the Christ, the Son of God."
64a. Jesus said to him, "You have said it yourself."

Matthew 27:54
Now the centurion, and those who were with him keeping guard over Jesus, when they saw the earthquake and the things that were happening, became very frightened and said, "Truly this was the Son of God!"

Mark 1:1

The beginning of the gospel of Jesus Christ, the Son of God.

Mark 15:39

When the centurion, who was standing right in front of Him, saw the way He breathed his last, he said, "Truly this man was the Son of God!"

John 1:11–13

11. He came to his own, and those who were his own did not receive Him.
12. But as many as received Him, to them He gave the right to become children of God, even to those who believe in his name,
13. who were born, not of blood nor of the will of the flesh nor of the will of man, but of God.

John 3:16

"For God so loved the world, that He gave his only begotten Son, that whoever believes in Him shall not perish, but have eternal life.

John 20:31

but these have been written so that you may believe that Jesus is the Christ, the Son of God; and that believing you may have life in his name.

Acts 2:36

"Therefore, let all the house of Israel know for certain that God has made Him both Lord and Christ--this Jesus whom you crucified."

Acts 9:18–22

18. And immediately there fell from his eyes something like scales, and he regained his sight, and he got up and was baptized;
19. and he took food and was strengthened. Now for several days he was with the disciples who were at Damascus,
20. and immediately he began to proclaim Jesus in the synagogues, saying, "He is the Son of God."
21. All those hearing him continued to be amazed, and were saying, "Is this not he who in Jerusalem destroyed those who called on this name,

and who had come here for the purpose of bringing them bound before the chief priests?"

22. But Saul kept increasing in strength and confounding the Jews who lived at Damascus by proving that this Jesus is the Christ

Acts 17:3
explaining and giving evidence that the Christ had to suffer and rise again from the dead, and saying, "This Jesus whom I am proclaiming to you is the Christ."

1John 4:15
Whoever confesses that Jesus is the Son of God, God abides in him, and he in God.

1John 5:5
Who is the one who overcomes the world, but he who believes that Jesus is the Son of God?

By this primary faith, anyone could (can) enter and be a citizen of the kingdom of God. This faith was asked first of the Jews during the ministry of Jesus by Jesus, himself. After Pentecost, the disciples asked it of both Jews and Gentiles. Therefore, to be clear about the meaning of being the people of God, we need to think separately of the Jews and the Gentiles. For the Jews, being the people of God through Jesus meant regeneration, rebirth, or being born again (John 3:1–10). Since the Jews were already the people of God, they could be the people of God again through primary faith from a physical sense to a spiritual sense (John 1:11–13) and from a superficial sense to a genuine and practical sense through repentance (Matthew 3:8–10). In addition, for the Jews, primary faith meant "believing the promise of God" because they had been waiting for the promised Messiah who was a descendent of David (2 Samuel 7:11–17, Acts 13:22–23, 32–33a). Whereas the Gentiles were neither the people of God nor waiting for the Messiah. Therefore, to them, primary faith meant (means) that the non-people of God become the people of God. The concept of regeneration, rebirth, or being born again could be applied to the Gentiles or the non-Jewish people in terms of the new life as the people of God (2 Corinthians 5:17); however, that cannot be the primary meaning of being the people of God to them. To the Gentiles, change of identity, status, nationality, or citizenship should take primacy.

	The primary meaning of being the people of God by primary faith
To the Jews	Being the people of God again: Regeneration, rebirth, or born again
To the Gentiles	Being the people of God: Change of identity, status, nationality, or citizenship

After someone joins the people of God through primary faith, he or she is asked to live the Christian life through another faith, to trust the power and mercy of the sovereign.

Secondary Faith: Trusting the Power and Mercy of Jesus who is the Son of God and the Christ (Messiah)

Primary faith necessarily entails secondary faith, to trust the power and mercy of Jesus. If a citizen of the new kingdom of God truly believes that Jesus is the Christ, the good sovereign, and the Son of God, the omnipotent sovereign, he or she should certainly trust the power and mercy of Jesus in time of sorrow, pain, adversity, and hardship. Not all citizens of the kingdom of God can live a peaceful, painless, happy, and blessed life. When a Christian faces adversity or hardships in life that he or she cannot resolve alone, primary faith, which is immanent, ideological, and qualitative in nature, incorporates secondary faith, which is external, practical, and quantitative in nature. Ideally thinking, if a Christian believes Jesus as the Christ and the Son of God, when he or she is in adversity or hardship, there is no need to worry, just pray, because the true Messiah will not abandon his people; the Son of God can do something to save him or her. In this ideal sense, primary faith entails 100% trust, or the full capacity of secondary faith. However, in reality, when primary faith entails secondary faith, most of the time a loss occurs due to the limited experiences of human existence. Since a Christian, even as a citizen of the kingdom and a child of God, is located in a particular land and society with limited existential experience, it is not easy for him or her to perceive the full saving capability of Jesus. They know intellectually that Jesus can do something for them; however, that trust is tinged with an element of doubt. Therefore, this secondary faith coupled with a loss of trust is called "little faith" in the Gospels (Matthew 6:30, 8:26, 14:31, 16:8, 17:20, Luke 12:28). On the contrary, the fully entailed secondary faith is called "great faith" (Matthew 8:10, 15:28). Generally speaking, the quantity of the secondary faith will be determined according to the quality of the primary faith, and both the primary and secondary faith work reciprocally in a dynamic way to enhance each other:

The Paradigm for the Dynamics of Faith

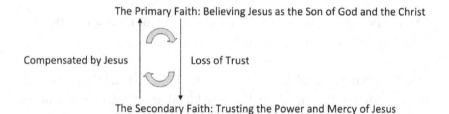

The Primary Faith: Believing Jesus as the Son of God and the Christ

Compensated by Jesus   Loss of Trust

The Secondary Faith: Trusting the Power and Mercy of Jesus

When primary faith entails secondary faith, in general, a certain loss of trust occurs due to the limited human experiences. However, that loss is compensated by Jesus, and the life of a Christian is restored as if he or she has 100% trust. In this process, a Christian usually experiences an unusual happening or senses a spiritual intercession of the sovereign. As a result, the Christian can have stronger primary faith and that reinforced primary faith produces greater secondary faith. As this dynamic reciprocal movement repeats in the Christian's life, both the quality of the primary faith and quantity of the secondary faith increase. The ultimate goal of this process is that the purest primary faith entails the full capacity of the secondary faith (100% trust). However, the journey to achieve that ultimate goal is the journey of a Christian life itself. I would like to present four examples to better illustrate this dynamics.

First example: Matthew 14:21–33

21. There were about five thousand men who ate, besides women and children.
22. Immediately He made the disciples get into the boat and go ahead of Him to the other side, while He sent the crowds away.
23. After He had sent the crowds away, He went up on the mountain by Himself to pray; and when it was evening, He was there alone.
24. But the boat was already a long distance from the land, battered by the waves; for the wind was contrary.
25. And in the fourth watch of the night He came to them, walking on the sea.
26. When the disciples saw Him walking on the sea, they were terrified, and said, "It is a ghost!" And they cried out in fear.
27. But immediately Jesus spoke to them, saying, "Take courage, it is I; do not be afraid."
28. Peter said to Him, "Lord, if it is You, command me to come to You on the water."
29. And He said, "Come!" And Peter got out of the boat, and walked on the water and came toward Jesus.
30. But seeing the wind, he became frightened, and beginning to sink, he cried out, "Lord, save me!"
31. Immediately Jesus stretched out his hand and took hold of him, and said to him, "You of little faith, why did you doubt?"
32. When they got into the boat, the wind stopped.
33. And those who were in the boat worshiped Him, saying, "You are certainly God's Son!"

In the text, we can find a good example of the reciprocal movement of the primary and secondary faith. The story happened right after feeding the five thousand. Before departing to the sea, the disciples had a certain degree of primary faith. We can assume that their primary faith became stronger than before since they witnessed that Jesus had such compassion for the people of God and performed the miracle of feeding them. When they were struggling on the sea because of the wind and the waves, they saw Jesus walking on the sea. Jesus declared himself as the Yahweh (ἐγώ εἰμι, I am). At first, Peter certainly had perfect primary faith (verse 28), and that faith immediately entailed the corresponding secondary faith (verse 29). He trusted the power of Jesus 100%; therefore, he could walk on the sea. However, while he was walking on the sea, he experienced a loss of trust and started to doubt his ability to walk on water. He had never experienced walking on the water before, and never saw and heard that a human being could do so. Gravity had limited Peter's experience as a human being on earth. However, Jesus did not let Peter sink when he asked for help. Jesus compensated for Peter's loss of trust: Jesus stretched out his hand and saved him. As a result, Peter's primary faith, as well as that of the disciples who witnessed the event, was enhanced. They worshiped Jesus in the boat and confessed, "You are certainly the Son of God."

During the ministry of Jesus, the disciples repeatedly experienced or witnessed this kind of dynamic, and through this process, their primary and secondary faith grew. We can arguably say that their primary faith became perfect, entailing the full capacity of their secondary faith when they witnessed and experienced the Resurrection of Jesus.

Second example: Mark 9:14–27

14. When they came back to the disciples, they saw a large crowd around them, and some scribes arguing with them.

15. Immediately, when the entire crowd saw Him, they were amazed and began running up to greet Him.

16. And He asked them, "What are you discussing with them?"

17. And one of the crowd answered Him, "Teacher, I brought You my son, possessed with a spirit which makes him mute;

18. and whenever it seizes him, it slams him to the ground and he foams at the mouth, and grinds his teeth and stiffens out. I told Your disciples to cast it out, and they could not do it."

19. And He answered them and said, "O unbelieving generation, how long shall I be with you? How long shall I put up with you? Bring him to Me!"

20. They brought the boy to Him. When he saw Him, immediately the spirit threw him into a convulsion, and falling to the ground, he began rolling around and foaming at the mouth.

21. And He asked his father, "How long has this been happening to him?" And he said, "From childhood.

22. "It has often thrown him both into the fire and into the water to destroy him. But if You can do anything, take pity on us and help us!"

23. And Jesus said to him, " 'If You can?' All things are possible to him who believes."

24. Immediately the boy's father cried out and said, "I do believe; help my unbelief."

25. When Jesus saw that a crowd was rapidly gathering, He rebuked the unclean spirit, saying to it, "You deaf and mute spirit, I command you, come out of him and do not enter him again."

26. After crying out and throwing him into terrible convulsions, it came out; and the boy became so much like a corpse that most of them said, "He is dead!"

27. But Jesus took him by the hand and raised him; and he got up.

This incident happened right after Jesus's Transfiguration on a high mountain, when the voice of God, the Father, testified to Jesus as his beloved Son. A certain degree of primary faith—unspoken and unexposed—was in those people who followed Jesus in the Gospels. Therefore, a certain degree of primary faith was immanent in the father who brought his son to Jesus. In general, weak primary faith is not strong enough to entail the full capacity of secondary faith. Therefore, the disciples could not expel the unclean spirit; Jesus points out their lack of faith in verse 19 and in Matthew 17:20 clarifies why not: "And He said to them, 'Because of the littleness of your faith; for truly I say to you, if you have faith the size of a mustard seed, you will say to this mountain, "Move from here to there," and it will move; and nothing will be impossible to you.'" When Jesus said "unbelieving" in verse 19, it could mean a lack of both primary and secondary faith, because they are inseparable. Jesus did not abandon the people of God in need despite their unbelief. When the disciples brought the boy to Jesus, the father of the boy revealed his lack of faith, too: "If you can do anything, take pity on us and help us!" (verse 22). If the father truly believed Jesus as the Christ and the Son of God and Jesus's mercy and power, he should not say "If." Jesus replied to him, "'If You can?' All things are possible to him who believes" (verse 23). "Believes" in verse 23 can mean both faiths; however, there is more emphasis on the entailed secondary faith than the primary because the faith of the father is related more to the capacity of Jesus's healing power than his identity. In verse 24, the father cried out to Jesus, "I do believe; help my unbelief." In this verse, "believe" and "unbelief" are more closely tied to secondary faith, too. Jesus compensated for the loss of trust of the disciples and the father. As a result, the boy marvelously recovered from the demonic possession by the mercy and power of Jesus. Even though the text is silent, we can reasonably assume that the primary faith of the disciples and the father became stronger than before since Jesus compensated for their lack of trust.

The following two examples demonstrate the fully entailed secondary faith.

Third example: Luke 18:35–43

35. As Jesus was approaching Jericho, a blind man was sitting by the road begging.
36. Now hearing a crowd going by, he began to inquire what this was.
37. They told him that Jesus of Nazareth was passing by.
38. And he called out, saying, "Jesus, Son of David, have mercy on me!"
39. Those who led the way were sternly telling him to be quiet; but he kept crying out all the more, "Son of David, have mercy on me!"
40. And Jesus stopped and commanded that he be brought to Him; and when he came near, He questioned him,
41. "What do you want Me to do for you?" And he said, "Lord, I want to regain my sight!"

42. And Jesus said to him, "Receive your sight; your faith has made you well."

43. Immediately he regained his sight and began following Him, glorifying God; and when all the people saw it, they gave praise to God.

In the text, the blind man identified Jesus twice as the Son of David (verses 38 and 39). This means that he truly believed Jesus was the promised Messiah of Israel; therefore, it can be said that primary faith was immanent in him. When Jesus asked him what he wanted Jesus to do for him, he did not say, "If you can" but directly and strictly, "Lord, I want to regain my sight!" His primary faith entailed the full capacity of his secondary faith: 100% trusting in the mercy and power of Jesus (verse 41). Jesus said to the blind man, "Receive your sight; your faith has made you well" (verse 42). In this verse, "your faith" means the fully entailed secondary faith, not simply positive thinking which can be produced without primary faith. Immediately the blind man regained his sight miraculously and became a disciple of Jesus, and those who witnessed the incident gave praise to God (verse 43).

The nature of this secondary faith is well illustrated in the similar story of two blind men in Matthew 9:27–31. In Matthew 9:28, when two blind men came up to Jesus and asked to be healed, just as the blind man in the previous text, Jesus directly asked them: "Do you believe that I am able to do this?" Here, Jesus did not ask, "Do you believe that I am the Messiah and the Son of God?" Since they already identified Jesus as the Son of David, it was assumed that primary faith was already immanent in them. When the two replied, "Yes, Lord," they clearly demonstrated the fully entailed secondary faith. Arguably, we can assume that the primary faith of the blind man, as well as that of the people who were witnesses, became stronger than before.

Fourth example: Matthew 8:5–13

5. And when Jesus entered Capernaum, a centurion came to Him, imploring Him,

6. and saying, "Lord, my servant is lying paralyzed at home, fearfully tormented."

7. Jesus said to him, "I will come and heal him."

8. But the centurion said, "Lord, I am not worthy for You to come under my roof, but just say the word, and my servant will be healed.

9. "For I also am a man under authority, with soldiers under me; and I say to this one, 'Go!' and he goes, and to another, 'Come!' and he comes, and to my slave, 'Do this!' and he does it."

10. Now when Jesus heard this, He marveled and said to those who were following, "Truly I say to you, I have not found such great faith with anyone in Israel.

11. "I say to you that many will come from east and west, and recline at the table with Abraham, Isaac and Jacob in the kingdom of heaven;

12. but the sons of the kingdom will be cast out into the outer darkness; in that place there will be weeping and gnashing of teeth."

13. And Jesus said to the centurion, "Go; it shall be done for you as you have believed." And the servant was healed that very moment.

Even during the ministry of Jesus, the gospel was mainly proclaimed to the Jews; however, the primary and the secondary faith were not limited to the Jews, but available to anyone (also see Matthew 15:21–28, Luke 17:11–19). In the text, a centurion, a Roman officer, came to Jesus for his paralyzed servant who was at home. Jesus intended to visit his house to heal his servant; however, the officer's reply amazed Jesus: "Lord, I am not worthy for You to come under my roof, but just say the word, and my servant will be healed" (verse 8). Even though the text does not say anything about the primary faith of the centurion explicitly, it is certain that he had it because otherwise, he could not respond to Jesus in such a way. Verse 8b "but just say the word, and my servant will be healed" clearly demonstrates the fully entailed secondary faith of the centurion. He understood the meaning of the authority clearly (verse 9); he knew that since Jesus is the Son of God, his words would summon a miracle. The amazed Jesus said to those who were following, "Truly I say to you, I have not found such great faith with anyone in Israel" (verse 10); and then Jesus said to the centurion, "Go; it shall be done for you as you have believed" (verse 13). Here, "great faith" (verse 10) and "have believed" (verse 13) certainly mean the fully entailed secondary faith of the centurion. And the servant was healed that very moment (verse 13b). As in all examples, it is likely the primary faith of the centurion and the people who witnessed became stronger than before.

Besides these four examples, we can find ample examples for this dynamic between primary and secondary faith throughout the Gospels: Matthew 6:25–34, 8:23–27, 9:27–31, 15:21–28, Mark 5:22–43 (24–34), Luke 7:36–50, 17:11–19.

Faith for Faith: Trusting the Accounts of the Life of Jesus

Finally, how can people access primary faith? When a person has primary faith, that faith necessarily entails secondary faith when it is needed. Therefore, the question can be rephrased as "How can people access both primary and secondary faith?" For the people during the ministry of Jesus, it was to believe what Jesus proclaimed. The people could directly access primary faith without any medium because they could see the evidence directly for what Jesus claimed and make a decision over it. For those who lived during the ministry of the Apostles, they had to trust what the first witnesses preached about Jesus. The Apostles' credibility became a medium to access primary faith. For the people after the Apostolic era, they had to trust the accounts regarding the life of Jesus. They placed their trust in what was written by the first witnesses or based upon their testimony, particularly, the accounts of the Gospels. I would like to call this type of faith "faith for faith."

The Bible should be defined as "the word about God which contains the word of God." If the Bible is simply defined as "the word of God," all inconsistencies and illogical things will be attributed to God. Therefore, even though we have the Christian canon, we should not interpret it literally, verse by verse. However, there is consistency about the life of Jesus in all four Gospels; at least, the claim regarding Jesus's sovereign identity (the Son of God and the Christ) is consistent and unanimous. Therefore, "faith for faith" should be to trust the accounts regarding the life of Jesus rather than simply trusting the accounts of the Bible. This "faith for faith" is the faith a person can possess gradually through the process of reading, hearing sermons, and experiencing a divine spiritual guidance.

Definition of Each Faith

Kind of Faith	Definition
The Primary Faith	To believe Jesus as the Son of God and the Christ (Messiah)
The Secondary Faith	To trust the power and mercy of Jesus who is the Son of God and the Christ
Faith for Faith	To trust the accounts of the life of Jesus

If a Christian says to a non-Christian, "Have faith," this faith will mean primary faith or "faith for faith." If a Christian says to another Christian who is in adversity, "Have faith," this faith points to secondary faith. These three faiths are inevitably related to each other and cannot be separated, because a person who trusts the accounts of the life of Jesus can have primary faith, in which secondary faith resides; therefore, as primary and secondary faiths grow, "faith for faith" grows accordingly.

Definition of faith as a whole
According to the accounts of the life of Jesus, to believe Jesus as the sovereign of the kingdom of God on earth and in heaven and, thereby, trust his total power and mercy.

Defining Salvation

Those Jews who had primary faith became members of the new kingdom of God, the Christian church, and were saved from the destruction of Jerusalem and Judea in AD 70. Therefore, salvation should be defined first in relation to judgment in three ways: in relation to Jews before AD 70, to the Gentiles before AD 70, and to all after AD 70.

Before AD 70

	Meaning of Salvation in relation to Judgment
To the Jews (particularly those who were in Judea)	To be saved from the destruction of Jerusalem and Judea by being a citizen of the New Kingdom of God which is eternally saved from the divine judgment of God by the atonement of Jesus
To the Gentiles	To be a citizen of the New Kingdom of God which would be saved from the destruction of Jerusalem and Judea and is eternally saved from the divine judgment of God by the atonement through Jesus

After AD 70

	Meaning of Salvation in relation to Judgment
To anyone	To be a citizen of the already saved New Kingdom of God which is eternally atoned from the divine judgment of God

According to the eschatological accounts in the New Testament, some Palestinian Jewish Christians who were martyred before AD 70 are assumed to have been resurrected and ascended to heaven in AD 70. Some who were alive in AD 70 are assumed to have been transformed and ascended to heaven without experiencing physical death. This assumption should be considered as part of the meaning of salvation for the Jews before AD 70.

Today, salvation means, "being a citizen of the eternal kingdom of God." Anyone who has primary faith can be a part of the Christian church, which is atoned for by the sacrifice of Jesus, and, therefore, eternally saved from the divine judgment of God. Because Christendom is the earthly kingdom of God, descended from the heavenly kingdom of God, both are intrinsically the same. The spirit and soul of those who become citizens of the Christian church will enter the heavenly kingdom after death (1 Peter 1:9). This aspect will be discussed further in Chapter 2, "The Christian Church as the Fulfilled Kingdom of God on Earth."

Since the judgment of God is based upon the sin of the people of God, the meaning of salvation is related to sin. God judged Jerusalem and Judea because of the sin of the Jews in the collective sense. On the contrary, God does not judge the Christian church as a whole since Jesus Christ already atoned for. Therefore, for the Jews (particularly those who were in Judea) before AD 70, "saved from sin" had a double meaning: primarily, "saved from sin of Judea" and secondarily, "saved from sin of the atoned Christian church." For the Gentiles, "saved from sin" meant only "saved from the sin of the atoned Christian church," not from their previous sin.

Before AD 70

	Meaning of Salvation in relation to Sin
To the Jews (particularly those who were in Judea)	1. To be saved from sin of Judea 2. To be saved from sin of the atoned Christian church
To the Gentile	To be saved from sin of the atoned Christian church

After AD 70

	Meaning of Salvation in relation to Sin
To anyone	To be saved from sin of the atoned Christian Church

b. Jesus as the Educator

Jesus Christ, the Son of God, presented himself as the educator to those who had primary faith. The images presented as the educator are a teacher (rabbi) and a prophet. Corresponding to these images, the image of Christians are the disciples. The English term "prophet" is the transliteration of Greek προφήτης (prophetes) which is the Greek translation of the Hebrew נָבִיא (Nabi). Even though the English "prophet" and the Greek προφήτης denote literally "forth-teller," the major task of "Nabi" (spokesperson) was to educate the people of God; in other words, to restore the Law to the lives of the people of God. In the process of educating people, "Nabi" sometimes foretold future events, which would happen by the divine will of God. Jesus foretold the imminent coming of the kingdom of God and the total destruction of Jerusalem and Judea; however, that prophecy was a part of his teaching to warn and prepare the disciples for the coming disaster (Matthew 24:1–5). In any case, simply foretelling the future events without any educational purpose isn't meaningful to people. Therefore, Jesus, who taught his people and was devoted to teaching, should be identified as an educator rather than a prophet or forth-teller.

Jesus as the sovereign means Jesus who is the Christ and the Son of God. Jesus as the educator means Jesus who taught those who believed his sovereign identity and became the people of God how to live as citizens of the new kingdom of God. When a nation is created, the laws are constituted, and the head of the nation certainly has a responsibility to educate the citizens according to the established laws. The history of Israel as a nation, which consisted of the descendants of the twelve tribes, started at the Exodus: the kingdom of God on earth was born. At the beginning of the kingdom, God, as the sovereign, set up the Ten Commandments to educate his people how to live as his people. Likewise, Jesus called out the Twelve Disciples and gave them the new commandment: "A new commandment I give to you, that you love one another, even as I have loved you, that you also love one another" (John 13:34); "This is My commandment, that you love one another, just as I have loved you" (John 15:12).[96]

We need to distinguish the new commandment from the eschatological ethics of Jesus. The main audience for Jesus's teaching consisted of two groups: the Palestinian Jews who would face soon the fatal destruction and his disciples who would face soon harsh persecution from the Jews and experience the birth of the new kingdom of God. Therefore, some teachings of Jesus in the Gospels should be understood in that unique, historical, geographical, and eschatological context. This eschatological context must be taken into account before applying these teachings to contemporary Christians. The following questions should be asked to properly understand the meaning of a teaching of Jesus: Was this teaching for the Jews who would soon face the total destruction? Was this teaching for the disciples who would face harsh persecution from their fellow Jews and close relatives? Was this teaching for the disciples who would greet and lead the new kingdom? For the disciples, therefore, Jesus directed his teachings to three areas of need: how to interact with outsiders in general, how to respond to fellow Jews who would persecute them, and how to interact with fellow Christians.

The first was well summarized in Matthew 5:16: "Let your light shine before men in such a way that they may see your good works, and glorify your Father who is in heaven." The second was well summarized in Matthew 5:44: "But I say to you, love your enemies and pray for those who persecute you." The last was perfectly summarized in the new commandment, which is one outstanding and timeless teaching to the Christian church. All Christians are obligated to observe it, regardless of time and circumstance. Jesus gave the new commandment repeatedly to the select group of disciples right before his crucifixion; it was the new Law which they must continue to observe. Therefore, when we think of Jesus's teachings, the new commandment, as the Law given to the Church, should have priority and superiority to all others.

The Summary of the ethical teachings of Jesus for the Christian Church

Object of Teaching	Content of Teaching
To outsiders in general	Practice good works.
To the ones who persecute	Love and pray for them.
To the fellow Christians	Love one another, just as I have loved you.

The texts related to the New Commandment:

John 13:34–35
34. "A new commandment I give to you, that you love one another, even
as I have loved you, that you also love one another.
35. "By this all men will know that you are my disciples, if you have love
for one another."

John 14:15, 21
15 "If you love me, you will keep my commandments.
21. "He who has my commandments and keeps them is the one who loves
me; and he who loves Me will be loved by My Father, and I will love
him and will disclose Myself to him."

John 15:9–12, 17
9. "Just as the Father has loved me, I have also d you; abide in my love.
10. "If you keep my commandments, you will abide in my love; just as I
have kept my Father's commandments and abide in his love.
11. "These things I have spoken to you so that my joy may be in you, and
that your joy may be made full.
12. "This is my commandment, that you love one another, just as I have
loved you.
17. "This I command you, that you love one another.

Uniqueness and Meaning of the New Commandment

Jesus gave the disciples only one commandment, the Law of Love.
However, this commandment summarizes all ethical teachings of Jesus
for all of Christendom.

Is there any nation that legislates love as a law? Has there been any king
or president who said to the citizens, "As I have loved you, love one
another"? Compared to all other nations and leaders, this Law of Love of
the New Kingdom of God is unique because of the abstract nature of the
component, love.

No nation has one law to govern the people. There is always a great collection of laws and, in most cases, those laws require specialized lawyers for interpretation. The Law of Love is unique because of its simplicity: Anyone can read, memorize, and understand the meaning. However, as far as ethics is concerned, this simple and abstract law summarizes all teachings of Jesus: If all citizens of the New Kingdom of God love one another as Jesus had loved his disciples, what other law is necessary?

This Law of Love is unique when compared with the Old Testament Law. Along with the Ten Commandments, Jesus summarized the Old Testament ethics:

Matthew 22:37–40

37. And He said to him, " 'YOU SHALL LOVE THE LORD YOUR GOD WITH ALL YOUR HEART, AND WITH ALL YOUR SOUL, AND WITH ALL YOUR MIND.'
38. "This is the great and foremost commandment.
39. "The second is like it, 'YOU SHALL LOVE YOUR NEIGHBOR AS YOURSELF.'
40. "On these two commandments depend the whole Law and the Prophets."

Matthew 7:12

"In everything, therefore, treat people the same way you want them to treat you, for this is the Law and the Prophets.

The Old Testament moral Law required the people of God to love God and their fellow citizens distinctively. However, the Law of Love uniquely relates "love of the citizens" to "love of God" through Jesus the Son:

John 15:9–10

9. "Just as the Father has loved Me, I have also loved you; abide in My love.
10. "If you keep My commandments, you will abide in My love; just as I have kept My Father's commandments and abide in his love.

John 14:11a, 21

11a. "Believe Me that I am in the Father and the Father is in Me."

21. "He who has My commandments and keeps them is the one who loves Me; and he who loves Me will be loved by My Father, and I will love him and will disclose Myself to him."

Jesus as the Son becomes the medium of love: The Father loves the Son, the Son loves his people, and his people love one another, which means, in turn, that his people love the Son, and the Father loves the people. "The Father loves the people" certainly implies that the people love the Father because the Son is in the Father and the Father is in the Son." The following diagram illustrates this love relationship:

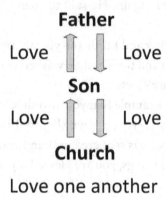

Unity in Love

Father

Love ⬆ ⬇ Love

Son

Love ⬆ ⬇ Love

Church

Love one another

Therefore, the Law of Love, in fact, includes "loving Jesus the Son of God" and "loving God," which is the great and foremost commandment.

Unlike the Old Testament moral Law, the Law of Love comes with a concrete example: the life of Jesus. His own life is the expression of "Love one another, just as I have loved you." To practice the Law of Love, therefore, we must see how Jesus loved his disciples or people. It was clear and vivid to the disciples who stayed with Jesus during his ministry and witnessed his death. However, contemporary Christians discover this by studying the texts. The New Commandment is fully expressed in John 13:34 and 15:12. By studying the immediate context of the fully expressed New Commandment, we have an idea of "how Jesus loved his people." In John 13, right before giving the New Commandment, during the Last Supper, Jesus washed the disciples' feet.

John 13:3–4, 12–17

3. Jesus, knowing that the Father had given all things into his hands, and that He had come forth from God and was going back to God,

4. got up from supper, and laid aside his garments; and taking a towel, He girded Himself.

5. Then He poured water into the basin, and began to wash the disciples' feet and to wipe them with the towel with which He was girded.

12. So when He had washed their feet, and taken his garments and reclined at the table again, He said to them, "Do you know what I have done to you?

13. "You call Me Teacher and Lord; and you are right, for so I am.

14. "If I then, the Lord and the Teacher, washed your feet, you also ought to wash one another's feet.

15. "For I gave you an example that you also should do as I did to you.

16. "Truly, truly, I say to you, a slave (δοῦλος) is not greater than his master, nor is one who is sent greater than the one who sent him.

17. "If you know these things, you are blessed if you do them.

Since, right after washing the disciple's feet, Jesus explicitly said that the disciples should wash one another's feet as he did to them, this example given by Jesus was contextually related to the New Commandment. Based upon the text, we can say that Jesus loved his disciples in an attitude as a slave who washed his or her master's feet. In this sense, the New Commandment can be rephrased as "Provide loving care for one another, as I have cared for you"; In other words, "love" is an action rather than an emotion or feeling. Jesus's teaching after washing the disciples' feet supports this practical aspect of love. Verse 14 defies any possible resistance to washing one another's feet: Since the Lord and the Teacher,

Jesus, washed the disciples' feet, Christians must wash one another's feet regardless of their feelings; it is not optional, but a mandatory action. In this regard, the Law of Love requires good characteristics such as humility, kindness, honesty, and patience; through these actions practitioners find rest for their souls (Matthew 11:29).

Another immediate context we need to consider is John 15:12–17:

John 15: 12–17
12. "This is My commandment, that you love one another, just as I have loved you.
13. "Greater love has no one than this, that one lay down his life for his friends.
14. "You are My friends if you do what I command you.
15. "No longer do I call you slaves, for the slave does not know what his master is doing; but I have called you friends, for all things that I have heard from My Father I have made known to you.
16. "You did not choose Me but I chose you, and appointed you that you would go and bear fruit, and that your fruit would remain, so that whatever you ask of the Father in My name He may give to you.
17. "This I command you, that you love one another.

The analysis of the text focused on the commandment:
13. "Greater love has no one than this, that one lay down his life for
his friends.
14. "You are My friends
if you do what I command you.
17. "This I command you,
that you love one another.
12. "This is My commandment,
That you love one another,
just as I have loved you.

The text belongs to the last discourse of Jesus (John chapter 14–16), spoken during the Last Supper immediately before his arrest. In the text, in-between the commandments (verses 12 and 17), Jesus exposed a reason for his immanent death and related his death with love and the commandment (verses 13–14). According to the analysis, the text can be summarized: I will lay down my life for you if you love one another the way I have loved you, because my love for you is the greatest.

The text should be also understood in the context of the following narrative (John 18:1–9), which describes how Jesus showed love for his people by choosing to go to the cross alone in order to save the lives of the disciples.

John 18:1–9
1. When Jesus had spoken these words, He went forth with his disciples over the ravine of the Kidron, where there was a garden, in which He entered with his disciples.
2. Now Judas also, who was betraying Him, knew the place, for Jesus had often met there with his disciples.
3. Judas then, having received the Roman cohort (σπεῖραν)[97] and officers from the chief priests and the Pharisees, came there with lanterns and torches and weapons.
4. So Jesus, knowing all the things that were coming upon Him, went forth and said to them, "Whom do you seek?"
5. They answered Him, "Jesus the Nazarene." He said to them, "I am He (Ἐγώ εἰμι)." And Judas also, who was betraying Him, was standing with them.
6. So when He said to them, "I am He (Ἐγώ εἰμι)," they drew back and fell to the ground.
7. Therefore He again asked them, "Whom do you seek?" And they said, "Jesus the Nazarene."
8. Jesus answered, "I told you that I am He; so if you seek Me, let these go their way,"
9. to fulfill the word which He spoke, "Of those whom You have given Me I lost not one."

According to this text, Jesus made it possible for the disciples to escape arrest. Taking verse 3 and Matthew 26:47[98] into consideration, we can arguably say that the well-trained several hundred armed soldiers and officers came to the garden to arrest not just Jesus but Jesus and his disciples. However, Jesus went forth before his disciples and, first, suppressed the power of the army by proclaiming "Ἐγώ εἰμι (I am)"[99] and asked the army to allow his disciples to go their way. Doubtlessly the suppressed army complied with the request.

John 15: 12–17 is summarized as "I will lay down my life for you if you love one another, just as I have loved you, because I love you greatest." Before the disciples proved that they loved one another, just as Jesus had loved them, Jesus showed the greatest love toward them first by going to the cross alone in order to save and preserve his people. Therefore, observing the Law of Love was not only the New Commandment, but also it became the debt to his people.

Going back to the question, "How did Jesus love his people?" Jesus loved his people so much that he lay down his life for them. In this regard, the New Commandment can be rephrased as "Love one another, just as I laid down my life for you."

Considering the immediate contexts of the New Commandment, we can draw a diagram of the New Commandment:

Diagram of the New Commandment

Laying down your life for one another

Washing one another's feet

The New Commandment can be rephrased as "Love one another, as I demonstrated by washing your feet" and "Love one another, as I loved you by dying for you." For both, Jesus showed an example and, thus, "love" here means a decisive "act" and "practice" rather than mere rhetoric. Since Jesus as the Lord and teacher washed the disciples' feet, "washing one another's feet" must be a basic practice of all Christians without question: each Christian should consider himself or herself as a servant to others. Practicing this servanthood requires disciplined character such as humility, kindness, honesty, and patience. Therefore, to practice the Law of Love, the Christian church should make a priority of developing the character of the members. On the other hand, "laying down your life for one another" represents the greatest love of the Christian church. Christians should not be satisfied with practicing servanthood. Their love should endeavor to reach the greatest love. It should be the ultimate goal of the Christian church that all Christians love one another to the point of death for one another or the church. The life of a Christian and the history of the Christian church should be the journey to keep this New Commandment.

The New Commandment and the Holy Sprit

Jesus as the educator gave the New Commandment to his people. However, is it possible for Christians to carry out that Commandment? Can the members of the Christian church really love one another, just as Jesus loved his people? Certainly, it is not an easy task for Christians to practice the Law of Love. That is why Jesus promised the Helper for his people. Let us read the relevant texts:

John 14:15–26
15. "If you love Me, you will keep My commandments.
16. "I will ask the Father, and He will give you another Helper, that He may be with you forever;
17. that is the Spirit of truth, whom the world cannot receive, because it does not see Him or know Him, but you know Him because He abides with you and will be in you.

18. "I will not leave you as orphans; I will come to you.

19. "After a little while the world will no longer see me, but you will see me; because I live, you will live also.

20. "In that day you will know that I am in my Father, and you in me, and I in you.

21. "He who has my commandments and keeps them is the one who loves Me; and he who loves Me will be loved by My Father, and I will love him and will disclose Myself to him."

22. Judas (not Iscariot) said to Him, "Lord, what then has happened that You are going to disclose Yourself to us and not to the world?"

23. Jesus answered and said to him, "If anyone loves me, he will keep My word; and My Father will love him, and We will come to him and make Our abode with him.

24. "He who does not love me does not keep My words; and the word which you hear is not Mine, but the Father's who sent Me.

25. "These things I have spoken to you while abiding with you.

26. "But the Helper, the Holy Spirit, whom the Father will send in My name, He will teach you all things, and bring to your remembrance all that I said to you.

John 15:26

"When the Helper comes, whom I will send to you from the Father, that is the Spirit of truth who proceeds from the Father, He will testify about me

John 16:7, 13

7. "But I tell you the truth, it is to your advantage that I go away; for if I do not go away, the Helper will not come to you; but if I go, I will send Him to you.

13. "But when He, the Spirit of truth, comes, He will guide you into all the truth; for He will not speak on his own initiative, but whatever He hears, He will speak; and He will disclose to you what is to come.

In these texts, the Holy Spirit is identified as the Helper and the Spirit of truth. The Holy Spirit as the Spirit of truth was (is) to testify about Jesus, who is truth, and guide his people into all truth (15:26, 16:13). How about the Holy Spirit as the Helper? The initial reason Jesus promised and identified the Holy Spirit as the Helper is found in John 14:15–16, 26. It was (is) to help his people keep his commandments and teach all the things Jesus taught. The Helper and the commandments are contextually closely related in the text.

John 14:15–16, 21, 23, 26

15. "If you love Me, you will keep My commandments.
16. "I will ask the Father, and He will give you another Helper, that He may be with you forever;
21. "He who has My commandments and keeps them is the one who loves Me; and he who loves Me will be loved by My Father, and I will love him and will disclose Myself to him."
23. Jesus answered and said to him, "If anyone loves Me, he will keep My word; and My Father will love him, and We will come to him and make Our abode with him.
26. "But the Helper, the Holy Spirit, whom the Father will send in My name, He will teach you all things, and bring to your remembrance all that I said to you.

We know that the most important commandment or teaching of Jesus related to love, the New Commandment, or Law of Love. Jesus knew that simply giving the Commandment, even with the example of his life, would not be sufficient for his people. Teaching, training, or education intrinsically implies a process, not just a one-time event, particularly when it is concerned with character, ethics, or morality. Jesus knew that keeping his Commandment would be a process, and that was why he promised the Helper, which would abide in his people forever (14:16–17). The Holy Spirit dwells in the Christian church forever, constantly helping the people of God love one another in the way that Jesus loved them. Therefore, it should be a conviction of the Christian church that Christians can love one another as Jesus did if they totally rely upon the help of the Holy Spirit. In this sense, the history of the Christian church should be an endless process of learning how to love one another through the guidance of the Holy Spirit. The following diagram will be helpful in understanding the relationship between the Holy Spirit and the Christian church:

Diagram of the Relationship between the Holy Spirit and the Christian Church

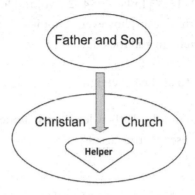

Through the New Commandment, we can see the vision of Jesus Christ, the Son of God, toward the earth. It was (is) to create the kingdom of God on earth in which the citizens truly love one another as the children of God, unconditionally and selflessly. The word "peace" will describe most properly the lives in that kingdom. Each local church, as a faith community holding to the New Commandment, would be a sign to the world of peace. If Jesus ever had a vision of the growing kingdom, certainly it was of a world in which all human beings, as the image of God, live peacefully. When a church grows, therefore, peace on earth grows, too.

c. Jesus as the Mediator

Jesus, who gave the commandments to his people, also atoned for their sin as the mediator. The images as mediator are the high priest and the sacrifice (Lamb). Corresponding to these images, the image of the Christians are the righteous or the saints.

Jesus as the sovereign means Jesus who is the Christ and the Son of God. Jesus as the educator means Jesus who taught those who believed and received his sovereign identity how to live as his people. Jesus as the mediator means Jesus who suffered and died on the cross for the people who live according to the New Commandment and his teachings. All four Gospels depict his last hours in detail (about twelve hours: six hours

inquiring and sentencing plus six hours on the cross): Matthew 26:57–
27:50, Mark 14:53–15:37, Luke 22:54–23:46, and John 18:12–19:30. The
suffering and death of Jesus, however, is not just related to the mediator,
but also to the sovereign and the educator, as well.

Suffering and Death as the Sovereign

As we already read in John 18:1–9, Jesus went alone to the cross in order
to let the disciples escape from arrest:

John 18:8–9
8.   Jesus answered, "I told you that I am He; so if you seek Me, let these
     go their way,"
9.   to fulfill the word which He spoke, "Of those whom You have given
     Me I lost not one."

In his last prayer, recorded in John chapter 17, Jesus confirmed that he, as
the leader, had kept and protected his people:

John 17:11–12
11. "I am no longer in the world; and yet they themselves are in the world,
     and I come to You Holy Father, keep them in Your name, the name
     which You have given Me, that they may be one even as We are.
12. "While I was with them, I was keeping them in Your name which You
     have given Me; and I guarded them and not one of them perished but
     the son of perdition, so that the Scripture would be fulfilled."

At the moment of arrest, Jesus fulfilled what he had prayed for the disciples
by saving their lives. Jesus was the true leader. He absolutely protected
the people who believed in him and belonged to him. If a disciple was
arrested and died with Jesus, we would certainly have doubt regarding his
sovereign identity. If Jesus could not protect his disciples at such a critical
moment, if he had abandoned his duty of protection to save his own life,
we would not call him the Christ or the Son of God. When we think of
his suffering and death, therefore, we should remember Jesus who chose

voluntarily the way of the cross to protect and preserve his people. The way to the cross was the ultimate expression of the sovereign love Jesus had for his people and, at the same time, the ultimate demonstration of the true leadership of the sovereign. Therefore, Christians can continue to confess Jesus as the sovereign and trust in his leadership.

Suffering and Death as the Educator

Not only did Jesus die as the true sovereign, but also as the true educator. Jesus taught his people to be perfect, like God the Father, and practice what they learned from him. During the last hours of his life, Jesus himself practiced what he taught his people. Let us read the relevant teachings of Jesus:

Matthew 5:11–12

11. "Blessed are you when people insult you and persecute you, and falsely say all kinds of evil against you because of Me.

12. "Rejoice and be glad, for your reward in heaven is great; for in the same way they persecuted the prophets who were before you.

Matthew 5:38–48

38. "You have heard that it was said, 'AN EYE FOR AN EYE, AND A TOOTH FOR A TOOTH.'

39. "But I say to you, do not resist an evil person; but whoever slaps you on your right cheek, turn the other to him also.

40. "If anyone wants to sue you and take your shirt, let him have your coat also.

41. "Whoever forces you to go one mile, go with him two.

42. "Give to him who asks of you, and do not turn away from him who wants to borrow from you.

43. "You have heard that it was said, 'YOU SHALL LOVE YOUR NEIGHBOR and hate your enemy.'

44. "But I say to you, love your enemies and pray for those who persecute you,

45. so that you may be sons of your Father who is in heaven; for He causes his sun to rise on the evil and the good, and sends rain on the righteous and the unrighteous.
46. "For if you love those who love you, what reward do you have? Do not even the tax collectors do the same?
47. "If you greet only your brothers, what more are you doing than others? Do not even the Gentiles do the same?
48. "Therefore you are to be perfect, as your heavenly Father is perfect.

Matthew 7:21–27

21. "Not everyone who says to Me, 'Lord, Lord,' will enter the kingdom of heaven, but he who does the will of My Father who is in heaven will enter.
22. "Many will say to Me on that day, 'Lord, Lord, did we not prophesy in Your name, and in Your name cast out demons, and in Your name perform many miracles?'
23. "And then I will declare to them, 'I never knew you; depart from me, you who practice lawlessness.'
24. "Therefore everyone who hears these words of Mine and acts on them, may be compared to a wise man who built his house on the rock.
25. "And the rain fell, and the floods came, and the winds blew and slammed against that house; and yet it did not fall, for it had been founded on the rock.
26. "Everyone who hears these words of Mine and does not act on them, will be like a foolish man who built his house on the sand.
27. "The rain fell, and the floods came, and the winds blew and slammed against that house; and it fell--and great was its fall."

Jesus taught his followers and the disciples not to resist an evil person but to love their enemies and pray for those who persecute them. In doing so he greatly emphasized "acting on" and "practicing" his teachings. He closed the teachings of the Sermon on the Mount (Matthew chapter 5 to 7) with an emphasis upon action, pointing out the problem of the scribes and the Pharisees as "not practicing what they say" (Matthew 23:1–3).

The true teacher or educator is the one who practices what he or she teaches. Jesus did not resist the evil ones and, instead, prayed for those who persecuted, even crucified him:

Matthew 27:11–14

11. Now Jesus stood before the governor, and the governor questioned Him, saying, "Are You the King of the Jews?" And Jesus said to him, "It is as you say."
12. And while He was being accused by the chief priests and elders, He did not answer.
13. Then Pilate said to Him, "Do You not hear how many things they testify against You?"
14. And He did not answer him with regard to even a single charge, so the governor was quite amazed.

Luke 23:33–34

33. When they came to the place called The Skull, there they crucified Him and the criminals, one on the right and the other on the left.
34. But Jesus was saying, "Father, forgive them; for they do not know what they are doing " And they cast lots, dividing up his garments among themselves.

Jesus was the true educator. When we think of his suffering and death, therefore, we should remember him as one who practiced what he taught his people. He suffered and walked to the cross as the true educator. Therefore, Christians can continue to cherish Jesus's teachings and are encouraged to imitate our Lord.

Suffering and Death as the Mediator

Jesus suffered and died as the true sovereign and educator; however, the most powerful identity related to his suffering and death should be as the mediator. Jesus, who presented himself as the sovereign and then gave the New Commandment to his people, finally gave up his own life for the sin of his people. He did so to save and reconcile the church with God. By this reconciliation, the Christian church was saved from the destruction of Jerusalem and Judea and became the eternal, holy kingdom of God on earth.

First, Jesus suffered and died for the nation, the Christian church, the New Kingdom of God on earth, or his people, without condition.

In the New Commandment, Jesus gave a new law to the Christian church. If the church does not observe this Law of Love, it would turn out to be as sinful as before the Lord, Jesus Christ. Mathematically speaking, if more than 50% of the members of the church do not love each other as Jesus loved his people, the church would be found to be sinners before God. In the Old Testament, when Israel did not observe the Law, God punished and eventually destroyed it. What would happen to the Christian church, then, when the church turns out to be sinful? Jesus himself suffered and died for the sin of his people. He is like the Passover lamb, saving the Christian church from the destruction of Jerusalem and Judea; he is the sacrifice on the Day of Atonement (the Yom Kipper), to preserve his church eternally as the holy kingdom of God on earth. Therefore, unlike ancient Israel and Judah, the Christian church is not punished and destroyed as a whole by God. Matthew 1:21 clarifies this redemptive role of Jesus set for him even before his birth: "She will bear a son; and you shall call his name Jesus, for he will save his people from their sins." When Jesus started his public ministry, John the Baptist identified Jesus as the sacrificial lamb for redemption: "The next day he saw Jesus coming to him and said, "Behold, the Lamb of God who takes away the sin of the world!" (John 1:29). Here, as we already studied in Section I, "the world" should be understood as the Jewish world, Judea, the world of the people of God.

In connection to the Old Testament, Jesus atoned for the sin of the Christian church as the Passover lamb and the high priest/sacrifices on the Day of Atonement.

1. Jesus suffered and died as the Passover lamb

Let us read the relevant Old Testament text to understand the meaning of the Passover lamb:

Exodus 12:1–14, 21–27, 43–47

1. Now the LORD said to Moses and Aaron in the land of Egypt,

2. "This month shall be the beginning of months for you; it is to be the first month of the year to you.

3. "Speak to all the congregation of Israel, saying, 'On the tenth of this month they are each one to take a lamb for themselves, according to their fathers' households, a lamb for each household.

4. 'Now if the household is too small for a lamb, then he and his neighbor nearest to his house are to take one according to the number of persons in them; according to what each man should eat, you are to divide the lamb.

5. 'Your lamb shall be an unblemished male a year old; you may take it from the sheep or from the goats.

6. 'You shall keep it until the fourteenth day of the same month, then the whole assembly of the congregation of Israel is to kill it at twilight.

7. 'Moreover, they shall take some of the blood and put it on the two doorposts and on the lintel of the houses in which they eat it.

8. 'They shall eat the flesh that same night, roasted with fire, and they shall eat it with unleavened bread and bitter herbs.

9. 'Do not eat any of it raw or boiled at all with water, but rather roasted with fire, both its head and its legs along with its entrails.

10. 'And you shall not leave any of it over until morning, but whatever is left of it until morning, you shall burn with fire.

11. 11. 'Now you shall eat it in this manner: with your loins girded, your sandals on your feet, and your staff in your hand; and you shall eat it in haste—it is the LORD'S Passover.

12. 'For I will go through the land of Egypt on that night, and will strike down all the firstborn in the land of Egypt, both man and beast; and against all the gods of Egypt I will execute judgments--I am the LORD.

13. 'The blood shall be a sign for you on the houses where you live; and when I see the blood I will pass over you, and no plague will befall you to destroy you when I strike the land of Egypt.

14. 'Now this day will be a memorial to you, and you shall celebrate it as a feast to the LORD; throughout your generations you are to celebrate it as a permanent ordinance.

21. Then Moses called for all the elders of Israel and said to them, "Go and take for yourselves lambs according to your families, and slay the Passover lamb.

22. "You shall take a bunch of hyssop and dip it in the blood which is in the basin, and apply some of the blood that is in the basin to the lintel and the two doorposts; and none of you shall go outside the door of his house until morning.

23. "For the LORD will pass through to smite the Egyptians; and when He sees the blood on the lintel and on the two doorposts, the LORD will pass over the door and will not allow the destroyer to come in to your houses to smite you.

24. "And you shall observe this event as an ordinance for you and your children forever.

25. "When you enter the land which the LORD will give you, as He has promised, you shall observe this rite.

26. "And when your children say to you, 'What does this rite mean to you?'

27. you shall say, 'It is a Passover sacrifice to the LORD who passed over the houses of the sons of Israel in Egypt when He smote the Egyptians, but spared our homes'" And the people bowed low and worshiped.

43. The LORD said to Moses and Aaron, "This is the ordinance of the Passover: no foreigner is to eat of it;

44. but every man's slave purchased with money, after you have circumcised him, then he may eat of it.

45. "A sojourner or a hired servant shall not eat of it.

46. "It is to be eaten in a single house; you are not to bring forth any of the flesh outside of the house, nor are you to break any bone of it.

47. "All the congregation of Israel are to celebrate this.

The meaning of the Passover lamb is stated in the verses 12, 13, and 27. The Passover lamb died for the people of Israel to save their lives from punishment; therefore, when God punished and destroyed the Egyptians due to their disobedience, the people of God were saved and preserved.

In the Gospels, Jesus identified himself as the Passover lamb in terms of his suffering and death. First, Jesus suffered and died on the day of the Passover (Nisan 14th): "You know that after two days the Passover is coming, and the Son of Man is to be handed over for crucifixion" (Matthew 26:2). Second, during the Last Supper, Jesus identified himself as the Passover lamb, which would be slain and consumed soon on the Day of the Passover. In anticipation of his imminent death, he identified his body and blood with the flesh and blood of the slain lamb by using the metaphor of bread and wine.

Matthew 26:26–28

26. While they were eating, Jesus took some bread, and after a blessing, He broke it and gave it to the disciples, and said, "Take, eat; this is My body."
27. And when He had taken a cup and given thanks, He gave it to them, saying, "Drink from it, all of you;
28. for this is My blood of the covenant, which is poured out for many for of sins.

Mark 14:22–24

22. While they were eating, He took some bread, and after a blessing He broke it, and gave it to them, and said, "Take it; this is My body."
23. And when He had taken a cup and given thanks, He gave it to them, and they all drank from it.
24. And He said to them, "This is My blood of the covenant, which is poured out for many.

Luke 22:17–20

17. And when He had taken a cup and given thanks, He said, "Take this and share it among yourselves;
18. for I say to you, I will not drink of the fruit of the vine from now on until the kingdom of God comes."
19. And when He had taken some bread and given thanks, He broke it and gave it to them, saying, "This is My body which is given for you; do this in remembrance of Me."

20. And in the same way He took the cup after they had eaten, saying, "This cup which is poured out for you is the new in My blood.

Further, when we compare the Old Testament text of the Passover and the Gospels' accounts regarding the death of Jesus, the corresponding symbols or typology are found:

Matthew 27:34
They gave Him to drink mixed with gall; and after tasting it, He was unwilling to drink.

Mark 15:23
They tried to give Him mixed with; but He did not take it.

Luke 23:36
The soldiers also mocked Him, coming up to Him, offering Him sour wine

John 19:28–36
28. After this, Jesus, knowing that all things had already been accomplished, to fulfill the Scripture, said, "I am thirsty."
29. 29. A jar full of sour wine was standing there; so they put a sponge full of the sour wine upon a branch of hyssop and brought it up to his mouth.
30. Therefore when Jesus had received the sour wine, He said, "It is finished!" And He bowed his head and gave up his spirit.
31. Then the Jews, because it was the day of preparation, so that the bodies would not remain on the cross on the Sabbath (for that Sabbath was a high day), asked Pilate that their legs might be broken, and that they might be taken away.
32. So the soldiers came, and broke the legs of the first man and of the other who was crucified with Him;
33. but coming to Jesus, when they saw that He was already dead, they did not break his legs.
34. But one of the soldiers pierced his side with a spear, and immediately blood and water came out.

35. And he who has seen has testified, and his testimony is true; and he
    knows that he is telling the truth, so that you also may believe.
36. For these things came to pass to fulfill the Scripture, "NOT A BONE
    OF HIM SHALL BE BROKEN."

Typology of the Passover lamb

Subject	Exodus chapter 12	Gospels
Taste of bitterness	Verse 8 eating bitter herbs	Matthew 27:34 tasting the wine mixed with gall Mark 15:23 tasting the wine mixed with myrrh Luke 23;36 tasting the sour wine John 19:28–29 tasting the sour wine
Red colored dripping hyssop	Verse 22 a bunch of hyssop dipped in the blood	John 19:29 a bunch of hyssop dripping the wine
Torn flesh	Verses 8–9 eating the flesh of the Passover lamb	John 19:34 pierced the side of Jesus with a spear
Unbroken bone	Verse 46 unbroken bone of the Passover lamb	John 19:33 unbroken bone of Jesus

Just as the Passover Lamb was killed for the people of Israel (Exodus
12:3, 27, and 47), Jesus was killed for the sake of the Christian church. In
other words, just as the people of God were saved by virtue of the death

of the Passover lamb when God punished and destroyed the Egyptians, Christians, as the new people of God, were saved by virtue of the death of Jesus when God punished and destroyed Jerusalem and Judea in AD 70. The following diagram of typology might be helpful for understanding:

Typology of Exodus

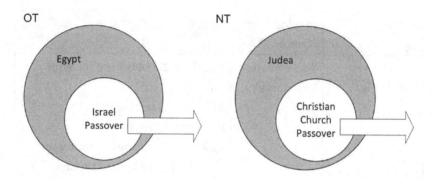

2. Jesus suffered and died as the sacrifice of the Day of Atonement (the Yom Kippur)

The Christian church was saved from the destruction of Jerusalem and Judea by virtue of the atonement of Jesus. What happened after that salvation? After Exodus, ancient Israel could be preserved as the holy kingdom of God by observing the Day of Atonement (the Yom Kippur), but she fell into idolatry and forsook her LORD. Likewise, Jesus suffered and died as the sacrifice of the Yom Kippur and, by virtue of that sacrifice, the Christian church is continuously preserved as the holy kingdom of God on earth.

Let us read the relevant Old Testament texts to understand the meaning of Yom Kippur:

Leviticus 16:3–34
3.   "Aaron shall enter the holy place with this: with a bull for a sin offering and a ram for a burnt offering.

4. "He shall put on the holy linen tunic, and the linen undergarments shall be next to his body, and he shall be girded with the linen sash and attired with the linen turban (these are holy garments) Then he shall bathe his body in water and put them on.

5. "He shall take from the congregation of the sons of Israel two male goats for a sin offering and one ram for a burnt offering.

6. "Then Aaron shall offer the bull for the sin offering which is for himself, that he may make atonement for himself and for his household.

7. "He shall take the two goats and present them before the LORD at the doorway of the tent of meeting.

8. "Aaron shall cast lots for the two goats, one lot for the LORD and the other lot for the scapegoat.

9. "Then Aaron shall offer the goat on which the lot for the LORD fell, and make it a sin offering.

10. "But the goat on which the lot for the scapegoat fell shall be presented alive before the LORD, to make atonement upon it, to send it into the wilderness as the scapegoat.

11. "Then Aaron shall offer the bull of the sin offering which is for himself and make atonement for himself and for his household, and he shall slaughter the bull of the sin offering which is for himself.

12. "He shall take a fire-pan full of coals of fire from upon the altar before the LORD and two handfuls of finely ground sweet incense, and bring it inside the veil.

13. "He shall put the incense on the fire before the LORD, that the cloud of incense may cover the mercy seat that is on the ark of the testimony, otherwise he will die.

14. "Moreover, he shall take some of the blood of the bull and sprinkle it with his finger on the mercy seat on the east side; also in front of the mercy seat he shall sprinkle some of the blood with his finger seven times.

15. "Then he shall slaughter the goat of the sin offering which is for the people, and bring its blood inside the veil and do with its blood as he did with the blood of the bull, and sprinkle it on the mercy seat and in front of the mercy seat.

16. "He shall make atonement for the holy place, because of the impurities of the sons of Israel and because of their transgressions in regard to all their sins; and thus he shall do for the tent of meeting which abides with them in the midst of their impurities.

17. "When he goes in to make atonement in the holy place, no one shall be in the tent of meeting until he comes out, that he may make atonement for himself and for his household and for all the assembly of Israel.

18. "Then he shall go out to the altar that is before the LORD and make atonement for it, and shall take some of the blood of the bull and of the blood of the goat and put it on the horns of the altar on all sides.

19. "With his finger he shall sprinkle some of the blood on it seven times and cleanse it, and from the impurities of the sons of Israel consecrate it.

20. "When he finishes atoning for the holy place and the tent of meeting and the altar, he shall offer the live goat.

21. "Then Aaron shall lay both of his hands on the head of the live goat, and confess over it all the iniquities of the sons of Israel and all their transgressions in regard to all their sins; and he shall lay them on the head of the goat and send it away into the wilderness by the hand of a man who stands in readiness.

22. "The goat shall bear on itself all their iniquities to a solitary land; and he shall release the goat in the wilderness.

23. "Then Aaron shall come into the tent of meeting and take off the linen garments which he put on when he went into the holy place, and shall leave them there.

24. "He shall bathe his body with water in a holy place and put on his clothes, and come forth and offer his burnt offering and the burnt offering of the people and make atonement for himself and for the people.

25. "Then he shall offer up in smoke the fat of the sin offering on the altar.

26. "The one who released the goat as the scapegoat shall wash his clothes and bathe his body with water; then afterward he shall come into the camp.

27. "But the bull of the sin offering and the goat of the sin offering, whose blood was brought in to make atonement in the holy place, shall be taken outside the camp, and they shall burn their hides, their flesh, and their refuse in the fire.

28. "Then the one who burns them shall wash his clothes and bathe his body with water, then afterward he shall come into the camp.
29. "This shall be a permanent statute for you: in the seventh month, on the tenth day of the month, you shall humble your souls and not do any work, whether the native, or the alien who sojourns among you;
30. for it is on this day that atonement shall be made for you to cleanse you; you will be clean from all your sins before the LORD.
31. "It is to be a Sabbath of solemn rest for you, that you may humble your souls; it is a permanent statute.
32. "So the priest who is anointed and ordained to serve as priest in his father's place shall make atonement: he shall thus put on the linen garments, the holy garments,
33. and make atonement for the holy sanctuary, and he shall make atonement for the tent of meeting and for the altar. He shall also make atonement for the priests and for all the people of the assembly.
34. "Now you shall have this as a permanent statute, to make atonement for the sons of Israel for all their sins once every year." And just as the LORD had commanded Moses, so he did.

On Yom Kippur (the tenth day of the seventh month, Tishri), the high priest annually made atonement for himself and for the people of Israel. The sacrificial animals used are as follows:

> For the high priest: A bull for a sin offering and a ram for a burnt offering (verse 3)
> For the people of Israel: Two male goats for a sin offering and one ram for a burnt offering (verse 5)
>
> One for the LORD and the other for the scapegoat (verse 7)

For atonement, the high priest went into the holy place, inside the veil, with the blood of the sacrificial animals for the sin offering (verses 11–17).

In the Gospels, Jesus is identified with the high priest and the sacrificial animals of the sin offering, because a text implies that Jesus entered the holy place right after or at the very moment of his death. Let us read the relevant verses of the Gospels:

Matthew 27:51
And behold, the veil of the temple was torn in two from top to bottom; and the earth shook and the rocks were split.

Mark 15:38
And the veil of the temple was torn in two from top to bottom.

Luke 23:45
because the sun was obscured; and the veil of the temple was torn in two.

The verses describe the event right after or at the very moment of the death of Jesus. Certainly, the torn veil denotes the high priest entering the holy place, inside the veil, with the blood of the sacrificial animals of the sin offering, because traditionally that was the only time that the veil was opened. Therefore, the torn veil implies that Jesus, as high priest, entered the holy place with his own blood at the moment of his death to atone for his people. This role of Jesus as the high priest and also as the sacrificial sin offering is theologized in Hebrews:

Hebrew 6:19–20
19. This hope we have as an anchor of the soul, a hope both sure and steadfast and one which enters within the veil,
20. where Jesus has entered as a forerunner for us, having become a high priest forever according to the order of Melchizedek.

Hebrews 9:11–15
11. But when Christ appeared as a high priest of the good things to come, He entered through the greater and more perfect tabernacle, not made with hands, that is to say, not of this creation;

12. nd not through the blood of goats and calves, but through His own blood, He entered the holy place once for all, having obtained eternal redemption.

13. For if the blood of goats and bulls and the ashes of a heifer sprinkling those who have been defiled sanctify for the cleansing of the flesh,

14. how much more will the blood of Christ, who through the eternal Spirit offered Himself without blemish to God, cleanse your conscience from dead works to serve the living God?

15. For this reason He is the mediator of a new covenant, so that, since a death has taken place for the redemption of the transgressions that were committed under the first covenant, those who have been called may receive the promise of the eternal inheritance.

The author of Hebrews theologized the death of Jesus by making the analogy with Yom Kippur. In this theologization, Jesus, as the high priest, entered into the veil of the spiritual tabernacle with his own blood, making a connection to the sacrificial blood of goats and bulls. Because Jesus was sinless, he did not need to atone for himself; therefore, his blood, his sin offering, must be for the people (Leviticus 16:9, 15, 18).

Also, Jesus is identified with the scapegoat in terms of the desertion and the Resurrection (Leviticus 16: 10, 21–22). What Jesus said on the cross right before his death echoed the voice of the deserted scapegoat:

Matthew 27:46
About the ninth hour Jesus cried out with a loud voice, saying, "ELI, ELI, LAMA SABACHTHANI?" that is, "MY GOD, MY GOD, WHY HAVE YOU FORSAKEN ME?"

Mark 15:34
At the ninth hour Jesus cried out with a loud voice, "ELOI, ELOI, LAMA SABACHTHANI?" which is translated, "MY GOD, MY GOD, WHY HAVE YOU FORSAKEN ME?"

Not only so these verses remind the Jews and the Christians of Psalm 22, but they also reflect the pain of desertion. The cry of the scapegoat, alone in the wilderness and in the face of danger, certainly typologizes the cry of Jesus on the cross at the brink of death. Further, this scapegoat, unlike other sacrificial animals, took away the sin of the people of God alive. The goat was not killed but lived, forever alive in the memory of the people of God. This immortal scapegoat certainly reminds the Christians of the resurrected Jesus. Isn't it true that not only did Jesus die for the sin of his people, but also the resurrected Jesus continues to bear the sin of the Christian church and take it away from the people of God?

Leviticus 16:24 says that the ram was to be offered as the burnt offering to make atonement for the people of God. Therefore, this ram is identified with Jesus, as well.

The whole point is that Jesus, as the high priest as well as the sacrifice of the Yom Kippur (two goats and one ram), made atonement for his people, the Christian church.

Typology of the Death of Jesus

Occasion	O.T.	N.T.
Passover	Flesh and Blood of the Passover lamb	Flesh and Blood of Jesus on the Cross
Yam Kipper	High Priest Death and blood of the goat of the sin offering Scapegoat of the sin offering Ram of the burnt offering Annually	Jesus Death and blood of Jesus Deserted and resurrected Jesus Death of Jesus Once for all or continuously

Therefore, Jesus suffered and died as the Passover lamb to save his people from the destruction of Jerusalem and Judea, and he did this once for all, or continuously, as the sacrifice of Yom Kippur, to preserve his people as the holy people of God; his kingdom as the New Kingdom of God.

Diagram of Jesus as the Mediator

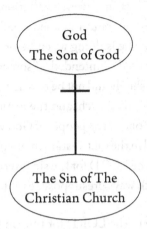

The suffering and death of Jesus as the Passover lamb, and the sacrifice of Yom Kippur, was for the sin of the nation, or the Christian church, and it was an act once and for all, without condition. How about the sin of an individual Christian? When a Christian sins unintentionally, how is he or she redeemed from that sin? The next section is devoted to this question.

Second, Jesus suffered and died for an individual Christian, a citizen of the New Kingdom of God, with condition of repentance.

The people of Israel were saved from the destruction of Egypt by virtue of the sacrifice of the Passover lamb. However, the blood of the slain lamb did not pardon the sin of an individual Israelite after the Exodus. After receiving the Law at Mount Sinai, Yom Kippur was institutionalized. However, the annual Yom Kippur sacrifice did not pardon the sins of an individual Israelite. For example, an individual who did any work on the Sabbath was to be put to death regardless of whether Yom Kippur was observed (Exodus 31:15). Both the Passover and Yom Kippur were related to the sin of the nation, not the individual: through it the nation was saved and preserved. After the covenant was made, an individual had to come to the LORD personally for pardon when he or she committed a sin unintentionally. How was an individual Israelite pardoned?

A corresponding analogy of atonement helps us understand how an individual Christian who is in covenant relationship with Jesus Christ would be pardoned for his or her unintended sin. Even though a Christian can recognize what he or she is doing when he or she commits a sin, still, that sin should be considered unintended. If someone sins against God or Jesus intentionally, he or she should not be considered as a Christian, rather as an enemy of the LORD or church, and the justice of the LORD will be done. A Christian sins as one of the people of God while he or she worships God. Two ways are found in the Old Testament for pardoning an individual: bringing the sacrifice to the LORD for the sin offering and appealing to the mercy of the LORD. Both ways presuppose repentance from a sinner.

1. Bringing the Sacrifice to the LORD for the Sin Offering

Leviticus chapter 4 describes how the sin offering proceeds when an unintentional sin is recognized. Four cases are stated: the priest (verse 3), the whole congregation of Israel (verse 13), a leader (verse 22), and anyone of the common people (verse 27). During Yom Kippur each year, the priest made a sacrifice for atonement for all the sins of the people of Israel. In-between the Yom Kippurs, however, whenever the congregation of Israel or an individual Israelite committed a sin and recognized it, the sin offering was given to the LORD for atonement and forgiveness.

Since all Christians are brothers and sister in Christ, the case of the common individual is most relevant to the subject. Let us read 4:1–2, 27–35 for the case of an individual:

Leviticus 4:1–2, 27–35
1.   Then the LORD spoke to Moses, saying,
2.   "Speak to the sons of Israel, saying, 'If a person s unintentionally in any of the things which the LORD has commanded not to be done, and commits any of them

27. 'Now if anyone of the common people sins unintentionally in doing any of the things which the LORD has commanded not to be done, and becomes guilty,

28. if his sin which he has committed is made known to him, then he shall bring for his offering a goat, a female without defect, for his sin which he has committed.

29. 'He shall lay his hand on the head of the sin offering and slay the sin offering at the place of the burnt offering.

30. 'The priest shall take some of its blood with his finger and put it on the horns of the altar of burnt offering; and all the rest of its blood he shall pour out at the base of the altar.

31. 'Then he shall remove all its fat, just as the fat was removed from the sacrifice of peace offerings; and the priest shall offer it up in smoke on the altar for a soothing aroma to the LORD. Thus the priest shall make atonement for him, and he will be forgiven.

32. 'But if he brings a lamb as his offering for a sin offering, he shall bring it, a female without defect.

33. 'He shall lay his hand on the head of the sin offering and slay it for a sin offering in the place where they slay the burnt offering.

34. 'The priest is to take some of the blood of the sin offering with his finger and put it on the horns of the altar of burnt offering, and all the rest of its blood he shall pour out at the base of the altar.

35. 'Then he shall remove all its fat, just as the fat of the lamb is removed from the sacrifice of the peace offerings, and the priest shall offer them up in smoke on the altar, on the offerings by fire to the LORD Thus the priest shall make atonement for him in regard to his sin which he has committed, and he will be forgiven.

When an individual Israelite sinned unintentionally in doing any of the things which the Lord had commanded not to be done, and recognized his or her sin, he or she was supposed to bring a female goat or lamb to the LORD for the sin offering (verses 28 and 32). Through the intercession of the priest, his or her sin was forgiven and atonement was made (verses 31 and 35). Regardless of Yom Kippur, an individual's sin had to be dealt with personally. Also, when an individual recognized his or her sin and brought a sacrifice to the LORD, that action certainly presupposed "personal repentance."

2. Appealing to the Mercy of the LORD

Unfortunately, we do not have any record in the Old Testament regarding how a common Israelite made atonement for himself or herself. However, two cases of the kings are outstanding: David and Manasseh. They were kings of Israel and Judah, however, their sins should be considered as of an individual, not of the nation, because their sins never represented the sin of Israel or Judah. Let us read the relevant texts:

2 Samuel 12:13–15

13. Then David said to Nathan, "I have sinned against the LORD" And Nathan said to David, "The LORD also has taken away your sin; you shall not die.
14. "However, because by this deed you have given occasion to the enemies of the LORD to blaspheme, the child also that is born to you shall surely die."
15. So Nathan went to his house.

Palm 51:16–17

16. For You do not delight in sacrifice, otherwise I would give it; You are not pleased with burnt offering.
17. The sacrifices of God are a broken spirit; A broken and a contrite heart, O God, You will not despise.

2 Chronicles 33:11–13

11. Therefore the LORD brought the commanders of the army of the king of Assyria against them, and they captured Manasseh with hooks, bound him with bronze chains and took him to Babylon.
12. When he was in distress, he entreated the LORD his God and humbled himself greatly before the God of his fathers.

13. When he prayed to Him, He was moved by his entreaty and heard his supplication, and brought him again to Jerusalem to his kingdom Then Manasseh knew that the LORD was God.

Isaiah 1:11–16
11. "What are your multiplied sacrifices to Me?" Says the LORD. "I have had enough of burnt offerings of rams And the fat of fed cattle; And I take no pleasure in the blood of bulls, lambs or goats.
12. "When you come to appear before Me, Who requires of you this trampling of My courts?
13. "Bring your worthless offerings no longer, Incense is an abomination to Me New moon and Sabbath, the calling of assemblies-- I cannot endure iniquity and the solemn assembly.
14. "I hate your new moon festivals and your appointed feasts, They have become a burden to Me; I am weary of bearing them.
15. "So when you spread out your hands in prayer, I will hide My eyes from you; Yes, even though you multiply prayers, I will not listen Your hands are covered with blood.
16. "Wash yourselves, make yourselves clean; Remove the evil of your deeds from My sight Cease to do evil,
17. Learn to do good; Seek justice, Reprove the ruthless, Defend the orphan, Plead for the widow.

We do not know whether or not David or Manasseh, as a leader of the nation, brought a sacrifice to the LORD for the sin offering according to Leviticus chapter 4. According to the texts, however, forgiveness granted to them was based upon their repentance and the mercy of the LORD without a sin offering. Considering Palm 51, which is believed to have been written by David right after he was notified by Nathan about his sin, it seems that David did not offer any sin offering for his sin (verses 16 and 17). Proto Isaiah (Isaiah 1–39), which is believed to have been written around time of Manasseh, also emphasizes the significance of status of mind and just actions rather than a mere offering (Isaiah 1:11–16). For both cases, Yom Kippur did not pardon their personal sins, but, the mercy of the LORD responded to a personal repentance.

It seems difficult to find any directly relevant account in the Gospels that relates the suffering and death of Jesus to the atonement of an individual Christian's sin. However, if we compare the requirements for atonement in the Old Testament, a case can be made that Jesus's suffering and death met the requirement of a sin offering for an Israelite. Because Jesus's suffering and death was once and for all and was already manifested in an action of mercy for his people, we can reasonably draw parallels between the two. In this context, Jesus suffered and died for an individual Christian, a citizen of the New Kingdom of God, upon the condition of repentance. In other words, when an individual Christian sins unintentionally by doing any of the things which Jesus had commanded not to be done, and recognizes his or her sin, he or she should repent the sin and will be forgiven by virtue of the mercy of the suffering and death of Jesus. Therefore, personal repentance is the condition upon which an individual Christian receives the benefit of atonement from the sacrifice of Jesus. If he or she does not repent his or her sin when it is recognized, or when he or she does not recognize his or her sin for long enough (from the perspective of Jesus and according to his justice), the proper divine actions will be taken in the life of an individual Christian. That engagement would include discipline, punishment, and judgment for the purpose of sanctifying a child of God. The process of sanctification consists of the dynamics of reciprocal movement of repentance and forgiveness:

The Paradigm for the Dynamics of Sanctification

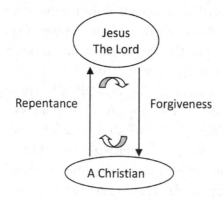

In conclusion Jesus, as mediator, suffered and died for the nation, the Christian church, once for all without condition, and he did so for an individual Christian upon the condition that he or she repents his or her sin. In other words, Jesus suffered and died as the Passover lamb to save the Christian church from the destruction of Jerusalem and Judea. It was as the sacrifice of Yom Kippur to preserve the Christian church. And it was as a female goat or lamb to forgive and sanctify individual Christians.

Before we move to the next section, Jesus as God, I will define the meaning of the Resurrection, which happened in-between his death and ascension.

The Meaning of the Resurrection

The relevant texts: Matthew 28:1–20, Mark 16:1–18, Luke 24:1–50, John 20:1–21:25

Since Jesus died as the mediator, logically he had to be raised from death to be able to return from where he came. However, beyond this logic, the Resurrection has an important theological meaning: The completion of the earthly life of Jesus.

A. The Completion of Jesus as the Sovereign

Jesus tried to prove his sovereign identity during his ministry. The signs and the miracles he performed played a significant role in proving this, and the Resurrection was the culmination of them. In other words, the Resurrection provided the most reliable evidence to the disciples that Jesus is the Son of God and the Christ (Messiah). Those who met the resurrected Jesus had no doubt about his sovereign identity. In addition, through the Resurrection, Jesus became the eternal sovereign, because from a human perspective one who is dead cannot reign as the Christ. If Jesus were not resurrected, no one could be sure whether or not his spirit continues to reign over his people.

B. The Completion of Jesus as the Educator

Jesus obeyed God, his Father, and taught his people how to live as the people of God according to the will of God. If Jesus was not resurrected, his commandment and teachings would not have any authority over his people, because they would see the result of obedience was merely suffering and death. Who would know what happened to the soul and spirit of Jesus? The Resurrection of Jesus proved that God ultimately rewarded the suffering and death of his obedient Son with glory. Therefore, on the basis of the Resurrection of Jesus, Christians can continue to observe his commandment and teachings with conviction.

C. The Completion of Jesus as the Mediator

Jesus suffered and died for his people as a redemptive sacrifice for their sin. To be this redemptive sacrifice, Jesus had to be sinless, otherwise, his suffering and death could be the result of his own sin. If Jesus was not resurrected, the possibility that Jesus died because of his own sin would remain. Through the Resurrection, that possibility was excluded and his innocence was proved by God; therefore, Christians can continue to be sure of redemption through Jesus Christ.

Thoughts on the Resurrection

The Christian church should celebrate the Resurrection of Jesus because it was Jesus who was resurrected, not merely because a human being overcame death. No Jew would celebrate if Herod the Great had been resurrected. As far as I know, no one wants Hitler to be resurrected. If a bad person is resurrected and continues to engage in this physical world, there is no reason to celebrate overcoming human death. In fact, we should remember that sometimes the world celebrates a death of a human being. But since merciful and powerful Jesus was resurrected, the Christian church celebrates his Resurrection, and Christians can continue to have hope for healing and restoration of their lives. Certainly, the world has a reason to join in that celebration.

Concluding that Christians will be resurrected in the future because Jesus was resurrected brings ambiguity to Christian theology. What is the difference between the immortal soul or spirit and the immortal resurrected being? Is one necessarily better than the other? To those who believe in the immortality of the soul and that their spirit will be in peace after death, is it really necessary for them to believe that they would also have a resurrected body after death?

It should be understood that the resurrection of the saints was a one-time event, which happened in AD 70 to those who were martyred in the Palestine region before hand, in conjunction with the Second Coming of Jesus and the destruction of Jerusalem and Judea. The same would hold true for the bodily ascension of the saints.

Therefore, Christian theology should focus upon the theological meaning and importance of Christ's Resurrection, rather than the resurrection of the Christians.

d. Jesus as God

In the Resurrection, Jesus completed his mission on earth and ascended to where he came from, to God the Father. The Ascension of Jesus completed his circle of life, and with his ascension, Jesus should be considered equal to God in authority. The image used in scripture for Jesus is the Word. Corresponding to this, the concept for Christians is human beings who bear the true image of God.

The Son of God is the sovereign identity of Jesus. However, whether the Son of God is God or the son of God has been a significant theological argument: The Arian Controversy.

Jesus = The Son of God < God / The Son of God

I do not want to spend space describing this age-old argument. Certainly, both sides have both logical problems as well as a biblical basis. If someone believes that the Son of God is God, in general, he or she would be regarded as a Trinitarian and inclined to faith. If someone believes that the Son of God is the son of God, in general, he or she would be regarded as an Unitarian and inclined to reason. I will approach this theological issue from a practical viewpoint for Christians. As I already stated in the previous section, "Jesus as the Sovereign," God handed over authority to his son to judge his people, forgive the sins of his people, and possess the belongings of God. Let us read the texts to refresh:

Matthew 9:6, 8
6.   "But so that you may know that the Son of Man has authority on earth to forgive sins"--then He said to the paralytic, "Get up, pick up your bed and go home."
8.   But when the crowds saw this, they were awestruck, and glorified God, who had given such authority to men.

Matthew 11:27
"All things have been handed over to Me by My Father; and no one knows the Son except the Father; nor does anyone know the Father except the Son, and anyone to whom the Son wills to reveal Him.

Matthew 28:18
And Jesus came up and spoke to them, saying, "All authority has been given to Me in heaven and on earth.

Mark 2:10
"But so that you may know that the Son of Man has authority on earth to forgive sins"--He said to the paralytic.

Luke 10:22
"All things have been handed over to Me by My Father, and no one knows who the Son is except the Father, and who the Father is except the Son, and anyone to whom the Son wills to reveal Him."

John 5:22, 26–27

22. "For not even the Father judges anyone, but He has given all judgment to the Son,
26. "For just as the Father has life in Himself, even so He gave to the Son also to have life in Himself;
27. and He gave Him authority to execute judgment, because He is the Son of Man.

John 10:18

"No one has taken it away from Me, but I lay it down on My own initiative I have authority to lay it down, and I have authority to take it up again This commandment I received from My Father."

John 16:15

"All things that the Father has are Mine; therefore I said that He takes of Mine and will disclose it to you.

John 17:2

even as You gave Him authority over all flesh, that to all whom You have given Him, He may give eternal life.

John 17:10

and all things that are Mine are Yours, and Yours are Mine; and I have been glorified in them

This handed-over authority is the primary claim of Jesus in the Gospels regarding the relationship between the Father and the Son. Moreover, Jesus claimed that the Father gave him the Father's own name (Yahweh), and even though a Christian prays to God, Jesus, himself, receives and answers that prayer:

John 14:13–14

13. "Whatever you ask in My name, that will I do, so that the Father may be glorified in the Son.
14. "If you ask Me anything in My name, I will do it.

John 16:23–24, 26

23. "In that day you will not question Me about anything Truly, truly, I say to you, if you ask the Father for anything in My name, He will give it to you. (NASB)

23. In that day you will no longer ask me anything. I tell you the truth, my Father will give you whatever you ask in my name. (NIV)

24. "Until now you have asked for nothing in My name; ask and you will receive, so that your joy may be made full.

26. "In that day you will ask in My name, and I do not say to you that I will request of the Father on your behalf.

John 17:11–12

11. "I am no longer in the world; and yet they themselves are in the world, and I come to You Holy Father, keep them in Your name, the name which You have given Me, that they may be one even as We are.

12. "While I was with them, I was keeping them in Your name which You have given Me; and I guarded them and not one of them perished but the son of perdition, so that the Scripture would be fulfilled.

According to the texts, the name "Jesus" is the name "Yahweh," and there is no difference between God, the Father, and Jesus, the Son, in terms of authority. From a practical viewpoint for Christians, therefore, there should be no problem for Jesus to be called God. The argument that Jesus is the "same substance" (ὁμοούσιος, homooúsios) with God, in fact, becomes meaningless. To Christians, Jesus is God.

The life of Jesus as a person can be summarized as follows: Jesus came from God as the Sovereign to his people; he taught as the Educator those who believed and received his sovereign identity; and he suffered and died as the Mediator for the sin of those who live according to his commandment and teachings. The images of Jesus and the Christians are as follows:

Image of Jesus and Christians

Life of Jesus	Image of Jesus	Image of the Christians
The Sovereign	King, lord, shepherd, groom, and friend	The people, children, sheep, bride, and friend
The Educator	Teacher (rabbi) and prophet	The disciples
The Mediator	The high priest and the sacrifice	The righteous or the saints
The God	The Word	The true image of God

B. Life as a Nation, the New Israel

The life of Jesus should be understood as a nation as well as a person. Jesus recapitulated the history of Israel.

Comparison of the History of Israel and Life of Jesus

The history of Israel started at the Exodus from Egypt; the crossing of the Red Sea marked that historical event. After the Exodus, Israel stayed in the wilderness for forty years. During that period, Israel was tempted for their faith to the LORD (Deuteronomy 8:2 and 16). Israel entered the Promised Land and established a kingdom; however, due to the sins of the nation, first, the northern kingdom, Israel, was destroyed by the Assyrians, and then the southern kingdom, Judah including the temple and Jerusalem, was destroyed by the Babylonians. The Davidic dynasty lasted until it was ended by the Babylonians in 587 BC. Israel (represented by Judah) entered the Babylonian captivity, marking the death of the nation with the sorrow and bitterness of the people of God. After about 70 years of captivity, however, Israel (represented by Judah) was restored by God and the temple and Jerusalem were rebuilt.

We observe an analogy of the history of Israel and the life of Jesus. Matthew 2:13–15 states: "Now when they had gone, behold, an angel of the Lord appeared to Joseph in a dream and said, 'Get up! Take the Child and his mother and flee to Egypt, and remain there until I tell you; for Herod is going to search for the Child to destroy Him.' So Joseph got up and took the Child and his mother while it was still night, and left for Egypt. He remained there until the death of Herod. This was to fulfill what had been spoken by the Lord through the prophet: 'out of Egypt I called my son.'"

The child, Jesus, was taken to Egypt to escape Herod and he came back to Palestine when Herod died. Matthew interpreted that incident as the fulfillment of Hosea 11:1 ("When Israel was a youth I loved him, and out of Egypt I called my son"), which was, in fact, a reminiscence of Exodus. Therefore, Matthew identified Jesus with the young nation of Israel. In the beginning of Jesus's ministry, John the Baptist baptized Jesus (Matthew 3:13–17, Mark 1:9–11, Luke 3:21–22, John 1:29–34). This "out of water" experience of Jesus may correspond to Israel crossing the Red Sea at the Exodus. Paul also interpreted the passing through the Red Sea as baptism in 1 Corinthians 10:1–2. Right after baptism, Jesus was led into the wilderness for forty days to be tempted (Matthew 4:1–11, Mark 1:12–13, Luke 4:1–13). During the period, Jesus quoted the words from Deuteronomy to respond to three temptations (Deuteronomy 8:3, 6:18, and 6:13). Therefore, when the number forty, the purpose of being in the wilderness (temptation), and Jesus's quotations are considered, it is clear that Jesus identified himself with Israel in the wilderness. After the forty days of temptation in the wilderness, Jesus proclaimed the coming of the kingdom of God and taught about that kingdom until the last days of his life. Therefore, in terms of the kingdom, Jesus's public ministry corresponds to the years of the ancient kingdom of Israel. Following this, Jesus suffered and died on the cross. His suffering and death correspond to the suffering and death of the nation Israel (Judah). Jesus stayed in the tomb for three days. These days correspond to the Babylonian captivity of Israel (Judah). After staying in the tomb, Jesus was resurrected by God according to his promise. His miraculous resurrection corresponds to the restoration of Israel (Judah) from the Babylonian captivity, brought about by God according to God's promise.

As I mentioned in the previous Section A, Jesus's life, when understood in the context of Isaiah 53 or the servant songs of Isaiah, is parallel to the nation Israel. The suffering and death of Jesus, as well as his resurrection, stand for the restoration of Israel from the Babylonian Captivity. In this context, the Christian church, as the new faith community that witnesses the Resurrection of Jesus, can be understood as the true restored Israel, the renewed kingdom of God.

In addition to this understanding, the suffering and death of Jesus can be understood as foreshadowing the destruction of Judea happened in AD 70 just as death of Judah who betrayed Jesus did. Likewise, the resurrection of Jesus can be understood as forecasting the Christian Church that was born on the Pentecost as the new Kingdom of God. In this regard, the Christian Church is spiritual like the resurrected Jesus; it is immortal as the resurrected kingdom; it is bodiless because it is not confined to a land like other nations. The prediction made by Jesus in Luke 23:28–30 may illustrate this viewpoint. When Jesus was on the way to the cross, a large crowd of the people, especially of women who were mourning and lamenting him followed him. However, Jesus turned to those women and said, "Daughters of Jerusalem, stop weeping for me, but weep for yourselves and for your children.

For behold, the days are coming when they will say, 'Blessed are the barren, and the wombs that never bore, and the breasts that never nursed.' Then they will begin to say the mountains, 'fall on us,' and to the hills, 'cover us.' For if they do these things when the tree is green, what will happen when it is dry?"

Certainly, Jesus was talking about the coming destruction of Jerusalem and Judea in AD 70. At the same time, it may be understood as that Jesus identified his death with the end of Judea. He foreshadowed the death of the nation over the death of an individual.

As the result of the life of Jesus, the Christian church was born. In the next chapter, I will define the Christian church

CHAPTER 2
The Christian Church as the Fulfilled Kingdom of God on Earth

The Christian church is the fulfilled kingdom of God on earth. During his public ministry, Jesus prophesied the imminent coming of the church and taught about the church in terms of the kingdom of God or the kingdom of heaven. The church as the kingdom began at Pentecost in the year Jesus was killed and was fulfilled in AD 70. Unlike Judah or Israel which were bound to the land, the church is the congregation of the people of God who hold the primary faith—land and location are not factors. Unlike Judah or Israel, the church as a whole was (is) not destroyed by God because Jesus atoned for the church. Since the church is the kingdom that came to earth from heaven and is not to be destroyed, the church is the eternal kingdom of God.

A. The Origin of the Christian Church

The Christian church started on Pentecost; however, it was neither simply created as another new kingdom on earth nor did it simply succeed the previous kingdom, Israel or Judah. It originated from the kingdom of God in heaven, the spiritual domain. In this sense, even though the Christian church should be understood in comparison to ancient Israel or Judah (Judea) for its tradition and components, the origin of the church should be distinguished from supersessionism that sees the church as the fulfillment of the Old Covenant. The Christian church, in a sense, replaced Judea in terms of the historicity of the kingdom of God on earth, but it did not fulfill the Abrahamic or Mosaic covenant. It is the new kingdom of God that came down from heaven to earth.

The Christian Church is not the Fulfillment of the Abrahamic Covenant
The Abrahamic covenant is described in Genesis 12:1–3, 13:14–17, 15:1–21, 17:1–22, 22:16–18, 26:1–5, 28:13–15, and 35:11–13. The most significant component of the covenant is the land. God promised a particular land to Abraham and his descendants. However, the Christian Church is not bound to that promised land, nor, in fact, to any land. In addition, descendants, multiplied like the stars of heaven, were promised in the covenant. However, Moses proclaimed that that promise was fulfilled right before the people of Israel entered the Promised Land: "Your fathers went down to Egypt seventy persons in all, and now the LORD your God has made you as numerous as the stars of heaven" (Deuteronomy 10:22). Therefore, the Christian church cannot be the fulfillment of the Abrahamic covenant.

The Christian Church is not the Fulfillment of the Mosaic Covenant
The Mosaic covenant is described in Exodus chapter 19 to chapter 24, verse 8. The most significant component of the covenant is law. When the people of Israel observed the Law, Israel could be the possession of God, the kingdom of priests, and the holy nation of God. The Christian church never fulfilled the Mosaic Law. It has its own Law (the New Commandment and teachings of Jesus) for which all Christians are bound. Moreover, its existence as the holy kingdom depends upon the eternal atonement of Jesus, not on observance of the Law of the Christian church. Since the annual atonement of Israel did not negate their obligation to observe the Mosaic Law (that was why God could destroy Israel and Judah), the eternal atonement of Jesus cannot be said to fulfill the Mosaic covenant. Jesus himself clearly talked about this issue in Matthew 5:1–48, the first chapter of the Sermon on the Mount. Verse 17 says, "Do not think that I came to abolish the Law or the Prophets; I did not come to abolish but to fulfill (πληρῶσαι)." Here, πληρῶσαι is Aorist-Infinitive-Active of πληρόω, which is translated as "I fill," "I fulfill," or "I complete." In chapter 5, Jesus

reinterprets the Mosaic laws and asks the disciples for higher ethics and morality rather than superficial observance of the Mosaic laws. Therefore, when Jesus said "I fulfill," that meant the completion of the nature of the law or ethics, not the Mosaic laws nor eternal atonement. In verse 20, Jesus even said, "For I say to you that unless your righteousness surpasses that of the scribes and Pharisees, you will not enter the kingdom of heaven." Therefore, there is no way for the Christian church to be the fulfillment of the Mosaic covenant.

The Christian Church Originated from Heaven as the New Kingdom of God or Heaven

Jesus came to the Jews as the promised Messiah, however, he was rejected by the Jewish authority and started the Christian church with a few who believed his sovereign identity. In this sense, Jesus fulfilled the Davidic covenant because of his eternal Messiahship. However, that fact does not mean that the Christian church is the fulfillment of the Abrahamic or Mosaic covenant, since the Davidic covenant was the personal covenant between God and David, not one that involved the land, the people, and the Law. In other words, the rejected, promised Messiah started the new kingdom, the Christian church, with the new people and the new Law. Therefore, in spite of a strong analogy between Israel (Judah) and the Christian church, the Christian church is not subject to the history of Israel or Judah, nor the fulfillment or result of that history. The fact that Jesus called twelve disciples manifests the intention of Jesus to start the new kingdom of God.

We can catch a glimpse of God's idea of starting a new kingdom in the Old Testament. According to Exodus 32:10, God wanted to start all over again with Moses even after the Abrahamic and Mosaic covenants: "Now then let Me alone, that My anger may burn against them and that I may destroy them; and I will make of you a great nation." Jesus also implied that the Christian church is the new kingdom, not the succession of the old kingdom, in the parable of a new garment and wine (Matthew 9:16–17, Mark 2:21–22, Luke 5:36–38). The Christian church originated from heaven, the spiritual domain. Jesus was the Son of God, not a human messiah. The Son of God came down on earth, the physical domain, to be the Sovereign of the Christian church where he continues to reign over his kingdom. The Holy Spirit came down on the Christians from heaven and continues to lead and help them. The first part of the Lord's Prayer also implies that the Christian church originated from heaven.

Matthew 6:9–10

9. "Pray, then, in this way: 'Our Father who is in heaven, Hallowed be Your name
10. 'Your kingdom come Your will be done, On earth as it is in heaven.

We see the contrast between heaven and earth and the prayer expresses the desire that the kingdom in heaven comes down on earth. Since the kingdom meant the Christian church by Jesus, this part of the Lord's Prayer was fulfilled through the Pentecost and AD 70 destruction (this aspect will be discussed in detail in the next section). Therefore, the Christian church originated from heaven, not from Israel or Judah. In addition, the kingdom of God in heaven and the Christian church on earth are intrinsically the same in terms of sovereignty: Jesus reigns over the kingdom of God in heaven as well as on earth. In this regard, the Christian church should be called the kingdom of heaven and a Christian is already in the eternal kingdom of heaven. Therefore, to Christians, death means simply a different mode of existence: a Christian always lives in the kingdom of heaven regardless of the mode of existence.

B. Prophesy and Fulfillment of the Christian Church

In the Gospels, Jesus prophesied and taught about the coming of the Christian church in terms of the kingdom of God or heaven. Moreover, as I stated in the previous section, Jesus taught the disciples the prayer for the coming of the Christian church: The Lord's Prayer. Jesus's prophesy about the Christian church was quickly fulfilled. The Christian church as the kingdom of God or heaven started at Pentecost, seven weeks after Jesus was resurrected, and was completed in AD 70, less than forty years after Jesus was resurrected. Therefore, Christians should not wait for the future fulfillment of the kingdom of God: The Christian church is not the unfulfilled entity that waits for the future fulfillment: It is the fulfilled kingdom of God or heaven.

Let us read the relevant Gospel texts:

Prophecy

Matthew 3:2
"Repent, for the kingdom of heaven is at hand."

Matthew 4:17
From that time Jesus began to preach and say, "Repent, for the kingdom of heaven is at hand."

Matthew 10:7
"And as you go, preach, saying, 'The kingdom of heaven is at hand.'

Mark 1:15
and saying, "The time is fulfilled, and the kingdom of God is at hand; repent and believe in the gospel."

Luke 4:43
But He said to them, "I must preach the kingdom of God to the other cities also, for I was sent for this purpose."

Luke 8:1
Soon afterwards, He began going around from one city and village to another, proclaiming and preaching the kingdom of God. The twelve were with Him.

Luke 10:9
and heal those in it who are sick, and say to them, 'The kingdom of God has come near to you.'

Luke 16:16

"The Law and the Prophets were proclaimed until John; since that time the gospel of the kingdom of God has been preached, and everyone is forcing his way into it.

Teaching

Matthew 5:3

"Blessed are the poor in spirit, for theirs is the kingdom of heaven.

Luke 6:20

And turning his gaze toward his disciples, He began to say, "Blessed are you who are poor, for yours is the kingdom of God.

Mark 4:26, 30

26. And He was saying, "The kingdom of God is like a man who casts seed upon the soil;

30. And He said, "How shall we picture the kingdom of God, or by what parable shall we present it?

Luke 13:18

So He was saying, "What is the kingdom of God like, and to what shall I compare it?

Matthew 13:18–52

18. "Hear then the parable of the sower.

19. "When anyone hears the word of the kingdom and does not understand it, the evil one comes and snatches away what has been sown in his heart. This is the one on whom seed was sown beside the road.

20. "The one on whom seed was sown on the rocky places, this is the man who hears the word and immediately receives it with joy;

21. yet he has no firm root in himself, but is only temporary, and when affliction or persecution arises because of the word, immediately he falls away.

22. "And the one on whom seed was sown among the thorns, this is the man who hears the word, and the worry of the world and the deceitfulness of wealth choke the word, and it becomes unfruitful.

23. "And the one on whom seed was sown on the good soil, this is the man who hears the word and understands it; who indeed bears fruit and brings forth, some a hundredfold, some sixty, and some thirty."

24. Jesus presented another parable to them, saying, "The kingdom of heaven may be compared to a man who sowed good seed in his field.

25. "But while his men were sleeping, his enemy came and sowed tares among the wheat, and went away.

26. "But when the wheat sprouted and bore grain, then the tares became evident also.

27. "The slaves of the landowner came and said to him, 'Sir, did you not sow good seed in your field? How then does it have tares?'

28. "And he said to them, 'An enemy has done this!' The slaves said to him, 'Do you want us, then, to go and gather them up?'

29. "But he said, 'No; for while you are gathering up the tares, you may uproot the wheat with them.

30. 'Allow both to grow together until the harvest; and in the time of the harvest I will say to the reapers, "First gather up the tares and bind them in bundles to burn them up; but gather the wheat into my barn."'

31. He presented another parable to them, saying, "The kingdom of heaven is like a mustard seed, which a man took and sowed in his field;

32. and this is smaller than all other seeds, but when it is full grown, it is larger than the garden plants and becomes a tree, so that THE BIRDS OF THE AIR come and NEST IN ITS BRANCHES."

33. He spoke another parable to them, "The kingdom of heaven is like leaven, which a woman took and hid in three pecks of flour until it was all leavened."

34. All these things Jesus spoke to the crowds in parables, and He did not speak to them without a parable.

35. This was to fulfill what was spoken through the prophet: "I WILL OPEN MY MOUTH IN PARABLES; I WILL UTTER THINGS HIDDEN SINCE THE FOUNDATION OF THE WORLD."

36. Then He left the crowds and went into the house And his disciples came to Him and said, "Explain to us the parable of the tares of the field."

37. And He said, "The one who sows the good seed is the Son of Man,

38. and the field is the world; and as for the good seed, these are the sons of the kingdom; and the tares are the sons of the evil one;

39. and the enemy who sowed them is the devil, and the harvest is the end of the age; and the reapers are angels.

40. "So just as the tares are gathered up and burned with fire, so shall it be at the end of the age.

41. "The Son of Man will send forth his angels, and they will gather out of his kingdom all stumbling blocks, and those who commit lawlessness,

42. and will throw them into the furnace of fire; in that place there will be weeping and gnashing of teeth.

43. "Then THE RIGHTEOUS WILL SHINE FORTH AS THE SUN in the kingdom of their Father He who has ears, let him hear.

44. "The kingdom of heaven is like a treasure hidden in the field, which a man found and hid again; and from joy over it he goes and sells all that he has and buys that field.

45. "Again, the kingdom of heaven is like a merchant seeking fine pearls,

46. and upon finding one pearl of great value, he went and sold all that he had and bought it.

47. "Again, the kingdom of heaven is like a dragnet cast into the sea, and gathering fish of every kind;

48. and when it was filled, they drew it up on the beach; and they sat down and gathered the good fish into containers, but the bad they threw away.

49. "So it will be at the end of the age; the angels will come forth and take out the wicked from among the righteous,

50. and will throw them into the furnace of fire; in that place there will be weeping and gnashing of teeth.

51. "Have you understood all these things?" They said to Him, "Yes."

52. And Jesus said to them, "Therefore every scribe who has become a disciple of the kingdom of heaven is like a head of a household, who brings out of his treasure things new and old."

Matthew 20:1–16

1. "For the kingdom of heaven is like a landowner who went out early in the morning to hire laborers for his vineyard.
2. "When he had agreed with the laborers for a denarius for the day, he sent them into his vineyard.
3. "And he went out about the third hour and saw others standing idle in the market place;
4. and to those he said, 'You also go into the vineyard, and whatever is right I will give you.' And so they went.
5. "Again he went out about the sixth and the ninth hour, and did the same thing.
6. "And about the eleventh hour he went out and found others standing around; and he said to them, 'Why have you been standing here idle all day long?'
7. "They said to him, 'Because no one hired us.' He said to them, 'You go into the vineyard too.'
8. "When evening came, the owner of the vineyard said to his foreman, 'Call the laborers and pay them their wages, beginning with the last group to the first.'
9. "When those hired about the eleventh hour came, each one received a denarius.
10. "When those hired first came, they thought that they would receive more; but each of them also received a denarius.
11. "When they received it, they grumbled at the landowner,
12. saying, 'These last men have worked only one hour, and you have made them equal to us who have borne the burden and the scorching heat of the day.'
13. "But he answered and said to one of them, 'Friend, I am doing you no wrong; did you not agree with me for a denarius?
14. 'Take what is yours and go, but I wish to give to this last man the same as to you.
15. 'Is it not lawful for me to do what I wish with what is my own? Or is your eye envious because I am generous?'
16. "So the last shall be first, and the first last."

Matthew 22:1–14

1. Jesus spoke to them again in parables, saying,

2. "The kingdom of heaven may be compared to a king who gave a wedding feast for his son.

3. "And he sent out his slaves to call those who had been invited to the wedding feast, and they were unwilling to come.

4. "Again he sent out other slaves saying, 'Tell those who have been invited, "Behold, I have prepared my dinner; my oxen and my fattened livestock are all butchered and everything is ready; come to the wedding feast."'

5. "But they paid no attention and went their way, one to his own farm, another to his business,

6. and the rest seized his slaves and mistreated them and killed them.

7. "But the king was enraged, and he sent his armies and destroyed those murderers and set their city on fire.

8. "Then he said to his slaves, 'The wedding is ready, but those who were invited were not worthy.

9. 'Go therefore to the main highways, and as many as you find there, invite to the wedding feast.'

10. "Those slaves went out into the streets and gathered together all they found, both evil and good; and the wedding hall was filled with dinner guests.

11. "But when the king came in to look over the dinner guests, he saw a man there who was not dressed in wedding clothes,

12. and he said to him, 'Friend, how did you come in here without wedding clothes?' And the man was speechless.

13. "Then the king said to the servants, 'Bind him hand and foot, and throw him into the outer darkness; in that place there will be weeping and gnashing of teeth.'

14. "For many are called, but few are chosen."

Matthew 25:1–30

1. "Then the kingdom of heaven will be comparable to ten virgins, who took their lamps and went out to meet the bridegroom.

2. "Five of them were foolish, and five were prudent.

3. "For when the foolish took their lamps, they took no oil with them,

4. but the prudent took oil in flasks along with their lamps.

5. "Now while the bridegroom was delaying, they all got drowsy and began to sleep.

6. "But at midnight there was a shout, 'Behold, the bridegroom! Come out to meet him.'

7. "Then all those virgins rose and trimmed their lamps.

8. "The foolish said to the prudent, 'Give us some of your oil, for our lamps are going out.'

9. "But the prudent answered, 'No, there will not be enough for us and you too; go instead to the dealers and buy some for yourselves.'

10. "And while they were going away to make the purchase, the bridegroom came, and those who were ready went in with him to the wedding feast; and the door was shut.

11. "Later the other virgins also came, saying, 'Lord, lord, open up for us.'

12. "But he answered, 'Truly I say to you, I do not know you.'

13. "Be on the alert then, for you do not know the day nor the hour.

14. "For it is just like a man about to go on a journey, who called his own slaves and entrusted his possessions to them.

15. "To one he gave five talents, to another, two, and to another, one, each according to his own ability; and he went on his journey.

16. "Immediately the one who had received the five talents went and traded with them, and gained five more talents.

17. "In the same manner the one who had received the two talents gained two more.

18. "But he who received the one talent went away, and dug a hole in the ground and hid his master's money.

19. "Now after a long time the master of those slaves came and settled accounts with them.

20. "The one who had received the five talents came up and brought five more talents, saying, 'Master, you entrusted five talents to me. See, I have gained five more talents.'

21. "His master said to him, 'Well done, good and faithful slave You were faithful with a few things, I will put you in charge of many things; enter into the joy of your master.'

22. "Also the one who had received the two talents came up and said, 'Master, you entrusted two talents to me. See, I have gained two more talents.'

23. "His master said to him, 'Well done, good and faithful slave. You were faithful with a few things, I will put you in charge of many things; enter into the joy of your master.'

24. "And the one also who had received the one talent came up and said, 'Master, I knew you to be a hard man, reaping where you did not sow and gathering where you scattered no seed.

25. 'And I was afraid, and went away and hid your talent in the ground. See, you have what is yours.'

26. "But his master answered and said to him, 'You wicked, lazy slave, you knew that I reap where I did not sow and gather where I scattered no seed.

27. 'Then you ought to have put my money in the bank, and on my arrival I would have received my money back with interest.

28. 'Therefore take away the talent from him, and give it to the one who has the ten talents.'

29. "For to everyone who has, more shall be given, and he will have an abundance; but from the one who does not have, even what he does have shall be taken away.

30. "Throw out the worthless slave into the outer darkness; in that place there will be weeping and gnashing of teeth.

First, the kingdom of God and the kingdom of heaven are exchangeable terminology (compare Matthew 3:2 with Mark 1:15 and Luke 10:9; and Matthew 5:3 with Luke 6:20; and Mark 4:26, 30 and Luke 13:18 with Matthew 13:18–52, 20:1–16, 21:1–14, and 25:1–30). The kingdom of heaven is the terminology Matthew coined for the kingdom of God.

Second, the kingdom of heaven in Matthew actually means the coming Christian church. Therefore, both the kingdom of God and the kingdom of heaven in the Gospels, in fact, mean the Christian church. The parables of the kingdom of heaven in Matthew clarify this fact.

The summary of the parables of the kingdom of heaven in Matthew

Text	Parable	Location	Possible Audience	Key Point
Matthew 13:18–52	The sower	The good soil	Farmers	Growth
	A man of good seed	The field	Farmers	False Christians
	A mustard seed	The field	Farmers	Growth
	Leaven	Three pecks of flour	Women	Growth
	A treasure	Field	Investor	Value
	A merchant	Economic world	Merchants	Value
	A dragnet	Under the water	Fishermen	False Christians
Matthew 20:1–16	A landowner	Vineyard	The disciples	Generosity
Matthew 22:1–14	A king	The wedding feast	The Jewish leaders	Invitation
Matthew 25:1–30	Ten virgins	The wedding feast	The disciples	Readiness
	The master	Economic world	The disciples	Diligence

Due to the word "heaven" in the term "the kingdom of heaven," some Christians assume that the kingdom of heaven in Matthew is the one a Christian will enter after death or the kingdom that the Christian church would meet in the future. However, when we read the relevant texts closely, we can find that all locations of the kingdom of heaven in the parables are earth-bound. In fact, the kingdom of heaven in Matthew means the coming Christian church on earth. As Jesus promised in Matthew 21:43

and Luke 12:32, the disciples received the kingdom, in other words, the Christian church:

Matthew 21:43

"Therefore I say to you, the kingdom of God will be taken away from you and given to a people, producing the fruit of it.

Luke 12:32

"Do not be afraid, little flock, for your Father has chosen gladly to give you the kingdom."

As prophesied in the parables, the Christian church grew rapidly: it started with twelve disciples, then seventy disciples and, then, about 120 disciples at Pentecost: Immediately, on Pentecost, three thousand were added and then soon, more than four thousand were added (Acts 2:41, 4:4). Even though we cannot know the number of the Christians by the first century, we can arguably assume from the accounts of Acts that there were many Christians all over the world by that time. This growth in number reminds us of God's promise to Abraham about his descendants (the stars of heaven). However, it should not be understood as the fulfillment of the Abrahamic covenant, but rather the fulfillment of the prophesy of Jesus. Also, as I stated in Section I, Jesus fulfilled his prophesy regarding the end described in the parables by returning in AD 70. When we take Acts and Epistles into consideration, we can assume that as the end of Judea approached, the Christian church grew in number; however, many lost faith due to persecution, false doctrine, and delayed Second coming. If we trust the accounts of the parables, we can assume that God's judgment on Judea not only saved the Christians from the destruction, but also purified the Christian church by distinguishing true from false.

Jesus certainly did not teach his contemporary Jews about a kingdom that would come two thousand years later. The kingdom Jesus taught should be relevant to his contemporary Jews. Basically, what Jesus said through the parables was: "The Good News was preached to everyone. However, only those who have a good heart receive the Good News and become the members of the church, which is priceless, more precious than all you have. The first Christian church will be very small but will grow quickly and be eventually great. There will be true and false Christians in the church; however, when Judea is destroyed, I will distinguish one from the other and I will certainly avenge those who persecuted the innocent Christians. The end of Judea might seem late to you, however, particularly you leaders must be sincere and patient. As the end approaches, the faith of many will be weakened. There is no privilege to being a Christian earlier than another: all Christians are equal and will be saved from the destruction of Judea."

C. The Purpose of the Christian Church

The purpose of the Christian church is simple and clear since it is the fulfilled kingdom of God on earth. Based upon the New Commandment given to the church by Jesus, loving one another should be the primary purpose. The Christian church is the new kingdom of God on earth; however, its purpose should not be different from the previous kingdom, Israel.

God's purpose to set up Israel on earth is clearly described in Genesis 18:19:

Genesis 18:19
"For I have chosen him, so that he may command his children and his household after him to keep the way of the LORD by doing righteousness and justice, so that the LORD may bring upon Abraham what He has spoken about him."

What God said to Abraham in Genesis 12:2–3 was a blessing, not just for himself but for humanity: "and in you all the families of the earth will be blessed" 12:3b. Therefore, Genesis 18:19 can be rephrased for the Christian church like this: "For I have chosen the twelve disciples, so that they may command the disciples after them to keep the way of Jesus by doing righteousness and justice, so that Jesus may bring a blessing upon the church to cover the whole earth."

In addition, Moses well summarized the purpose of Israel in Deuteronomy 10:12–13:

Deuteronomy 10:12–13

12. "Now, Israel, what does the LORD your God require from you, but to fear the LORD your God, to walk in all his ways and love Him, and to serve the LORD your God with all your heart and with all your soul,

13. and to keep the LORD'S commandments and his statutes which I am commanding you today for your good?

What the LORD God required from Israel is certainly what Jesus Christ requires from the Christian church, and that should be the purpose of the church: To fear the Sovereign, to walk in all ways of Jesus Christ, to love Jesus, to serve the Sovereign with all our heart and soul, and to keep Jesus's commandments and statutes.

The Christian church should not exist just for its own good. It should exist for the world and humanity. It should not be the task of the Christian church to condemn the world and humanity. It should set up a model community of love and justice and invite the world and all humanity into that community. As the church grows, therefore, the world should be a better place for humanity to live. In short, to be the true kingdom of God or heaven on earth, is to practice love and justice for the sake of the whole of human society.

D. Rights and Obligations of the People of God

Since the Christian church is the fulfilled kingdom of God (heaven), all Christians should have rights and obligations as citizens of the holy nation.

Rights

All Christians should have right to be protected as a citizen of the kingdom. John 1:12 says, "but as many as received him, to them he gave the right to become children of God, even to those who believe in his name." Since God created the kingdom, and Christians became brothers or sisters of Jesus, God is considered the Father, and the citizens, the children of God. Therefore, not only as citizens in the legal and political sense, but also as children, all Christians have the right to be loved and nurtured. Jesus as the Sovereign is obligated to protect, love, and nurture Christians. In addition, when a Christian leaves this physical domain, his or her spirit has the right to enter the kingdom of God (heaven) in the spiritual domain, because both are the same kingdom ruled by the same Sovereign, Jesus, who should be obligated to observe and allow this entering.

Obligations

To worship:
The primary obligation of the Christians is to worship the Sovereign. Worship clarifies the relationship between the sovereign and the people, the one who governs and the ones who are governed. The psalmist invited the people of God to worship their Maker: "Come, let us worship and bow down, Let us kneel before the LORD our Maker" (Psalm 95:6), just as the magi worshiped the baby Jesus (Matthew 2:11) and the disciples worshiped the resurrected Christ (Matthew 28:17). Jesus clarified the nature of worship: in spirit and in truth: "But an hour is coming, and now is, when the true worshipers will worship the Father in spirit and truth; for such people the Father seeks to be his worshipers. God is spirit, and those who worship Him must worship in spirit and truth" (John 4:23–24). Whom should Christians worship? The Christians should worship the One who sits on the throne, the Sovereign who reigns over the church, in spirit and truth. Father and Son are one.

To observe the Law:

The citizens of the kingdom of God are obligated to observe the Law of the nation. For the Christian church, the Law is the New Commandment and teachings of Jesus. The fact that Christians cannot practice the Law perfectly does not mean that they are not obligated to observe. All churches and Christians should do their best to observe the Law with the help of the Holy Spirit, the Helper.

To observe the communion:

Jesus himself set up this obligation; therefore, all Christian churches should observe the communion regularly to remember the suffering and death of Jesus, in conjunction with remembering the Christian church as the eternal holy kingdom of God on earth.

To evangelize the world:

Based upon the Great Commission given by Jesus in Matthew 28:18–20 and Acts 1:8, Christians have eagerly evangelized the world. The Doctrine of Total Depravity, derived from the Original Sin, and the imminent Second Coming of Jesus, in association with the end of the world, have been the most important tools for evangelizing the world. It is time, however, for the Christian church to present a new evangelical method because these two tools have no biblical or Christological basis. As presented in Section I, they are the result of the distortion that happened in the process of universalization when Judea "became the world." True and biblical evangelism should not condemn or threaten the world, but rather invite people to a better place. Following is an exemplar approach consisting of two principles.

An Exemplar Approach for Evangelism

I. Jesus, who is the Son of God, reigns over the kingdom of God on earth as the Christ (Messiah) of his people.

Reference: Matthew 16:16, John 20:31, Acts 2:36; 9:19–22; 10:42–43

II. Anyone who believes this and is baptized becomes a citizen of that kingdom and receives the proper benefits of the Messianic reign.
Reference: John 1:12, Acts 2:38–39

List of the Benefits:
1. Will have a fellowship with the people of God who are humble and gentle.
2. Will be taken care of by the ministers who are called by God to serve his people.
3. Will have peace in mind because you live up to the teachings of Christ.
4. Will experience a deliverance by the power of Christ when you are in adversity.
5. Will be forgiven by the merciful Christ when you sin and repent.
6. Will enter the kingdom of God in the spiritual domain when you leave this physical temporal world.

There will be many more benefits that cannot be described here.

Conclusion

For the last two thousand years, Christianity has been a powerful and influential religion for humanity. Missionaries devoted their lives to converting people to Christianity. Along with evangelizing the world, the Christian church has built many institutions and organizations such as schools, hospitals, and orphanages all over the world. Also, the church has been the major voice to the world for justice, love, equality, and peace. In spite of these wonderful and positive works the church has done for the world, the division of the Christian church and skepticism about Christian theology also became visible. Ironically the major theological forces for evangelism such as the Doctrine of Total Depravity and the Eschatology associated with the imminent Second Coming of Jesus have provided the major causes for theological ambiguity that resulted in divisions and skepticism over the past centuries. Living in a pluralistic and electronic age, the world has become narrower than ever before. Anyone can access all kinds of information. As a Christian pastor living in such an age, I think it is time for the Christian church to look into itself and be honest to the world. If the church is not able to present a logical explanation for its claims and cannot show unity, any evangelical effort for the kingdom of God will be in vain and lose the power to persuade the world.

The theological ambiguity has contributed to the divisions of the church and caused conflict between Christian doctrine and reason. The work I presented in this book is an effort to search for an unequivocal theology for the future of the Christian church. Section I, Rapid Universalizing of Christianity: Judea Became the World, and Section II, Thoughts on Distortions, focus on deconstruction that tries to analyze the traditional and conventional theological views that hold strongly to these problematic doctrines. In the Section III, The Restored Christianity: Christianity without the Total Depravity and with the Fulfilled Eschatology, I have tried to introduce a new Christian theology, but much work is left to be done. I hope that Section III will inspire future scholars to finish this work for the kingdom of God. I believe the same amount of effort theologians have devoted to construct a theology with the Total Depravity and the future eschatology should be devoted to reconstructing one without them.

If the distortion is not clearly addressed, we risk losing some biblical truths. I do believe the Virgin Birth and the Resurrection of Jesus and the work of the Holy Spirit. However, I do not believe that the world is Judea and vice versa or that all human beings are the Jews and vice versa. I think that the writers of the New Testament were sincere and genuine, and they did their best for the kingdom of God on earth. I believe the distortion happened naturally and that no one should be blamed. Today, the responsibility to know the truth is on the readers of the Bible. I am confident that if one reads the New Testament, recognizing how what Jesus said was distorted by the disciples, one would find more helpful insights for faith rather than confusion.

Once a sound theology is constructed without Total Depravity and with the fulfilled Second Coming of Christ, theologians should readdress the relationship between the Christian religion and other religions, and between the Christian church and a secular state. Study in these areas is constantly improving. However, as long as the Christian church sticks to false doctrines, the improvement will be limited because the nature of the Church is ambiguous and incomplete, with the state and other religions fundamentally viewed as sinful. A new theology will provide a new perspective to the issues involved in that study.

The Christian church should be the kingdom of God on earth, one that does not threaten the world but inspires it. Though we can name several individual Christians who continue to inspire the world, we seem to be in a time in which the church is losing the power and capacity to do so. The Protestant churches just celebrated the five hundredth anniversary of the Reformation. Now is the time not just to celebrate but to evaluate the pain and loss caused by division after division and to ponder how the power and dignity of the Christian church can be recovered. When Christians cannot be in unity and do not love one another sincerely, the pain will not heal, and the power and dignity will not be restored. I hope this book provides the reader an opportunity to look carefully into the Christian Church and imagine ways to energize the faith.

End Notes

1. In 1 Timothy 2: 5–7, Paul presents Jesus as the only savior of the world and himself as a teacher of the Gentiles.

   "For there is one God, and one mediator also between God and men, the man Christ Jesus, who gave Himself as a ransom for all, the testimony given at the proper time.

   For this I was appointed a preacher and an apostle (I am telling the truth, I am not lying) as a teacher of the Gentiles in faith and truth."

2. When Christianity was born and spread in the first century, the nation it belonged to was Judea. Therefore, when universalizing of Christianity is concerned, it should be said that Judea became the world. However, the religious tradition of Judea is hardly separated from that of Israel in the Old Testament. Therefore, when I talk about sin of Judea, I feel more comfortable to write in Judea/Israel.

3. Hebrews 11:4 "By faith Abel offered to God a better sacrifice than Cain, through which he obtained the testimony that he was righteous, God testifying about his gifts, and through faith, though he is dead, he still speaks."

4. Deuteronomy 30:14 "But the word is very near you, in your mouth and in your heart, that you may observe it."

5. Matthew 1:21 "She will bear a Son; and you shall call His name Jesus, for He will save His people from their sins."

6. Westermann, *Genesis*, 26. In the sentence on Adam, death is perceived not as punishment, but as a matter of course. It is part of the span of life that extends from birth to death.

7. Westermann, *Genesis*, 25. See Trible, 124. In verse 15, the clause "... he will strike your head, and you will strike his heel" has been traditionally interpreted as having a proto-evangelical or eschatological connotation by identifying "he" with Christ and "you" with Satan. However, that particular interpretation seems irrational because the "seed" of the woman and the serpent refers to the generations to come in the collective sense of progeny, not in the sense

of an individual. The pronoun "he" is used for both genders throughout the Pentateuch.

8. Exodus 3:13–15

    13.Then Moses said to God, "Behold, I am going to the sons of Israel, and I will say to them, 'The God of your fathers has sent me to you.' Now they may say to me, 'What is His name?' What shall I say to them?"

    14. God said to Moses, "I AM WHO I AM"; and He said, "Thus you shall say to the sons of Israel, 'I AM has sent me to you.'"

    15. God, furthermore, said to Moses, "Thus you shall say to the sons of Israel, 'The LORD, the God of

    your fathers, the God of Abraham, the God of Isaac, and the God of Jacob, has sent me to you ' This is My name forever, and this is My memorial-name to all generations.

    Exodus 6:2–3

    2. God spoke further to Moses and said to him, "I am the LORD;

    3. and I appeared to Abraham, Isaac, and Jacob, as God Almighty, but by My name, LORD, I did not make Myself known to them.

9. Westermann, *Genesis*, 25. Verses 14–19 consist of the judgments upon the serpent, the woman, and Adam. It is descriptive, identifying human existence apart from God, as perceived by an author (J). The real sentence that God imposes, which should follow the trial directly, is expulsion from the garden. Westermann insists that expulsion is actually the only punishment that fits the crime in the text. The insertion of verses 14–19 is more clearly seen by first reading the narrative without them. Then, when considering those verses as a separate unit, the interpretation of death as the result of disobedience is confined to the expulsion from Eden.

10. E. A. Speiser, *Genesis* (TAB; Garden City, New York: Doubleday & Company, Inc., 1964), xxi.

    The documentary hypothesis in its classic form comprises J (Jehovah), E (Elohim), P (Priestly), and D (Deuteronomy), as well as R for redactors or compilers.

11. Hermann Gunkel, *The Legends of Genesis: The Biblical Saga and History* (New York: Schocken Books, 1970), vii.

12. Gunkel, *The Legends of* Genesis, p. viii.

13. Gunkel, *The Legend of Genesis,* pp. 10–11.

14. Gunkel, *The Legend of Genesis,* p. 3.

15. Gunkel, *The Legend of Genesis,* pp. 4–5.

16. Gunkel, *The Legend of Genesis,* pp. 8–9.

17. Gunkel, *The Legend of Genesis,* p. viii.

18. Claus Westermann, *Genesis: A Practical Commentary* (Grand Rapids: William B. Eerdmans Publishing Company, 1987), 3.

19. Gunkel, *The Legend of Genesis*, p. viii.

20. Gunkel, *The Legend of Genesis*, p. 13.

21. Speiser, *Genesis*, p. liv.

22. Speiser, *Genesis*, p. liii.

23. Gunkel, *The Legend of Genesis*, pp.14–16.

24. Gunkel, *The Legend of Genesis*, pp.17–18.

25. Speiser, *Genesis*, liv.

26. Westermann, *Genesis*, 2.

27. Westermann, *Genesis*, 3–4.

28. Gunkel, *The Legend of Genesis*, ix.

29. Speiser, *Genesis*, xxiii.

30. Speiser, *Genesis*, p. xxvii.

31. Speiser, *Genesis*, p. xxviii.

32. Gunkel, *The Legend of Genesis*, p. 2.

33. Gale A. Yee, "Gender, Class, and the Social-Scientific Study of Genesis 2–3," Semeia 87 (2006): 179.
    Refer to 1 Kings 4: 7–19: "Solomon had twelve deputies over all Israel, who provided for the King and his household; each man had to provide for a month in the year...."

34. Yee, "Gender, Class, and the Social-Scientific Study," 187–188.

35. Speiser, *Genesis*, lv.

36. Westermann, *Genesis*, 22.

37. Westermann, *Genesis*, 23.

38. See, ANET, 75.

39. See, ANET, 77.

40. Speiser, *Genesis*, 26–27.

41. Westermann, *Genesis*, p. 27.
    A variant is found in the Gilgamesh epic, where Gilgamesh, stricken by his friend's death with a horror of death, sets off in search of the "plant of life" that will protect him from death.

42. Speiser, *Genesis*, 28.

43. ANET, 101ff.

44. Speiser, *Genesis*, 27. Refer to the web site: http://faculty.gvsu.edu/websterm/Adapa.htm

45. Speiser, *Genesis*, 27.

46. Refer to Acts 5:1–11
    1. But a man named Ananias, with his wife Sapphira, sold a piece of property,

2. and kept back some of the price for himself, with his wife's full knowledge, and bringing a portion of it, he laid it at the apostles' feet.

3. But Peter said, "Ananias, why has Satan filled your heart to lie to the Holy Spirit and to keep back some of the price of the land?

4. "While it remained unsold, did it not remain your own? And after it was sold, was it not under your control? Why is it that you have conceived this deed in your heart? You have not lied to men but to God."

5. And as he heard these words, Ananias fell down and breathed his last; and great fear came over all who heard of it.

6. The young men got up and covered him up, and after carrying him out, they buried him.

7. Now there elapsed an interval of about three hours, and his wife came in, not knowing what had happened.

8. And Peter responded to her, "Tell me whether you sold the land for such and such a price?" And she said, "Yes, that was the price."

9. Then Peter said to her, "Why is it that you have agreed together to put the Spirit of the Lord to the test? Behold, the feet of those who have buried your husband are at the door, and they will carry you out as well."

10. And immediately she fell at his feet and breathed her last, and the young men came in and found her dead, and they carried her out and buried her beside her husband.

11. And great fear came over the whole church, and over all who heard of these things.

47. Since Paul divides all human beings into three groups: the Jews, the Greeks, and the Christians, we should notice that the term Gentiles and Greeks are exchangeable in Paul's writings.

48. In Korea, a kind of universal expressions is often said by the elders when they refer to the young generation sarcastically. When the young generation did some improper from their viewpoint, the elders say, "the world comes to an end."

49. The Day of Atonement
In the Old Testament, the enactment of this season is described in detail in chapter 16 of the Leviticus, but keeping it for a holy day is introduced in the Leviticus 23:26–32. This ceremony symbolizes the pinnacle of the New Testament doctrine of the atonement of Christ.

50. John 1:1–3
1. In the beginning was the Word, and the Word was with God, and the Word was God.

2. He was in the beginning with God.

3. All things came into being through Him, and apart from Him nothing came into being that has come into being.

51. John 3:1 Now there was a man of the Pharisees, named Nicodemus, a ruler of the Jews.

52. Deuteronomy 21:8–9 Then the LORD said to Moses, "Make a fiery serpent, and set it on a standard; and it shall come about, that everyone who is bitten, when he looks at it, he will live."
    And Moses made a bronze serpent and set it on the standard; and it came about, that if a serpent bit any man, when he looked to the bronze serpent, he lived.

53. Gospel of John was written in AD 80s.

54. Refer to Matthew 21:33–46. In the parable, Jesus makes it clear that God sent His Son into Judea and later the Gentiles would be beneficiaries.

55. Paul divides the Gentile into two groups in Romans 1: 14: Greeks and barbarians, the wise and the fool: 14. I am under obligation both to Greeks and to barbarians, both to the wise and to the foolish. However, Greeks represent the Gentiles in 1:16; 2:9–10, 12.
    1:16. For I am not ashamed of the gospel, for it is the power of God for salvation to everyone who believes, to the Jew first and also to the Greek.
    2:9. There will be tribulation and distress for every soul of man who does evil, of the Jew first and also of the Greek,
    2:10. but glory and honor and peace to everyone who does good, to the Jew first and also to the Greek.
    2: 12. For all who have sinned without the Law will also perish without the Law, and all who have sinned under the Law will be judged by the Law;

56. Romans 11:3 identifies "Christians in Rome" as the Gentiles: "But I am speaking to you who are Gentiles. Inasmuch then as I am an apostle of Gentiles, I magnify my ministry."

57. http://christianbookshelf.org/pamphilius/church_history/index.html

58. The first Jewish-Roman War started in AD 66 and ended in AD 70 when Jerusalem was destroyed. The last Jewish stronghold, Masada, was conquered in AD 73. Therefore, "four years before the war" might mean AD 62.

59. F.F. Bruce, *Paul: Apostle of the Heart Set Free* (Grand Rapids, Michigan: William B. Eerdmans Publishing Company, 1983), 441–455.
    Walter A. Elwell, ed., Evangelical Dictionary of Theology *Peter the Apostle* by A.F. Walls (Grand Rapids, Michigan: Baker Book House, 1990), 848–849.
    Both of them presumably died after AD. 64 the Great fire of Rome.

60. William Whiston trans., *The Works of Josephus* (Peabody, Massachusetts: Hendrickson Publishers, 1991), 537–538.
    According to Josephus James was stoned to death by Ananus ben Ananus.

61. Luke T. Johnson, *The Writings of the New Testament* (Philadelphia: Fortress Press, 1986), 256–267, 442.

62. Canon Leon Morris, Tyndale New Testament Commentaries *Revelation* (Grand Rapids, Michigan: William B.
    Eerdmans Publishing Company, 1989), 27–41.
63. http://christianbookshelf.org/pamphilius/church_history/chapter_xviii_the_apostle_john_and.htm
64. Matthew 19: 27–29

    27. Then Peter said to Him, "Behold, we have left everything and followed You; what then will there be for us?"
    28. And Jesus said to them, "Truly I say to you, that you who have followed Me, in the regeneration when
    the Son of Man will sit on His glorious throne, you also shall sit upon twelve thrones, judging the twelve tribes of Israel.
    29. "And everyone who has left houses or brothers or sisters or father or mother or children or farms for My name's sake, will receive many times as much, and will inherit eternal life.

    Luke 22: 28–30

    28. You are those who have stood by Me in My trials;
    29. and just as My Father has granted Me a kingdom, I grant you
    30. that you may eat and drink at My table in My kingdom, and you will sit on thrones judging the twelve tribes of Israel.

65. Revelation 2:26–27

    26. 'He who overcomes, and he who keeps My deeds until the end, TO HIM I WILL GIVE AUTHORITY OVER THE NATIONS;
    27. AND HE SHALL RULE THEM WITH A ROD OF IRON, AS THE VESSELS OF THE POTTER ARE BROKEN TO PIECES, as I also have received authority from My Father;

    Revelation 3:21

    'He who overcomes, I will grant to him to sit down with Me on My throne, as I also overcame and sat down with My Father on His throne.

    Revelation 20:4

    Then I saw thrones, and they sat on them, and judgment was given to them And I saw the souls of those who had been beheaded because of their testimony of Jesus and because of the word of God, and those who had
    not worshiped the beast or his image, and had not received the mark on their forehead and on their hand; and they came to life and reigned with Christ for a thousand years.

66. Revelation 1:9

    I, John, your brother and fellow partaker in the tribulation and kingdom and perseverance which are in Jesus, was on the island called Patmos because of the word of God and the testimony of Jesus

67. http://christianbookshelf.org/pamphilius/church_history/chapter_xviii_the_apostle_john_and.htm
68. 68. http://en.wikipedia.org/wiki/Seven_hills_of_Rome
69. Matthew 1:21 "She will bear a Son; and you shall call His name Jesus, for He will save His people from their sins."
    Luke 2:11 "for today in the city of David there has been born for you a Savior, who is Christ the Lord."
70. Refer to John 4:42. The Samaritans shared the territory of the Jews and a part of their tradition. In this sense, the world in John 4:42 should be understood as the Jewish-Samaritan world. John 4:42: and they were saying to the woman, "It is no longer because of what you said that we believe, for we have heard for ourselves and know that this One is indeed the Savior of the world."
71. Refer to Acts 2:40 what Peter preached to the Jews. Acts 2:40: And with many other words he solemnly testified and kept on exhorting them, saying, "Be saved from this perverse generation!"
72. If we take the record of the New Testament seriously, I think, some Christians who were martyred before AD 70 might be resurrected in AD 70 and some Christians who were alive in Jerusalem in AD 70 might not taste the physical death and both were taken up into God, and the majority of Christians who saved from the destruction of Judea constituted the primitive Christian Church.
73. Eusebius Chapter 5 paragraph 5: But it is necessary to state that this writer records that the multitude of those who were assembled from all Judea at the time of the Passover, to the number of three million souls, were shut up in Jerusalem "as in a prison," to use his own words.
74. http://en.wikipedia.org/wiki/Council_of_Jerusalem
75. For this argument, "the kingdom of God" or "the kingdom of heaven" proclaimed by Jesus in the Gospels should be understood as the coming Christian Church. "Already, but also not yet," the common phrase for the Christian eschatology, implies the kingdom of God as the future event. However, based upon my arguments, the kingdom of God meant the Christian Church in contrast to Judea. From the perspective of Jesus, the kingdom of God was present and started when he proclaimed the gospel and called his disciples, but the birth of the Christian Church was still in imminent future. It might be said that "the kingdom of God" was accomplished at the Pentecost when the Holy Spirit came upon 120 Christians and the church of Jerusalem was born or when the Christian Church became free from the Jewish persecution in AD 70, or at least, when the Christian Church became free from the Roman persecution in AD 313. This subject will be discussed further in section III.

76. Since Jerusalem represented the Judea as its capital, the restoration of Jerusalem meant the restoration of the Judea or the people of God. Refer to Ezekiel 34, particularly verse 15 for the reign of God.

77. Paul writes "that if you confess with your mouth Jesus as Lord, and believe in your heart that God raised Him from the dead, you will be saved" in Romans 10:9. This expression might be the closest definition of faith to the identity of Jesus as the son of God and Christ. In the previous chapters of Romans and Galatians, most terms of faith are contrasted with the Law and works implying faith as believing atonement.

78. It was futuristic to Jesus, but should be not after the Pentecost.

79. 1:18 For the wrath of God is revealed from heaven against all ungodliness and unrighteousness of men who suppress the truth in unrighteousness
2:2 And we know that the judgment of God rightly falls upon those who practice such things
2:17 But if you bear the name "Jew" and rely upon the Law and boast in God
3:9b for we have already charged that both Jews and Greeks are all under sin
3:19b so that every mouth may be closed and all the world may become accountable to God
3:23 for all have sinned and fall short of the glory of God
5:12 Therefore, just as through one man sin entered into the world, and death through sin, and so death spread to all men, because all sinned

80. Refer to Exodus 12:48 "But if a stranger sojourns with you, and celebrates the Passover to the LORD, let all his males be circumcised, and then let him come near to celebrate it; and he shall be like a native of the land. But no uncircumcised person may eat of it."

81. Jesus as the son of David was lost when the gospel was preached to the gentiles.

82. Refer to 2 Samuel 7: 1–16.

83. Refer to Genesis 17:10–14 and John 7:22
Genesis 17:10–14
    10. "This is My covenant, which you shall keep, between Me and you and your descendants after you: every male among you shall be circumcised.
    11. "And you shall be circumcised in the flesh of your foreskin, and it shall be the sign of the covenant between Me and you.
    12. "And every male among you who is eight days old shall be circumcised throughout your generations, a servant who is born in the house or who is bought with money from any foreigner, who is not of your descendants.
    13. "A servant who is born in your house or who is bought with your money shall surely be circumcised; thus shall My covenant be in your flesh for an everlasting covenant.

14. "But an uncircumcised male who is not circumcised in the flesh of his foreskin, that person shall be cut off from his people; he has broken My covenant."

John 7:22 "For this reason Moses has given you circumcision (not because it is from Moses, but from the fathers), and on the Sabbath you circumcise a man."

84. Refer to Deuteronomy 6:4 (Shema Israel) "Hear, O Israel! The LORD is our God, the LORD is one!

85. Refer to Leviticus chapter 16: The Sin Offering and The Day of Atonement.

86. Refer to John 13:34; 15:12; Matthew 5:21–48. Matthew 5:1–7:29.

87. Refer to Acts 1:12–26; 2:1.

88. Refer to Acts 1:16–26.

89. Refer to Revelation 4:4,10; 5:8; 11:16; 19:4; 7:4–8; 14:1, 3; 21:10–21.

90. Paul does not say much about the casuistic law of the Old Testament. His concept of the Law is mainly of the apodictic law, by which he claims that no one is righteous.

91. The Old Testament and Gospels' viewpoint regarding this subject will be further discussed in the next chapter.

92. I Corinthians 9:21 "to those who are without law, as without law, though not being without the law of God but under the law of Christ, so that I might win those who are without law."

Galatians 6:2 "Bear one another's burdens, and thereby fulfill the law of Christ."

93. John 14: 15–21

   15. "If you love Me, you will keep **My commandments.**

   16. "I will ask the Father, and He will give you another **Helper**, that He may be with you forever;

   17. that is **the Spirit of truth**, whom the world cannot receive, because it does not see Him or know Him, but you know Him because He abides with you and will be in you.

   18. "I will not leave you as orphans; I will come to you.

   19. "After a little while the world will no longer see Me, but you will see Me; because I live, you will live also.

   20. "In that day you will know that I am in My Father, and you in Me, and I in you.

   21. "He who has **My commandments** and keeps them is the one who loves Me; and he who loves Me will be loved by My Father, and I will love him and will disclose Myself to him."

94. Paul mentions about the role of the Holy Spirit in helping in terms of prayer in Romans 8:26: "In the same way the Spirit also helps our weakness; for we do not know how to pray as we should, but the Spirit Himself intercedes for us with groanings too deep for words." However, since Paul's writing is not systematic,

all words of Paul cannot be taken into consideration. His explicit emphasis should be taken into consideration for analysis.

95. The relationship between Jesus and God will be discussed later in chapter 1 under the section Jesus as God.

96. When the New Commandment was given, according to the Gospel of John, there were eleven apostles because Judas was out. However, the number twelve should be interpreted as the people of God rather than the literal numerical meaning.

97. http://en.wikipedia.org/wiki/Cohort_%28military_unit%29
During the first century AD, the command structure and make-up of the legions was formally laid down, in a form that would endure for centuries. The first cohort was now made up of five double-strength centuries totalling 800 men, the centurion of its first century automatically being the most senior in the legion. This century was known as the *primus pilus* (first file), and its centurion was known as the *primus pilus* (first file).

98. Matthew 26:47
While He was still speaking, behold, Judas, one of the twelve, came up accompanied by a large crowd with swords and clubs, who came from the chief priests and elders of the people.

99. In the Gospel of John, Ἐγώ εἰμι (I am) has a certain divine power. It might be related to the holy name of God, Yahweh.

Printed in the United States
By Bookmasters

Printed in the United States
By Bookmasters